Love and Beauty

Love and Beauty

by GUY SIRCELLO

Princeton University Press
Princeton, New Jersey

Published by Princeton University Press, 41 William Street,
Princeton, New Jersey 08540
In the United Kingdom: Princeton University Press, Guildford, Surrey

Publication of this book has been aided by the Whitney Darrow Fund of Princeton
University Press

This book has been composed in Linotron Garamond

Clothbound editions of Princeton University Press books
are printed on acid-free paper, and binding materials are
chosen for strength and durability. Paperbacks, although satisfactory
for personal collections, are not usually suitable for library rebinding

Printed in the United States of America by Princeton University Press,
Princeton, New Jersey

Library of Congress Cataloging-in-Publication Data

Sircello, Guy.
Love and beauty / Guy Sircello.
p.   cm.
Includes index.
ISBN 0-691-07335-X (alk. paper)
1. Love.   2. Aesthetics.   I. Title.
BD436.S54   1988   128—dc19   88-14005   CIP

Contents

CONTENTS

DESIRE

1. *Reviving Love*

Beauty is the best and most delightful part of our world, and in loving the best of the beautiful, we are the happiest and best of creatures. Without the love of even the slightest kind of beauty, we are less happy and less good than we otherwise might be, and of nothing other than beauty can this be said. Loving beauty is therefore of the utmost importance.

Thoughts like these are not new in the West, even if the above formulation of them is. Plato already probably had such thoughts, even if he did not express them in these terms.[1] Yet to most persons in our civilization who entertain thoughts at all about such things the ideas in the first paragraph will seem outrageous in many ways: perhaps grossly false, absurd, or downright meaningless; possibly naive or silly or pretentious or effete; clearly useless and pointless; definitely out of style. For several centuries now in the West, but especially since the middle-class revolutions of the late eighteenth century, the love of beauty, both the fact of it and the idea of it, has been losing prestige among vulgar and learned alike.[2] The style of bourgeois civilization, governed as it is by personal ambition—whether for power, status, wealth, or moral rectitude—is a natural enemy of the love of beauty.[3] This personal ambition in the social, political, and economic sphere has its intellectual counterpart in the various forms of skepticism and subjectivism beginning with Descartes. These intellectual forms are ultimately expressive of the desire to let nothing have dominion over "me," to submit to nothing outside of "myself," to be completely in charge of "my" own world[4]—the ultimate fantasy, we might say, of merchants with ships at sea. In such circumstances, I think, it is easy to see why desires to love the

3

world might give way to desires to win over the world, to control the world, to make the world, or to remake it.

It is not surprising therefore to see that civilization lay siege to the idea of the love of beauty, weakening it by stages and abandoning it finally for dead. A first stage in this siege was to shrink the domain of beauty itself down from the whole natural, intellectual, and moral universe to the purely sensory world; to further restrict it then to a single province within the sensory, namely, "art"; and simultaneously to refine the world of art itself down into a kind of treasure chest for a small class—the rich and knowing. A further stage in the attack was to call the love of this impoverished beauty "aesthetic pleasure," or later, and worse, "the aesthetic attitude." Another stage was to isolate this attitude, making it an alternative to, even a competitor of, other attitudes, feelings, and activities, such as the practical, the intellectual, the religious, the moral, the political, the sexual. Yet another stage was the realization and acceptance that even the tiny domain to which the love of beauty in this disfigured form had been banished, namely, art, was itself by the twentieth century disowning it. The idea nevertheless retained a precarious life in the cultural backwater of some midcentury academic circles until even the keepers of the ancient flame huddled there proclaimed the aesthetic attitude to be merely a "myth." With that, the old and grand idea of the love of beauty, now a mutilated, disinherited, and homeless waif, was expected simply to die.[5] And anyone asserting its ancient power—as in the first paragraph of this book—could with impunity be assumed to be intellectually, politically, morally, or spiritually effete.[6]

But what if in the face of such a siege you believe, as I, that there is a single concept of beauty that ranges, not only over seashells and symphonies, but over the highest reaches of wis-

4

dom and justice, the sublimest laws of the physical universe, and the most ordinary of everyday activities—like lighting a fire, or cooking a soup—as well? And what if you also believe that there is a joy to be taken in such beauties that is like enough to love? Well, if you do *not* think such beliefs are effete, and if you wish to show that you are right, you must construct a theory of beauty and of the love of beauty that will both justify your beliefs and revive that old concept of the love of beauty and its power. For, though on the verge of death as a cultural force, the idea of the love of beauty is not yet finished. It lives in its exemplifications, which are all around us, even if they go for the most part unrecognized. What it needs— though not all that it needs—to be revived is formulation in a clear, sound, articulate, and coherent theory. It has never had that benefit. The writer who had the best intuitions about the love of beauty—Plato—left no theory of beauty at all and only ravishing intimations of a theory of love.[7] We can even speculate that it was the very absence of such a theory that left the idea of beauty so apparently defenseless against its modern enemies.

Though it is late in the day, therefore, even for the owl of Minerva, I attempt in this book to produce such a theory. The theory builds, as it must, on a theory of beauty, which I have already supplied in *A New Theory of Beauty*. But of what precisely do I construct a theory in this book? Of more, it will turn out, than simply the love of beauty. It will be a theory of the love of everything beautiful as well as of the love of all that is, in even the slightest degree, on the way to being beautiful. But what does that include? What does "love" here refer to? It refers, first of all, to every kind of love, for persons, places, things. It refers to the love of art and to the love of virtue and to the love of the gods. It refers to friendships and to "likings"

5

of all kinds. It refers to sex and to the love of duty. It refers to all enjoyments, high and low. From a pretheoretical point of view, it refers to a great heap of unlike things, an unlikely subject matter for a single theory perhaps. But no more unlikely, I am trusting, than all that which the New Theory of Beauty comprehends. Some will insist that what is in this great heap has no single name, and they may be right. But I shall choose the name "Love"—because it is like the English word "love." My theory, then, I shall call the New Theory of Love.

But how begin to make a theory of such a heap? I want to analyze some relatively small piece of this vast and diverse subject matter and generalize from it. But which piece? Ideally, that piece should have a common, not to say vulgar, name. It should also be as untangled in theoretical controversy as possible, as free from conflicting values as possible, and as accessible to as many readers' experience as possible. It will, therefore, boot nothing to try to find new grounds for an ambitious theory in an analysis of the concepts of, for example, "love (of persons)," or "the aesthetic attitude," to name only two historically important pieces in the heap. The latter, besides denoting a kind of experience much too esoteric, is itself a creature of theory and hence lives almost exclusively in an atmosphere of (unprofitable) theoretical controversy.[8] The former is a veritable cultural battleground, fought over not only by conflicting theorists, but by fundamentally divergent world views and value systems.[9] Indeed, the concept of love is so embattled that it seems often not to be a single concept at all, generating doubt that "love," in any of its meanings, denotes an experience common to present members of our own culture, to say nothing of the human race throughout history.

I take as my starting point an analysis of enjoyment. The prima facie suitability of an analysis of enjoyment as a ground for what follows rests on these considerations: (1) Though not all analysts of enjoyment agree entirely about the concept, there are no large-scale philosophical, let alone cultural, battles raging about it. (2) Everyone—young, old, rich, poor, moral, immoral, friend or alien—experiences enjoyment, and I am aware of no one who is concerned to deny that. (3) There is an obvious relationship between enjoyment and other phenomena in the heap that this study takes as its subject matter; for example, enjoyment is pleasant, if not pleasure itself, beauty is eminently enjoyable, and some forms of love are paradigmatically enjoyable. (4) Enjoyment occurs, or has been held to occur, in the most diverse contexts: in sensual activities as well as in practical and intellectual ones; in the exercise of moral character and in the pursuit of animal lusts; in snuggling up in sleep and in the contemplation of the divine. Enjoyment seems to go into as many nooks and crannies of experience as does beauty itself and may appear therefore to be not such a small portion of the "heap" of Love after all. (5) Finally, a nearly ubiquitous, if somewhat colloquial, synonym for "enjoy" is "love," and generations of junior high school English teachers have been unable to stamp this usage out. If the New Theory of Love turns out to be anywhere near right, it may provide reason for seeing wisdom in this common usage.

2. Pleasure and Enjoyment

Because enjoyment is close kin to pleasure, it can seem to be the same thing. What we enjoy, after all, is what we take pleasure in, and our taking pleasure in it seems, on the face of it, to come to nothing but our enjoyment of it. Moreover, whatever is pleasant seems preeminently, even necessarily, enjoyable, so much so that "pleasant" and "enjoyable" can function as synonyms in some contexts. It is possible to speak of either a pleasant or an enjoyable day at West Street Beach, or visit to the French Quarter, or encounter with a stranger in Central Park, and have exactly the same experiences in mind. Furthermore, it seems universally true that it is pleasant to enjoy a thing, and true not simply on factual grounds. It may not in every case be *nothing but* pleasant to enjoy a thing, of course. After all, doing that enjoyable thing might involve sacrifice, hard work, or discipline that in itself is not pleasant. But presumably the pleasantness of the activity is enough to outweigh the unpleasantness. If not, how could we reasonably be said to enjoy it?

For all this, pleasure and enjoyment are not simply identical.[10] Many arguments could demonstrate this, but I prefer to develop a line that contrasts a particular form of pleasure with enjoyment.[11] That form of pleasure I shall label "propositional pleasure." Propositional pleasure is that pleasure I have insofar as I am *pleased that* our side won, the day turned sunny, or we all escaped unscathed by scandal. It is the pleasure we take in the (at least alleged) existence of a state of affairs, describable in a "that" clause. Propositional pleasure, however, is not marked in language only by the word "pleased" and its variants, such as "I take pleasure in the fact that . . ." I can also be *delighted* that the job turned out so well, *overjoyed* that my opponent fell flat on his face, *relieved* that the party is over, *gratified* that my worth is finally recognized. I may also be *glad* or *happy* that any of the above occurred. Insofar as I am any of these, however, it seems to me to follow that I am also *pleased* that the corresponding state of affairs obtains. Being delighted that, overjoyed that, relieved that, gratified that, happy that, and so forth sometimes indeed amount to no more than being pleased that. On the other hand, sometimes different *ways* of being pleased that . . . are indicated by differences in the terms used. Thus, generally speaking, to say that I am over-joyed that . . . or that I am delighted that . . . may indicate that my pleasure is accompanied by fairly strong *feelings* of pleasure, whereas simply to say that I am pleased or happy that. . . usually implies very mild feelings of pleasure, or none at all. As I shall later argue, however, the presence or absence of pleasurable feelings, and *a fortiori* their intensity, is inessential to propositional pleasure.

My main purpose in calling attention to propositional pleasure is to bring to light, by way of contrast, certain features of enjoyment. One might begin by observing a difference in their grammatical objects. Whereas propositional pleasures are *defined* in terms of statements taking "that" clauses as their grammatical objects, "enjoyment" and its cognates *cannot*, grammatically, take such objects. But to some this will seem a merely superficial difference, for the following reasons. First, all cases of enjoying "objects" other than the enjoyer's own activities can be reduced to cases of enjoying such activities. For example, if I enjoy scotch, then I enjoy drinking scotch, serving scotch, looking at scotch, buying scotch, or some combination of these and probably of other activities as well. Similarly, if I enjoy gardens, then I enjoy one or more of the following activities and probably some others: looking at gardens, wandering in gardens, working in gardens, designing gardens, studying gardens. Moreover, there is nothing to my enjoyment of scotch or of gardens other than some such activity, condition, or state of mine with respect to them. This kind of reduction, moreover, works quite universally, it seems to me. For "object" here can be taken in the widest possible sense. Thus I may be enjoying (the state of) *being in Laguna Beach*, or (the state of) *having a word processor*. I may even be currently

9

enjoying (my former state of) *having been the parent of very small children*. But even the enjoyment of such "objects" can be reduced to the enjoyment of one or more activities that I am engaging in vis-à-vis those "objects." Thus I may now be enjoying *watching* the crowds in Laguna, or enjoy *working* on my word processor, or enjoy *remembering* the curiosity and ingenuousness of my children.[12]

Now, if that is so, it might be reasonable to suppose that each case of enjoyment just *is* a case, or a set of cases, of some specific form, or forms, of propositional pleasure. For after all, it seems undeniable that if I am enjoying wandering in the garden, then I am *pleased that* I am wandering in the garden, and that if I am enjoying drinking scotch, I am *pleased that* I am drinking scotch. Here, too, generalization to a universal principle seems right. But if so, then enjoyment is apparently no different from being delighted, relieved, overjoyed, gratified that . . . ; enjoyment would then seem to be a specific form of propositional pleasure. To demonstrate that it is not, I shall have to analyze propositional pleasure more closely.

Start with another simple grammatical point: the verb "enjoy" can occur in the past, present, and future continuous tenses, but no way of describing propositional pleasure can take such forms. The following are perfectly grammatical: *I was enjoying gardening until the rain started; I am now enjoying the unusual summer storm; I hope I will be enjoying a long, hot bath between four and five this afternoon, so don't call.* But phrases like "I am being pleased that . . . ," "I was being happy that . . . ," and "I hope I will be being delighted that . . ." either have no use in English or are incorrect ways of saying "I am pleased, was glad, or will be delighted that . . ." In fact, some continuous tense is necessary to describe actual or possible *occurrences* of enjoyment. For the simple present tense of "enjoy" is always

10

used to describe only what happens generally or for the most part: "I enjoy waltzing" indicates that, in general, whenever I waltz, I enjoy it. Examples of analogous past and future forms are "I used to enjoy waltzing" and "When my cast comes off, I shall enjoy waltzing again."

This grammatical feature of "enjoy" makes it seem like a verb for an *activity*, like, indeed, all those activities that can themselves be enjoyed. And also like those enjoyable activities, enjoyment can be the object of resolve and of effort. Thus I can try to forget my fear of flying and to enjoy the rest of the trip; I can resolve to enjoy the camping trip despite the relentless mosquitoes. But resolve and effort are powerless to produce propositional pleasure. Why?

3. *Enjoyment and Desire*

The reason involves no limitations of body or will. The reason is a categorial limitation; propositional pleasure is not the sort of thing, conceptually speaking, that is directly effectable by resolve or effort. The reason for this, in turn, is reflected in another grammatical feature of propositional pleasure: it is described in the *passive voice*. Thus my being pleased, delighted, overjoyed, and so forth seems, simply in virtue of the grammatical form in which I must describe it, not something that I do, but something that *happens to me*. Of course, my propositional pleasures do not just happen to me out of the blue, like my being hit by a golf ball while driving the freeway. There may indeed be some ingredient in our propositional pleasure that is a circumstance beyond our control. But such a circumstance affects us, that is, *affords us the pleasure*, only if we ourselves are appropriately preconditioned. The question is, What is this sort of circumstance, and what is the sort of condition

11

in us that, combined with the circumstance, constitutes a necessary and sufficient condition of our being pleased that . . . ?

One component of propositional pleasure that is neither this circumstance nor this condition is a *feeling* of pleasure. Such a feeling, of course, varies with the variety of propositional pleasure; sometimes it is merely a warm glow, sometimes high excitement. Sometimes it is merely inwardly experienced; sometimes it shows in our behavior, from a simple relaxation of our facial muscles to a literal jump for joy. But whatever the form such feelings take, they are not necessary components of propositional pleasure. There are, after all, many things at any given moment about which we are pleased but which do not occasion any feelings of pleasure. This is obscured, however, by the fact that, typically, when we notice or have occasion to remark on a propositional pleasure of our own, we do experience and manifest some feeling of pleasure. But such feelings come and go, even when the propositional pleasures that are their sources do not. Thus I may be pleased today, when I receive the news, that I got the promotion; I may also be pleased next week, when you ask me about it, that I got the promotion; and I may be pleased next month, when I see the increase on my paycheck, that I got the promotion. On each of these occasions I may also have (and show) feelings of pleasure, though probably somewhat different feelings each time. Nevertheless, even though there may be three different feelings of pleasure I experience and show with respect to my having been promoted, I am not pleased *three times* that I have been promoted, as if I had ceased to be pleased in between the times I had the feelings of pleasure. Rather, I was pleased all along, and I still am, even when, as now, I neither experience nor show *feelings* of pleasure. Whereas propositional pleasures thus seem to be something like *states* of ourselves, the feelings they can sometimes and intermittently occasion seem to be something like *occurrences*.

What *is* an essential condition for the existence of any of our propositional pleasures, on the other hand, is a desire. Specifically, a desire for the state of affairs *about* which I am pleased is a necessary precondition of my being so pleased. Thus if I am pleased that I was promoted, I must have desired that I be promoted. We can distinguish, moreover, two kinds of conditions for satisfying such a desire. The fact that I was actually promoted is an *objective condition* for the satisfaction of the desire that I be promoted. A *subjective condition* for the satisfaction of that desire is that I believe that some objective condition for the satisfaction of the desire obtains. A desire cannot be satisfied without both of these conditions obtaining. But for me to have a given propositional pleasure requires only that I have a correlative desire and the *belief* that the desired state of affairs obtains. I claim then that if I am pleased that p, then I either have or have had a desire of which p's being the case is an objective condition of satisfaction, and I believe that p.[13]

Let me explain a key term—"desire"—in the above formula, for I am using it in a special sense, somewhat different from its ordinary sense but quite in line with the senses philosophers traditionally have implicitly given it. I use the term to cover clear and unambiguous cases of desire, mere "wants," explicit or vague wishes, hopes—fervent and well formed as well as mild and barely conscious—and also "would likes." This rather wide extension of "desire" allows us to see how the formula at the end of the last paragraph might be true. There is no doubt that sometimes when we are pleased that p, we clearly and explicitly wanted or even desired it to be the case that p. But there are many other cases of being pleased that . . . I may be pleased, for example, when a well-liked student of ten years

13

ago, of whom I have heard and thought little since, tells me of her receiving the doctorate. But that is surely because I have some vague wish or hope for the general success of people whom I remember fondly. Again, I may be pleased to hear that Aunt Tillie's plane is arriving two hours later than scheduled, even though it had not occurred to me to desire, want, or hope that it would. For now I'll be able to avoid the rush-hour traffic. The source of my pleasure is, of course, that I always would like to avoid such traffic if possible; I have, as it were, a standing desire to do so. Or suppose that I wake up one July morning and am pleased that it is raining. Now, I had neither desired, wanted, nor hoped that it would rain, simply because, in my experience, it *never* rains in July in Laguna Beach. On the other hand, it had not rained for eight months; things were dusty and dangerously dry. Before it rained it was certainly true that I *would have liked*, in an abstract kind of way, those conditions to be different.

The last three examples of "desire" also tell us something more about objective conditions of the satisfaction of a desire. If I am pleased that p, then I have or had a desire of which p's being the case is an objective condition of satisfaction. That desire may be, but need not be, a desire that p. The reason is, as the preceding discussion suggests, that p's being the case may be an objective condition of satisfaction not only of the desire that p, but also of more generally described desires. For example, that my former student received the Ph.D. may please both me and her mother. But whereas her mother desired in the strongest, most explicit, and specific way that she receive the Ph.D. (and was therefore pleased when she did so), I only vaguely hoped that she would do well in the future. But since receiving the Ph.D. is, in my opinion, an instance of her doing well in her future, the fact that she did the former is an objective condition of the satisfaction of my desire that she do the latter. Thus, believing that she did the former, I am pleased that she did. Generally speaking, I am pleased that p only if, having or having had a desire that q, I believe both that p and that p implies q, either directly or with the addition of other relevant propositions. And thus it is that, though I had no kind of desire that Aunt Tillie's plane arrive late, I can nevertheless be pleased that it does, if its coming in late means to me that I shall avoid traffic that I desire to avoid.

Thus far I have described necessary conditions of being pleased that . . . Now I want to state a related sufficient condition:

Either
(a) if I have a desire that p and I believe that p
   or
(b) if, believing that p, I have had a desire that p up to the point of my beginning to believe that p[14] and do not now desire that $-p$,[15]
then I am pleased that p.

I believe that this statement conforms to our intuitions concerning the relation between the satisfaction of our desires and an important category of our pleasures, even if it allows into the category of propositional pleasure some "pleasures" that are mild indeed. But my claim is justified simply thus: once it is seen that a necessary condition of propositional pleasure is the believed satisfaction of a desire, and once it is also seen that *feelings* of pleasure are not essential to propositional pleasure, it should be obvious that the essential pleasantness of propositional pleasure lies precisely in the subjective conditions of satisfaction of the correlative desire.

The foregoing analysis of propositional pleasure allows us to see why such pleasure cannot be had as a result of effort or resolve. Granting that I have a desire that p, I can be pleased that p only if it seems to me that p is the case. Furthermore, granting such a desire that holds through my believing in p's having become the case, I cannot but be pleased that p, once it seems to me, to the point of conviction, that p *is* the case. Thus, given certain desires in me, my being pleased simply comes to me as an "inevitable" effect of the way the world is believed by me to be at the moment. I may try or resolve to bring it about that p, but once it seems to me, to the point of conviction, that the world is such that p, my being pleased that p simply "happens" willy-nilly. If, then, the essentially *pleasurable* feature of propositional pleasure lies precisely in the subjective conditions of satisfaction of a relevant desire, propositional pleasures cannot be had by dint of effort or resolve. And since the latter is not the case with enjoyment, enjoyment, however pleasant, cannot be simply identical with propositional pleasure.

The above result, however, still leaves open the following possibilities: (1) that enjoyment is a *kind* of propositional pleasure, for example, that kind of propositional pleasure that *does* generate pleasant feelings; and (2) that enjoyment necessarily includes or presupposes some kind of propositional pleasure. On the basis of the first of these possibilities one might entertain the hypothesis that the *pleasantness* of enjoyment is identical with the pleasant feelings generated by certain propositional pleasures. The second possibility might lead one to entertain the hypothesis that enjoyment itself is identical with such feelings. But both of these hypotheses are false.

The pleasant feelings that are sometimes generated by propositional pleasures come to us, like those pleasures themselves, *simply* as a result of our believing a particular desire of ours is

16

realized. *That* they occur is a function of the character of the relevant desire and our relationship to the objective conditions of its satisfaction. Such feelings cannot therefore be generated by resolve or effort. But it is not merely enjoyment itself, but the pleasantness of enjoyment, that can be the effect of resolve or effort. Indeed, that is the point of resolving or trying to enjoy a thing—precisely to get pleasure out of it. Thus the pleasantness of enjoyment is not identical with the pleasant feelings generated in some propositional pleasures.[16]

But neither is enjoyment itself identical with such pleasant feelings. For we can either enjoy or not enjoy these pleasant feelings. Not to enjoy them would be, for example, to repress them, try to ignore them, or try to forget they occurred. On the other hand, it is not possible *not* to enjoy some actual (occurrent) case of enjoying a thing. For to say I enjoyed some case of enjoyment is always redundant; to direct someone to enjoy a case of enjoyment is pointless. There is no way to comply with such a direction except to do what one is doing, but in such a case the *direction* to do so is unnecessary.[17]

I turn next to a more direct analysis of (occurrent) enjoyment, seeking answers to two questions: (1) What is enjoyment? and (2) What constitutes its pleasantness? But before I do, I want to make clear what I believe I have established in the present section about possible answers to these two questions. To the first question it is not reasonable to answer that enjoyment is (a) propositional pleasure, (b) the pleasant feelings generated in some propositional pleasure by the belief that a desire has been satisfied, or (c) any subset of propositional pleasures that is defined in terms of some *sort* of objective conditions of satisfaction of desire, such as whatever I am doing right now, "now" being applicable to any time whatsoever.[18] To the second question it is not reasonable to answer that the *pleasantness* of enjoyment is (a), (b), or (c). Finally, it is not reasonable to give as an answer to the first question that which assumes or implies that the pleasantness of enjoyment is (a), (b), or (c).

4. *The Experience of Enjoyment*

But even if my enjoying a thing cannot simply be a way of being pleased that, say, I am doing that thing, we cannot deny that desire and its satisfaction have parts to play, however complex, in a complete analysis of enjoyment.[19] Our experience of our own enjoyment tells us so. Take lovemaking, for example, and the enjoyment thereof. Lovemaking, one would think, is the last place to look for desireless pleasure, and of course that is right. A common scenario is: I see the beautiful beloved from afar, burn with desire for him, scheme to meet him, touch him, bed him—and *that* is where the satisfaction takes place. But even in this scenario, that is not all there is to the *enjoyment* of making love. For there is more pleasure in making love than that constituted by the satisfaction of the desire to make love. When lovemaking is enjoyed, it perhaps satisfies a desire precisely to make love, but it also *generates* a desire—for making love. The first caress leads to more caresses and to the desire for more, with variations and repeats. The possession of the beloved in one position leads to the desire for possession in yet another, and on and on—when enjoyment is at its highest—with neither orgasm nor exhaustion the natural or predictable terminus of any of the desires thus generated.

At least these three features mark our experience of enjoyable lovemaking: the desire to make love, aroused by the very act itself; the satisfaction of that desire in the act itself; and, finally, the impetus to *go on* making love, consisting of what

feels like the continuous motion of desire-begetting-satisfac-
tion-begetting-desire. All of these elements, furthermore, are
quite independent of any desire to make love antecedent to the
first touch of lovemaking. Plato may indeed have had precisely
this phenomenon in mind when he had Diotima represent Love
as a mixture of Poverty and Riches—of, we might say, want or
desire *and* its satisfaction (*Symposium*, 203b–204b).

These features of the enjoyment of lovemaking can be generalized. We sometimes do want to run or to garden in advance
of doing it, and we look forward to it eagerly because, among
other things, we expect to enjoy it. But once we are running
or gardening and enjoying it, we have already satisfied those
antecedent desires. And yet if we are enjoying the running or
the gardening, we want to keep at it, not because we wanted
to run or garden *before* we started doing so, but precisely because we are now enjoying doing so. And when we stop, if it
is not because of exhaustion or boredom—that is, because we
have *stopped* enjoying the activity—we wish we could continue,
as if the desire to run or to garden, which in some way of course
has been satisfied, were also still there, but frustrated now.
Thus, too, when the mountains that appear around the bend,
or the legs that stride past our beach blanket, quite unbidden
and unexpected, disappear again from view, we feel the loss
although, but also because, we enjoyed the sight of them so
much. It is as if, when we are enjoying a thing, we cannot get
enough of it, as if the desire to possess it is always outliving its
own satisfaction.[20]

Thus far I have argued that even if enjoying a thing is a sort
of pleasure, it is not simply the sort of pleasure that consists in
being pleased that something is the case. On the basis of our
experience of enjoyment, however, it seems that a *desire* that
something be the case is in some way ingredient in the phe-

nomenon of enjoyment. Such a desire, furthermore, need not precede the enjoyed activity, for it is generated by the enjoyment itself, and even if it does precede the enjoyed activity, it is regenerated by the enjoyment itself. In addition, in the course of the enjoyment such a desire is satisfied in one respect, but in another respect is not satisfied. These results generate four questions: (1) What kind of desire can this desire be? (2) Can we construct a plausible theory of enjoyment that comprehends a desire of this kind? (3) Can such a theory avoid implying that enjoyment is merely a kind of propositional pleasure? (4) Can such a theory account for the fact that enjoyment can be the result of effort or resolve?

5. *The Desire for Immortality*

As a step toward answering these questions, suppose the following: In enjoying a thing it is both necessary and sufficient that the enjoyer be engaged in an activity R that *causes the enjoyer to desire to continue doing it indefinitely*. If R exists and we can identify it, then we can answer questions 2 through 4 affirmatively. For we can construct a theoretical definition of enjoyment as an *activity*, which, like most activities, we can try or resolve to do. Furthermore, although under these conditions enjoyment would have to be understood partially in terms of desire partially satisfied, enjoyment would not be *defined* as desire (or a particular type of desire) believed to be satisfied and hence would not be identified with propositional pleasure or a subset thereof. Finally, such a desire would explain the experiential facts described in the preceding section, and more besides. I shall elaborate these points, but first I wish to explain the ambiguous term "indefinitely" in the description of R italicized above.

My desiring to continue to do something indefinitely may be one of two things. It may be that, for all future times t, I desire not to stop doing that something at t. Or it may be that, for all future times t, I do not desire to stop doing that something at t. Whereas the first desire is a desire to keep on doing the thing "forever," the second is merely a desire that does not have any stopping point "in mind." I intend the second interpretation of "indefinitely," as it seems to me to capture our experience without committing my theory to anything excessive.

Yet it is easy to overlook, in our experience, the difference between the two kinds of desire. For one thing, sometimes in enjoying a thing we do feel as if we could and would go on forever. Moreover, the *absence* of a term to our desire can certainly feel like the *presence* of a desire to go on forever. It apparently felt like that to Plato, or so I surmise, since he introduces the term "forever" into his conception of love without the breath of an argument (*Symposium*, 206a), as if there were no other possibility.[21] More is probably going on in this case, of course, than a mere misreading of experience. For immortality was important to Plato in many philosophical contexts. Thus it does not seem out of philosophical character for him to believe, apparently, that love is the desire for immortality (207a) as well as for the beautiful, even if this seems not quite justified by anything in the experience ostensibly being discussed in the *Symposium*.[22] I, however, have no philosophical commitment to immortality and hence choose what I consider a more careful reading of our experience of enjoyment suggesting that in Love lies, not a desire for our own *im*mortality, but at most a (momentary) forgetting of our mortality.

I want now to draw attention to several features of this hypothetical desire to continue doing R indefinitely. First, having such a desire presupposes being already engaged in R or having been engaged in R in the very recent past. Second, therefore, the desire need not antedate the beginning of the occurrence of enjoyment, since by hypothesis engagement in R, whose continuation is desired, is sufficient for the occurrence of the enjoyment. Third, the desire to continue doing R presupposes the desire to do R; for continuing to do R is simply doing R "on," as it were. But since, again by hypothesis, the enjoyer is engaged in R, the enjoyer is, in enjoying, satisfying a desire to do R as well as desiring to do R. Furthermore, at any given time during the enjoyment the enjoyer both has satisfied (and is satisfying) the desire to do R and has (still) the desire to do R "on." Therefore at each such moment, including the "last," the enjoyer has satisfied in part but has not completely satisfied the desire raised by doing R. This, then, is the sort of desire our experience of enjoyment seems to contain. I shall henceforth call this desire to continue indefinitely doing R aroused by R itself "intrinsic desire." All other desires I shall refer to as "extrinsic desires." Thus, according to my earlier discussion, all propositional pleasures consist in the (subjective) satisfaction of *extrinsic* desires. Intrinsic desires are, like Platonic *eros*, never satisfied (objectively or subjectively). For at any time during my being engaged in R I have done R precisely up to that time, but my desire all along has been and is now precisely to go on doing R indefinitely. My desire could at any time be satisfied only if my desire had been to go on doing R *only up to that time.* But such a desire, no matter how aroused, would not be an intrinsic desire.

But, after all, *is* there such an activity as R? Do intrinsic desires exist? In the next several sections I shall construct a theoretical model of enjoyment. In that model I shall identify an activity that gives rise to intrinsic desire and claim that it is a necessary and sufficient condition of (occurrent) enjoyment. I have put another requirement on such a model, namely, that it explain what is pleasant about enjoyment. After all, it has been the search for what is pleasant about enjoyment that has motivated much of the discussion to this point. It is that search which in part explains the temptation to see enjoyment as a kind of propositional pleasure. In addition to accounting for the pleasantness of enjoyment, a satisfactory theory of enjoyment should account for the fact, mentioned earlier, that if I am enjoying doing a thing, then I am also *pleased that* I am doing that thing, even if my being so pleased is not identical with my enjoying doing that thing.

6. *The Enjoyment of Experience*

When, on a particular occasion, I enjoy cooking, dancing, or hiking, hardly ever do I enjoy everything about that cooking, dancing, or hiking. I do not enjoy, for example, the hot oil splashing on my arm, the heel wound on my toe, the mosquito bites. So it is relevant to ask, of any particular activity or state or condition that I enjoyed or am enjoying, just *what* I enjoyed or am enjoying *about* it. There are a wide variety of possible answers to this kind of question, and in what follows I shall try to make some sense of that variety.

First, answers to the question may be given by naming concrete or abstract objects. Thus I may say about today's hike that I enjoyed the "scenery," or "the outdoors," or "the green hills." As I noted earlier, however, the enjoyment of any "object" that is not an activity of mine can be reduced to the enjoyment of one or more activities I engage in with respect to that object. Answers of the above sort should be taken, then, as shorthand ways of saying, for example, "*observing* the scenery," "*walking*

23

in the outdoors," "*wandering over* the green hills," "*seeing* and *hearing* the colorful crowd and *feeling* its excitement," "*smelling* the cooking food," "*working with* fresh ingredients," "*experiencing* the organized chaos of the kitchen." Since it is always our own acts or activities that are, properly speaking, enjoyed, what we enjoy *about* such acts or activities can be phrased in terms of other acts or activities.

Furthermore, the latter acts and activities may themselves be rather complex and, though enjoyed, not enjoyed in all their aspects. We may therefore ask of them, in turn, what we enjoyed or are enjoying about them. Indeed, I may go on asking this question about every act or activity that this procedure brings to light until I come to acts or activities that fall into one of three categories. One category consists of relatively simple perceptual acts of the "external senses," like smelling, tasting, seeing, hearing, and feeling (by touch). Thus, what I enjoyed about cooking yesterday may have been smelling the herbs and spices, seeing the colors of the fresh produce, feeling its firmness and tenderness, and tasting the progress of the meal at each of its stages. What I enjoyed about the hike may have been hearing the rural stillness, the chatter of the birds, the rustle of the pine needles in the wind, or feeling the hard rocks beneath my heels, or seeing the clean atmosphere and fresh foliage. And what I enjoyed about dancing last night, besides seeing the color of the crowd's costumes and feeling the crowd's excitement, may have been seeing the intensity of their faces and the abandon of their bodies, or smelling their sweat and feeling my own drenched clothes.

A second category consists of what we may call perceptual acts of our "interior senses." These are acts in which we sense or feel or experience our own bodily or mental states, acts, or occurrences. Thus, when I enjoy hiking I may enjoy feeling the rhythm of my stride, of my heartbeat, and of my breathing, or feeling my own exhilaration. When I dance I may enjoy the feeling of my own excitement, enthusiasm, and abandon, experiencing the rhythms and convolutions of my own body. When I enjoy cooking, I can also enjoy my own mock-dramatic bustle, can enjoy feeling my own confidence, my own control, my own organization.

The third category of acts that can contribute to my enjoyment of more complex activities consists of those acts of remembering, thinking, imaging, imagining, or fantasizing that may accompany or be stimulated by the primarily enjoyed activities. What I enjoy, in part, about cooking may be the memories it stirs up in me of my mother's kitchen, or of helping my father prepare lunch. What I enjoy about hiking may be the images of absolute space or of limitless landscapes it conjures up in my mind. What I enjoy about dancing may be the fantasy it provokes in me of myself as a theatrical figure.

Let us put these categories together and draw up a list of terms designating relatively simple kinds of acts, instances of which can be what it is we enjoy about other, more complex, acts and activities:

> seeing
> hearing
> tasting
> smelling
> feeling (by touch)
> sensing
> perceiving
> experiencing
> feeling (internally)
> imaging

remembering
imagining
fantasizing
thinking (of)

This list is not meant to be exhaustive. Some of the terms, furthermore, may be used in some contexts interchangeably with others. I have, moreover, not listed obvious and straightforward synonyms. It should be obvious, furthermore, that frequently, if not always, when we are engaged in one of the above kinds of acts, we are also engaged in some of the others, often with respect to the same "object." In such cases, especially, it seems appropriate to describe our activity by the most generic of the above terms: *experiencing*. In honor of this fact, I shall henceforth use the term "experience" and its cognates to refer to this whole class of acts: an instance of feeling, seeing, remembering, and so forth will be called an instance of experiencing or, alternatively, of experience, or it will be called an experience. Later in this study I shall find it necessary to distinguish between "experience," "an experience," and "experiencing," but when that time comes, I shall clearly signal it.

I now want to claim that all of my enjoyment can be reduced to enjoyment of my experience. This claim means (1) that if I progressively ask about every enjoyed activity that is not itself an experience what I enjoyed or am enjoying about it, I shall eventually answer in terms of one or more enjoyed experiences; and (2) that there is no enjoyment of any object, act, activity, state, or condition *other than* the enjoyment of the experiences that are involved in the enjoyment of the object, act, activity, state, or condition. This claim implies that if we understand what it is to enjoy experiences, we shall understand every case of enjoyment because we shall understand everything that is enjoyable about every case of enjoyment. To put this implication in another way: to understand what it is to enjoy experience is to understand all the enjoyment there is.

Now, this reducibility claim is a large one, and it is crucial to my enterprise. The best deductive argument that I can invent for the claim is the following: I cannot enjoy anything unless I am aware of it. Furthermore, I can enjoy a thing only insofar as I am aware of it and only in those respects in which I am aware of it. But being aware of what I am enjoying is precisely having some experience of it. This experience itself must be enjoyable and enjoyed, or nothing is, and furthermore such enjoyment must be identical with the enjoyment of what I am enjoying. The crucial premise in this argument, of course, is that we can enjoy a thing only insofar as, and in those respects in which, we are aware of it. The truth of the premise may seem to some to depend precisely on the truth of my reducibility claim. But one can, alternatively, see my reducibility claim as articulating the implications of the more "primitive" intuition expressed in the premise.

One may also see my reducibility claim as a generalization from a few cases in our (or my) own experience in which the reduction works satisfactorily. I can think of nothing that the above reduction technique "leaves out" of any of my own enjoyments that I try it on. Furthermore, I can think of no reasons why it would not work in other cases. Anyone who balks at accepting the claim is invited to present counterexamples to it. Or, of course, a counterargument. Until it is shown to be untenable, I shall adopt it as a principle. It may turn out, too, that the ultimate theoretical advantages of accepting the claim as a principle outweigh the disadvantage of its not being founded on bedrock (whatever *that* might be thought to be). As a final statement to the skeptical, however, I point out that the number and variety of enjoyed experiences to which, under my claim, the enjoyment of some "object" (thing, condition, state, act, or activity) is reducible can be very large, and therefore my claim does not imply a simple-minded reduction that in any *obvious* way misses some of the enjoyability of our everyday enjoyments.

THE BELOVED

7. *Experience and Quality*

The enjoyment of enjoyed experiences may be further reduced to a special kind of enjoyed experience—an experience whose "object" is a special property that I call in *A New Theory of Beauty* a property of qualitative degree, or PQD.[23] Of the examples of enjoyed experiences I have already given, the following are experiences of PQDs: feeling the firmness of the fresh produce, feeling the tenderness of the produce, hearing the rural stillness, seeing or hearing the excitement of the crowd, seeing the intensity of the other dancers' faces, seeing the abandon of the other dancers' bodies, feeling the abandon of my own dancing body, feeling my own excitement, enthusiasm, confidence, control, organization. All the other examples of enjoyed experiences I gave earlier are not experiences of PQDs.

My new claim of reducibility has two parts: (1) we can ask of all enjoyed experiences that are not experiences of PQDs what is enjoyed about them and get answers, if not immediately, then ultimately, by repeated applications of the question, in terms of experiences of PQDs; (2) by this process we can reveal *everything* that is enjoyed about the original enjoyed experience. Let me give some illustrations of (1) using examples I have already given of enjoyed experiences of "objects" that are not PQDs:

. . . What I enjoy about smelling the herbs and spices when I cook may be smelling their sweetness and pungency, or it may be thinking of the exoticism and romance of the stores, or lands, where I bought them.

. . . What I enjoy about seeing the colors of the produce may be seeing the freshness, the vividness, the vibrancy of the colors.

. . . What I enjoy about tasting the meal as it progresses may be tasting the harmony of its flavors, tasting the subtlety of its blends and changes, or sensing my own canniness as I add just the right touch of cinnamon to the sauce.

. . . What I enjoy about hearing the birds' song may be hearing its sweetness, its sauciness, its boldness, its complexity, its simplicity.

. . . What I enjoy about hearing the rustle of the pines may be sensing the mysteriousness of the forest, its sinisterness, or its calm.

. . . What I enjoy about seeing the green foliage may be seeing its freshness, its cleanness, its nonurban wholesomeness.

. . . What I enjoy about feeling hard rocks beneath my heels may be sensing nature's solidity, or experiencing my own security inside my sturdy boots, or feeling my own strength and hardness responding to the rock.

. . . What I enjoy about seeing the color of the costumes in the dancing crowd may be seeing their boldness, their gaiety, their raucousness.

. . . What I enjoy about smelling the sweat of the crowd and feeling my own drenched clothes may be sensing the animality and sexuality of the crowd and feeling my own.

. . . What I enjoy about the rhythm of my stride, of my heartbeat, of my breathing while I hike may be its regularity, its calm, its serenity.

. . . What I enjoy about feeling the rhythms and convolutions of my own body while dancing may be feeling my own energy, my abandon, or my sexiness.

. . . What I enjoy about recalling my mother's kitchen may be remembering the warmth, the comfort, the security it used to give me.

. . . What I enjoy about remembering helping my father

prepare lunch may be the pride or the companionship I felt in those experiences.

. . . What I enjoy about imaging absolute space and limitless landscapes while on my hike may be the feeling of calm and detachment it gives me.

. . . And what I enjoy about fantasizing myself as a theatrical performer may be feeling my own power, my own sexuality, or precisely my own theatricality.

These examples show how enjoyed experiences of PQDs can explicate the enjoyment of experiences that are not ostensibly of PQDs. But the second part of my (last) reducibility claim is that there is no enjoyment of the latter kind of experience that is not simply the enjoyment of one or more of the former kind of experiences. What reasons do I have for this claim? I have no deductive argument to offer like the one for my earlier reducibility claim. My only reasons for making the claim are that (1) the enjoyment of my own actual enjoyed experiences seems completely explicable in terms of enjoyed experiences of PQDs, as, for example, in the illustrations given immediately above; (2) I can see no reason why the enjoyment of other enjoyed experiences I may have should not be equally susceptible to such a reduction; and (3) I can see no reason why my own enjoyment should be in this respect unlike that of others. Now, I consider this reducibility claim, like my earlier ones, challengeable in principle by counterexamples. But I also believe that treating the claim as a *principle* will lead to a theory of Love that is interesting and powerful enough to constitute, by that very fact, an argument in favor of the claim that could outweigh at least some kinds of counterexamples.

My three reducibility claims together amount to this: the enjoyment I have of any "object" that is not itself an activity is the sum total of the enjoyment of all activities of mine vis-à-vis that "object," and the enjoyment I take on any given occasion in any activity of mine is, in turn, nothing but the total enjoyment I take in *all* of my experiences of PQDs that constitute, either proximately or ultimately, what it is *about* that original activity that I enjoy. It is this combined claim that I shall henceforth refer to as the reducibility claim, the reducibility principle, or the reducibility technique.

I should note here four features of enjoyed experiences of PQDs. The first feature is in effect an important addition to my reducibility claim. The PQDs to the experience of which our enjoyment is reducible belong to a limited class of all possible PQDs. In *A New Theory of Beauty* I define beauty as a high degree of any PQD *of a certain sort*. That sort is determined negatively, namely, as all PQDs except those of "deficiency, lack, or defect" (such as unhealthiness, deformedness, rustiness, fadedness, and rottenness) and those of the "appearance" of defiency, lack, or defect (such as sick-acting, rusty-looking, faded-looking, rotten-tasting, and rotten-smelling).[24] Just as it is only to PQDs of this limited class that the beauty of "objects" is reducible, so, I want to claim now, is it to our experiences of PQDs of this same class that our enjoyments are reducible. The reasons for this qualification of my reduction principle are that (1) it seems to me that generally we do not, as a matter of fact, enjoy experiences of PQDs of deficiency, defect, or lack or PQDs of the "appearance" of these; and (2) the enjoyment that we might have of such experiences can in turn be reduced to the enjoyment of experiences of PQDs of the "beautiful" sort. Later, when discussing applications of my general theory of Love, I shall illustrate how the latter kind of reduction is possible. At this point, however, I want to introduce a technical term—"quality"—to refer to that sort of PQD a high degree of which accounts for all the beauty in "objects" and the enjoyment of the experience of which constitutes all our enjoyment. I should have introduced this term already in *A New Theory of Beauty*; "PQD" is too ugly a term to use as frequently as I must. Moreover, my irony in defining beauty by means of such an ungainly and hypertechnical piece of nomenclature has escaped nearly everyone's notice. Why carry on with it?

The second thing to note about our enjoyed experiences of qualities is that it is not necessary that the enjoyed quality be present in some "object" to a high degree.[25] In other words, an enjoyable experience of a quality is not necessarily an experience of beauty.[26] Third, an enjoyable experience of a quality need not be a veridical experience. For example, even though I may enjoy dancing in part because of the feeling it gives me of my own sexiness, I may not be sexy at all when I dance; I may actually just be klutzy—however it may ultimately be determined or determinable whether I am "in fact" sexy or klutzy. Similarly, I may enjoy hearing the birds' song because I enjoy hearing its sweetness. Yet neither the truth of the preceding statement nor my actual enjoyment depends upon the birds' song being "in fact" sweet. Likewise, my enjoyed nostalgia for the comfort and security of my mother's kitchen may really be all that my enjoyment of (an occasion of) cooking amounts to, even if I never actually felt comfortable or secure in that kitchen (even if, say, my ostensible memory of that comfort and security is really pure fantasy). A fourth feature, related to the third, is that the quality of which I have an enjoyed experience may, in that experience, be attributed to an "object" that does not and never did exist. We can, after all, be led to fantasize completely invented "objects" when we enjoy a thing. I have enjoyed Berlioz's "Symphonie Fantastique" by imagining grotesque, calm, humorous, and violent scenes "in my head," and my enjoyment of the music on those occasions has consisted, in some part, of those enjoyable experiences.[27]

8. *Eschewing the Metaphysics of Qualities*

My theory of Love, like my theory of beauty, rests squarely on the notion of quality. Many questions might be raised about what we can roughly call the metaphysics of qualities: *Are* there qualities? What is it for an "object" to *have* a quality? What makes the experience of an "object" having a quality *veridical* or not? Can any distinction ultimately be made between a veridical and a nonveridical experience of a quality? Do all sentient beings experience all of the "same" qualities? Any of the "same" qualities? Do all *human* beings? *Can* they experience the "same" qualities? What, after all, are the criteria for sameness of quality? Are there qualities that some sentient beings never experience? Are there qualities that no sentient beings have ever experienced? Are there qualities that sentient beings could never in principle experience? I have an interest in trying to answer these and related questions, but I have no answers to them now. I intend therefore to avoid presupposing answers to these questions in constructing my theory of Love, as I did in constructing my theory of beauty.

Some may object that I cannot avoid answering or presupposing answers to at least some of the questions. Does not a theory that rests on qualities already presuppose, for example, that they exist? No, not necessarily. As for the theory of Love, it presupposes only that there are *experiences* of qualities. And the New Theory of Beauty, were it to be discovered in a metaphysical inquiry that there are no qualities, could be construed as a theory of "objects" *as we experience them in a certain way*, namely, as possessing qualities present in varying degrees.

Some may protest, however, that points made in just the last section already presuppose distinctions between qualities that truly belong to "objects" and those that do not. Why otherwise say, as I did, that enjoyment may be reduced to enjoyable experiences of qualities whether or not those experiences are veridical? Two responses to this objection are relevant. First, the point may be construed as guaranteeing the reducibility of enjoyment to enjoyable experiences irrespective of the results of an inquiry into the metaphysical status of qualities. Second, the point may also refer to the possibility—which I take it no one is interested in denying—of distinguishing *within our experience* between qualities that do and qualities that do not belong to their "objects." To admit that we make such a distinction in our own experience is not to imply, I take it, that we do so on good, consistent, or systematic grounds, that we all do so on the same grounds, or that such a distinction has any metaphysical import.

Finally, some may think that the metaphysical caution I am professing here conflicts with the "objectivity" that I claim for my theory of beauty. It does not. In *A New Theory of Beauty* I professed the same agnosticism with respect to most conceptions of the subjectivity or objectivity of qualities that I do here. My claim, then and now, is that the New Theory of Beauty defines a conception of beauty that is objective only in that it is *not subjective* in several ways. In particular, "beauty," in that theory, is *not* defined in terms of any properties belonging to a class I called "properties of psychological effect." A prime and apposite example of that class is the property of being *pleasant*.[28]

In the next several sections I shall describe what I call "the world of qualities." But I interpret this phrase in terms of the metaphysical asceticism I have been claiming here. Under that rubric I shall discuss qualities only as they are experienced by a certain type of sentient being, namely, human beings. I leave it open whether other kinds of sentient beings, known to us or unknown, experience qualities and, if they do, whether the "worlds" of their qualities are like ours in structure. I also leave it open whether there are unexperienceable qualities, which would not, therefore, be included in our "world." In speaking of "our" world of qualities I do not, furthermore, assume that all human beings, or even some of them, experience all the same qualities, or even some of the same qualities. For I shall be speaking only of the *categories* of qualities and of their *interrelationships*, which together structure all the particular qualities into something like a world. I also do not *assume* that the *structure* of the world of qualities is the same for all human beings. I am, however, claiming that it is. If I am wrong, no doubt I shall be offered counterexamples.

9. *The World of Qualities*

We can categorize the qualities of our world in many ways. The way I choose is both illuminating of our experience of qualities, as I shall show later, and useful for my theoretical purposes, as I shall eventually argue. My way of structuring this world starts with a person who is an experiencer of that world, for example, myself. I describe the categories in terms of some particular (human) experiencer of qualities, but I mean the structure of categories to apply to all (human) experiencers of qualities.

(1) One kind of quality of which I have experience comprises the qualities that qualify my own actions: my grace as a I dance, my gentleness as I speak, my efficiency as I work. In this category also belong those qualities which, while ostensi-

38

bly attributed to me, my body, or my mind, are in fact thus indirectly attributed to acts, or collections of acts, of mine. Thus, the experience I may have of my own incisiveness of mind is the experiences I have of the incisiveness of (many) mental acts of mine that form a pattern. Similarly, my experience of my own bodily grace can only be the experiences of the gracefulness of one or more of my own bodily actions. Summary judgments like "I am incisive," "I am graceful," or "I am honest" may or may not *mean* more than that I act incisively, gracefully, or honestly on a set of occasions. But my *experience* of such qualities of mine can be nothing but my experiences of the qualities of particular acts of mine.

Excluded from this category are such qualities as, say, the roughness (to the touch) of my beard, the smoothness of my skin, the nobility of my jawline, the elegant length of my fingers, and the sturdiness of my legs. For the latter sort of qualities are not interpretable as qualifying *acts* of mine. Such qualities as the nobility in the carriage of my head, the elegance of my hand when it is in motion, and the animation of my eyes are included here, however, because they are just the nobility of the way I *carry* my head, the elegance of the way I *move* my hands, and the animated way I *use* my eyes when I glance at you, smile at you, tease you, react to your news, and so forth. Similarly, the sturdiness of my stride belongs in this category even if it may, in certain cases, depend upon the sturdiness of my legs, which does not belong.

I also include my health (healthiness) in this category. My reason for doing so is that my health is completely reducible, not precisely to the way in which *I* do anything, but to the way in which parts and systems of my body *function*, namely, healthily. If we were comfortable with the ancient idea of the soul as a living body's functioning at all levels of its capability, we would have no trouble seeing my healthiness in the same category as my grace, my kindness, and my imaginativeness. For it, like the others, is a way in which *this* soul (myself) does some of the things of which it is capable. Think of this category if you can, then, as consisting of qualities insofar as they are experienced by a (human) soul as belonging to an act or acts of that soul or to an act or acts of a part or parts of it.

(2) The second category of qualities comprises qualities that are experienced by me as qualifying the acts—of just the varieties described above—of sentient beings other than myself. These sentient beings may be human or otherwise. This category also includes qualities that I experience as belonging to the acts of sentient beings in representations—in photographs, motion pictures, paintings, drawings, dramatic productions, and so forth.

(3) The third category comprises qualities insofar as an "I" experiences them as belonging to parts or aspects of "my" experienced world that are "tracks" of the acts either of "myself" or of other sentient beings. Let me explain the notion of a "track." A track can be any "object" except the act of a sentient being. A track may be an "object" produced by an act or acts of a sentient being, though it need not be. But whether it is so produced or not, it is always made to be a certain way by an act or acts of a sentient being. The way it is made to be is always describable as a quality or qualities. And what it is about the act or acts that made the track that way is always describable as a quality or qualities of the track itself.

Examples of tracks will be helpful. A graceful motion of your hand through the sand can leave a graceful mark in the sand. Move energetically through the dark with a Fourth of July sparkler in your hand and leave energetic streaks of light on the night. Have the dancers move intricately around the

Maypole, and the ribbons in their hands will weave intricate patterns.

Perhaps more important and interesting examples of tracks occur in art and artlike constructions. The sentimentality in a poem, the directness in a portrait, the anger in a diatribe written two millenia ago, the wit in an opera, the boldness in the interior design of a room, often qualify tracks. They do so under two conditions: (a) that they qualify "artistic acts" detectable in the work itself, and (b) that such artistic acts resemble in those qualities actual "originating acts" of the artists done at the time the work was actually produced.[29] Such tracks, moreover, are not confined to art. All elaborate verbal productions, especially—including historical writing, other types of scholarship, natural and social science, and philosophy—can exhibit tracks that are qualified by, for example, boldness, imaginativeness, inventiveness, intellectual elegance, patience, responsibility, or moral earnestness.[30]

(4) The fourth category of qualities is parasitic upon the last two. Qualities in this category are those experienced by a given person as belonging to an "object" of any sort, but only under the following conditions: (a) the "object" is experienceable by that person as in some respect or respects like either some act of a sentient being—human or nonhuman, real or fantastic—some representation of an act of such a being, or some track of such a being; and (b) the experienced quality is experienceable by that person as belonging to that act or track. "Objects" so experienced are characteristically natural "objects" that are not acts, but they may also be artificial or artistic "objects" or aspects of such "objects." They may also be aspects or parts of sentient beings that are not, and are not reducible to, their acts.

Some examples of seeing inanimate "objects" as acts, real or represented: El Capitan's boldness might be seen as if the rock were standing boldly at the entrance to Yosemite Valley. A calm sea might be seen as if it were calmly resting. In the delicate rustling of the leaves of a tree we might see the tree as delicately moving its limbs. The happy, open vista that spreads before us as the cloud uncovers the sun we might experience as if the landscape were suddenly smiling in a happy, open way. Other examples: The healthy and vigorous tree we can fairly easily see as a higher-order being whose constituent parts, like our own in health, are functioning healthily and whose branches "reach" vigorously for the light and air. Even the clarity of a color or a light source we can experience as the vivid "assertion" of some living energy. And the same is true of purity or brilliance of sound, or the strength or vivacity of the characteristic smells and tastes of things.[31]

Some examples of seeing "objects" as tracks: The subtlety of the changes in sunset colors might be seen as the effect of subtlety in the *coloring* of the sunset. Delicacy in the form of an insect might be seen as the mark of delicacy in the *formation* of that insect. The wonderful harmony of color in the chaparral landscape might be experienced as the effect of a harmonious *blending* of colors. The boldness of El Capitan might be seen as the result of a bold *shaping* and *placing* of that rock. The sea's calm can be experienced as the effect of a calming *touch* on the waters; the water's turbulence in the cove might be seen as the track of a turbulent *stirring* of the waves. So, too, can a dancer's elegant neckline seem like the effect of an elegant *sculpturing*; the lyrical lines of her body can appear to be lyrically *drawn* or *contoured*.

It is important to notice in my description of this category the modality of the "experience." I do not claim that qualities in this category are all and always in fact *experienced* as belonging—even "as it were"—to acts, represented acts, or tracks.

They may be. But it may also be that only in retrospect, on reflection, or on reconsideration are they judged, by the experiencing persons, to be *experienceable* by themselves in those ways.

Now, this category is important in that upon the qualities in it depends a great deal of beauty, especially natural beauty. The only natural beauty that does not depend upon this category of qualities is that which belongs to acts of nonhuman sentient beings and noncultural acts of human beings. In fact, some people might say that many of the qualities that we often attribute to animal behavior—such as sadness or cleverness—are really only the result of "anthropomorphic" imagining. These persons would thus place such experienced qualities in the fourth category rather than in the second. Other persons, with generally antiexpressive views of art, might tend to see many qualities in art, not as *actual* qualities of tracks, but at most as being *experienceable* as qualities of tracks. Such persons, then, would want to place many of the aesthetic qualities of art in this category instead of the third category.[32]

The extent and significance of this fourth category may remind us, incidentally, of a general implication of "the aesthetic point of view," if this phrase is taken to denote an interest in, as well as a tendency to seek out and find, beauty of all kinds. Taking the aesthetic point of view, as both its friends and foes have often more or less explicitly recognized, implies an ability and willingness to experience the world in large part as either animated, the product of animation, or both.[33]

10. *Sameness of Quality: A Problem*

The above four categories show us, incidentally, that qualities, as a class of properties, can belong to an enormous range of "objects": natural and artificial, human and nonhuman, mental and nonmental, real and unreal. But not only are there great differences among the kinds of "objects" to which qualities in general can belong; there are also great differences among the "objects" to which a single quality can belong. The last fact is reflected in, though it is not identical with, the fact that the same quality-words apply to "objects" in all four of the above categories. I can jump boldly into the pond to rescue the puppy, as can you; I can boldly add a streak of brilliant red to a pastel painting and produce thereby a bold red streak on a pastel ground; El Capitan can stand boldly at the entrance to Yosemite Valley. I could adduce other examples without improving the point. There probably are, indeed, few quality-words that cannot be applied to "objects" in all four of the categories distinguished earlier.

Some readers are sure to object that the use of the same quality-word across categories does not reflect sameness of quality across those categories. For the differences between, say, boldness in my puppy rescue, in the red streak, and in El Capitan seem clearly too great; these diverse "objects" therefore do not seem to share a quality that could be reflected in the single quality-word. If they do not, then the single word used across categories is explainable in terms of metaphorical extension. Since we can explain the fact that a single quality-word can designate qualities that seem quite different by resorting to the notion of metaphor, the objection goes, we need not admit that the same quality often, or ever, appears in highly diverse "objects." Such an objection suggests, then, that this version of the one-and-many problem is only a function of the way qualities are classified by language and does not therefore constitute a problem in the phenomena themselves. I think the suggestion is wrong, and I shall explain why.

Such facile talk about metaphorical uses of quality-words

presupposes that there is a class of cases of qualities to which any given quality-term is *literally* applicable. It further presupposes that in at least some of these cases, the quality is "the same" quality as in other of these cases. I want to argue, however, that even among "core" cases of a quality there is often, if not always, at least as much prima facie diversity as there appears to be across categories of "objects." Let us look at a characteristic case of a quality belonging to a complex "object," namely, a whole human body in action. To simplify the analysis let us imagine that body "frozen" at a single instant of time. Such imagining has, in fact, already been done for us millions of times—in paintings, photographs, and sculpture. So let us look at the quality of what I shall call "Olympian imperturbability" in the big bronze Poseidon of the fifth century B.C. from Artemisium, now in the National Museum at Athens (the one with the arms outstretched and with the about-to-be-hurled weapon and the eyeballs missing). Now, although the figure is represented, apparently, at a peak of strenuous activity, there is no sense of strain and no emotion. There is no eagerness to succeed in the action and no fear of failure; the figure exhibits a sense of unquestioned and easy power. There is every sense of the "rightness" of the act, in both the physical and the moral sense. This complex quality also seems to pervade the figure. But it shows especially in the serious but composed face, in the powerful, flexed but untense muscles, in the graceful lines and the open, undefended stance of the nude body.

The sort of overall attribution of a quality I have made to this represented figure is a common kind of attribution. And *if* we disregard the fact that the figure is an artistic representation of a man(-god), it is as clear a case of nonmetaphorical attribution as we are likely to discover (which is not yet to say

45

that it *is* nonmetaphorical). Nevertheless, it raises in a pregnant way the problem of "sameness" and "difference" of quality. For while, on the one hand, the whole figure seems to
instantiate the single quality of "Olympian imperturbability,"
that very instance of the quality appears to consist, on the other
hand, of instances of a quality (or qualities) that may or may
not be the same as that Olympian imperturbability. As I have
analyzed the figure, its overall quality seems to consist of the
"seriousness" and "composure" of the face, the "easy power" of
the muscles, the "grace" of the body lines, and the "openness"
of the body's stance. Are all these qualities of aspects of the
figure just the "same" Olympian imperturbability, described
in different terms and instantiated in various "parts" of the
figure? Are they like the greenness of the four quadrants of a
tablecloth that is overall a uniform green? In favor of this hypothesis is (1) the intuition that the Olympian imperturbability of the whole "shows in" the described qualities of its aspects; (2) the fact that "Olympian imperturbability" can
equally well describe the face, the muscles, the body lines, and
the stance; and (3) the fact that were any of the latter aspects
of the figure lacking in their qualities, there would be *less* of
the quality of Olympian imperturbability in the whole figure,
which implies that the qualities of the parts are incremental
constituents of the quality of the whole.

But against the hypothesis is the consideration that the differences between imperturbability in the face, in the muscles,
in the stance of the body, and in the lines of the body appear
to be, when considered "abstractly," at least as great as that
between the imperturbability of the figure and that, say, of the
becalmed Adriatic Sea. If the former differences seem smaller,
one can think, it is only because the "objects" bearing the imperturbability in the former cases are more obviously intercon-

nected. For the imperturbability certainly does *not* show up in all aspects of the bronze figure in just the way the green of the tablecloth shows up in each of the quadrants. One could, after all, recognize the green equally well in a quadrant that had been cut off and widely separated from the whole cloth. Of course, it would be impossible so to separate the body stance and lines from the whole figure (though not to separate the face from the figure). Still, we can *imagine* the "same stance" in a figure with different muscles, lines, and facial expressions that would not be imperturbable at all. The "same" facial expression on a different body in a different position doing a different thing might show, not imperturbability, but pensiveness or even vacuity.

Finally, another thought experiment can convince us that, however similar to or different from one another the qualities of the various aspects of the figure in bronze are, they are no more or less so than any of them are similar to or different from qualities belonging to "objects" in the other categories distinguished earlier. Imagine creating a scene in a film around a figure with just the Olympian imperturbability of our Poseidon figure. Imagine the scene as one in which the god's effort is not to hurl a weapon but to exert some other divine power to bring the sea back under his influence by becalming it. And imagine the sea before him gradually taking on that "same" Olympian imperturbability we see in the face and body of the divine figure, while behind him we see great austere bluffs overlooking the sea, like great stone faces of the gods themselves, with the "same" imperturbable look to them, and above we see the clouds recede, revealing, like a veritable image of the god's own face, a sky of the clearest, deepest, and serenest blue.

47

11. *Sameness of Quality: A Solution*

The result of this discussion is that if we experience sameness of quality at all among different "objects," there is no reason why we cannot experience sameness in quality, in general if not in every particular case, across all the four categories distinguished earlier. On the other hand, even clearly and indubitably experienced sameness of quality can seem, upon analysis, to be groundless. But if so, what is the correct determination of sameness among qualities in our world?

The question is not simply, or even primarily, of abstract metaphysical interest. It is centrally relevant to the experience of enjoyment and important therefore in constructing a theory of enjoyment. What I enjoy at a time is, generally, what I want to continue experiencing and what I would want to experience again. That being so, a certain part of my practical life is ruled by my past (including my immediately past) enjoyments. I thus make all kinds of daily choices on the assumption that I am able to determine when an experience of a quality is an experience of the "same" quality I enjoyed once and am seeking again. Our experience, furthermore, assures us that we not only can but do make such determinations. Moreover, we make them quite reliably; that is, we are regularly satisfied in our quest for further enjoyments of a particular kind, and when we are frustrated, it is *hardly ever* because we are unsure whether the experiences of quality we are having are the same as what we were hoping for. (When we are frustrated, in fact, it is usually because we know for certain that they are *not* the same.) Finally, we make such determinations, generally speaking, without effort, without deliberation, and in the twinkling of an eye. As theorists of enjoyment we need, then, not only some principle of sameness of quality, but one that will explain the above facts about our experience—as enjoyers—in determining sameness of quality.

Fortunately, however, the principle we require does not need to be a principle determining sameness of quality from *every* point of view. It need only be a principle rich enough to determine sameness among the qualities in our world, that is, as they appear to us in our experiences of them. For it is only in this respect—whether or not there *is* any *other* respect—that qualities matter to our enjoyment. Notice, too, that our principle need not be powerful enough to allow us—either as theorists or as enjoyers—to say, at a given moment, of *all* the qualities in a given person's complete world of qualities, which are the same as which. On the contrary, the principle that we require for a theory of enjoyment need be no more powerful than what we require as enjoyers. In particular, it need tell us only which of a (relatively) few qualities *at hand* and *in mind* are the same as which others. And, of course, once again we are lucky in not needing for present purposes a more potent principle of sameness, since neither we as theorizers nor we as enjoyers are in a position to survey panoramically, as it were, the whole of anyone's world of qualities (including our own) with an eye to pigeonholing all the qualities in it correctly.

I offer then the following principle of sameness of quality. I mean for it to apply to all human beings and to all the qualities in their world of qualities: *If any qualities P and Q, of which a human being S has experiences, seem to S to be the same quality, then they are the same quality.*

Notice, first, that this principle gives only a sufficient condition for sameness. It thus leaves it open whether that condition, or some others, or none at all, are necessary conditions of sameness of quality. The modesty of the principle in this respect also leaves undetermined, in accord with my earlier expressed metaphysical agnosticism, a legion of issues. The principle leaves it open, for example, whether two or more human beings can, or ever do, have experiences of the same qualities. It leaves undetermined whether any quality experienced by a human being even "exists" independently of that experience. Notice, second, that the principle of sameness has no companion principle of *difference* of quality. I present no such principle because I know no convincing one and because my present purposes do not require one. It may well be that it is impossible to state an adequate principle of difference of quality without being clear about the necessary conditions of sameness of quality. It might even be that, ordinary intuition heavily to the contrary, there *are* no differences among any of the qualities experienced by human beings. But whatever may turn out to be the truth status of such an apparently far-fetched proposition, it is not prejudiced by the above principle of sameness.

But what are the arguments in favor of my principle of sameness of quality? I hope it is clear that I think there is no question of this principle of sameness of quality, or of any other, being simply true or false. Indeed, one of the results of my analysis of the *problem* of sameness of quality in the preceding section is that there are no clear "facts" of the matter with respect to sameness and difference of quality. If we need such a principle for theoretical purposes, then, we must *adopt* a principle. There are three reasons in favor of adopting the principle I have set down. (I have not, so far, been able to think of any plausible reasons *not* to adopt it.) First, the world of qualities of any human being includes, prominently, experiences such as memories, fantasies, and images of the external real world as well as of made-up worlds. It also includes experiences of private feelings, emotions, and sensations. The qualities experienced in such experiences, *as* they are experienced, are not accessible to beings other than the ones in whose experiences they appear. Consequently the only human beings capable of determining sameness among those appearing qualities are the ones to whom they appear. More "public" principles of sameness among qualities would very likely leave many such privately accessible qualities simply indeterminate with respect to sameness, either among themselves or with others. Again, such a result might well be acceptable and even desirable from some points of view. But recall that one motive for being concerned with sameness of quality is that determinations of such sameness are important to enjoyers in their enjoyments. And it is precisely in enjoyment that an enjoyer's "private" ideas of qualities are crucially important. Moreover, determinations of sameness are made, reliably and easily, by these same enjoyers, whether their enjoyed experiences are "private" or not. The principle of sameness I have adopted accounts for this fact. The third reason is that the authority that the above principle of sameness gives to the enjoyers in determining sameness of quality in their world of qualities matches the authority that the enjoyers have with respect to their own enjoyment. Since an enjoyer is in an especially authoritative position to know whether she is enjoying something and, especially, what it is about that something she is enjoying, then since enjoyment depends crucially upon identifying "the same" qualities in the enjoyer's experience, the enjoyer ought to be in at least an equally authoritative position in making the latter identifications.

Now, I do not intend this last reason to imply that in all cases the enjoyer has the last word about *whether* he enjoys a thing or not. I do not believe that is so; sometimes others can tell better than we whether we enjoy an activity or condition or not. This is especially true when we have reason to deceive ourselves about our own enjoyments. Nevertheless, public appearances of enjoyment are indeterminate in a great many cases when *we* know, as surely as we know anything, that we enjoy a thing. More importantly, however, when it comes to analyzing what we enjoy *about* a thing, it is very difficult for an external observer and considerably easier for us to determine that. *Our* word here therefore counts for practically everything.

TUMESCENCES OF
THE SOUL

The above principle of sameness of quality does not entail or, if carefully applied, result in randomness, irrationality, or even unmanageable irregularity. Human beings being pretty much alike in their physical makeup and operations, we should find in the realm of experiencing qualities, when we assume the above principle, generally what we in fact find: a fair amount of sharing of enjoyments, a fair amount of communicating thoughts about qualities via language, and a fair amount of reliable prediction of one another's enjoyments in particular cases, even when we do not share those enjoyments. In this and succeeding sections I shall explain that regularity. In particular, I shall argue that there are certain regularities in the ways that qualities seem the same to us, and develop accounts of *why* we determine sameness in these ways. None of my claims will be based merely on an analysis of concepts; they are grounded, rather, on introspectively gained experience.[34] Obviously, I use my own experience and present an analysis of that; indeed, much of the analysis of this book is similarly grounded. But I assume that I share the forms of my experience with all beings likely to be my readers and therefore that general claims based on an analysis of such experience can be tested, though in ways that are too complex to explore here and that are, in any case, beside the present point.

The ways I shall describe of determining sameness among qualities are *forms* of experience. As such they do not determine the content of that experience. My claims in the following pages, therefore, are consistent with the possibility that many, or even all, of the actual qualities that any particular person experiences are experienced, indeed even experience*able*, only by that person.

My principal claim is that *qualities that seem the same to us do so because we can and do experience them as parts of certain more complex experiences, which I call "expansion experiences."* I shall leave the meaning of this claim unexplicated until I have introduced the concept of "expansion experiences." Although such experiences are quite common, virtually nothing has been done to describe and analyze them, to sort them out and categorize them, and to assess their importance for philosophy.[35] Now, expansion experiences, as they come to us, vary immensely among themselves. Accordingly, I shall introduce expansion experiences by describing their varieties. I intend in these descriptions (1) to remind readers of certain common kinds of experiences, (2) to describe salient features of such experiences suggestive of a general characterization of expansion experiences, and (3) to show, in particular, how the character of these experiences is such as to render peculiarly explicable the fact that part of what we experience in them is a *sameness* of quality amidst an apparent *diversity* of quality.

13. *Arousals*

I shall call expansion experiences of one type "arousals," or "arousal experiences." The objects of such experiences are, characteristically, *our own* emotions, moods, feelings, or sentiments and anything else sufficiently like these. But the experiences I am calling arousals are distinguishable in three ways from the general class of experiences of our own emotions, moods, feelings, and sentiments. First, they are experiences of these things from the "inside" only; they are not experiences of our own behavior that we might have by seeing, hearing, or touching ourselves as we are expressing or acting out such emotions, moods, feelings, or sentiments. In Humean terms, arousals are constituted entirely by "ideas of reflection," not by "ideas of sensation." Second, in the interest of my overall presentation of expansion experiences, I limit arousals to our "internal" experiences of our own emotions, moods, feelings, or sentiments insofar as the latter are not (or are not yet) expressed or manifested or are not, at any rate, expressed or manifested "externally" in any more or less voluntary actions. And, third, arousals are experiences of ourselves *coming to have* an emotion, mood, feeling, or sentiment, whether because of some external occurrence alone or because of our own mere thought of an actual or possible external occurrence, in such a way that the emotion, mood, feeling, or sentiment in us "grows" greater, stronger, or more intense. Let us consider four examples.

(a) Imagine reading an (unjustly, of course) accusatory letter to yourself detailing the alleged offenses you gave to the writer and the dire consequences that shall be visited upon you. In a short time you go from not being angry to a state in which you feel anger in virtually every part of yourself. The feeling may start in your face, around your mouth and nose, and spread up to your eyes and the top of your head, simultaneously descending to your jaws, rapidly then to your thorax, and from there laterally through your shoulders to your arms and downward through your abdomen to your lower extremities, until you are "burning" all over with rage. And all of this *before* you spring up angrily, crumple the paper fiercely, and kick the wall.

(b) Imagine leafing idly through some snapshots and coming unexpectedly upon one of a long gone lover, a reminder of loss and the passage of time. Melancholy seeps into you until you are saturated with it. You feel it first in your mouth and jaw; it rises to your eyes, then descends through your neck and shoulders, down through your arms into your gut and through your legs into your very toes. And this all happens *before* your reveries on other losses begin, *before* you rise from your chair slowly and drag yourself listlessly through some small chores, and so on.

(c) Imagine having weighed for days the decision whether to bring up before your faculty colleagues a controversial issue, certain to bring disapproval—even wrath—down upon you, even though you feel ethically bound to raise the subject. But as you sit, refuting to yourself, one by one, the *moral* objections to bringing up the issue, so that finally your ethical course seems to you unequivocal, you feel a certain feeling of boldness creep over you, into your chest and shoulders, up to your jaw and eyes, down through your spine, until you feel yourself filled with resolve, in the face of the risks, to do what your intuition and your reason tell you is right.

(d) You may have avoided even thinking seriously about the awful disease, preferring to imagine it as something that affects and can affect only "other people." And when an acquaintance is stricken, you persist in the denial. You do not visit him, in large part out of fear of witnessing its ravages and in part out of a fear—though an irrational one—of exposing yourself. Finally, though, a mutual friend persuades you to make a visit, and when you see the once lively and robust figure reduced to an aged, shrunken waste, you melt completely. Compassion invades you, first through your eyes, and from there in a rush throughout your body you feel your muscles "soften" and "melt" and you are hurrying to embrace him and break down in sobs.

In (a) through (d) I have described four "arousals" in comparatively raw, or preanalytic, terms. In order to see how they can perform the function I am claiming for them, we must be able to construe these arousals in the primitive terms of my theoretical analysis—in particular, in terms of "experiences" of "qualities" of "objects." Let us, therefore, construe the quality in (a) as anger (angriness), in (b) as melancholy or sadness, in (c) as boldness or courage (courageousness), and in (d) as compassion (compassionateness). The mode of experience in which all these qualities are apprehended is "feeling." Thus in the examples we *feel* the anger, the melancholy, the boldness, or the compassion as it wells up in us, creeps over us, suffuses us, rushes through us. But what are the "objects" of these felt qualities? The obvious answer with respect to (a) through (d) is "ourselves." In these experiences we feel *ourselves* to be angry, sad, bold, or compassionate. Such an answer, however, even though true, will not allow us to make as fine-grained, as general, and ultimately therefore as useful a theoretical analysis of expansion experiences as I am seeking. But what other answer can we give that is both true—or at least reasonable—and theoretically useful?

The correct answer is—in a phrase—"act-beginnings." In arousals, we feel the anger, melancholy, and so forth of acts of our own, but acts that are not overt, that are not, for the most part, even accomplished—acts that are so close to their beginnings in our nervous systems that it is only we, for the most part, who can detect them at all. Consider:

(a′) Before my face actually or recognizably hardens in anger, I can feel its muscles begin to stiffen. Before the curse contorts my mouth, I can feel the impulse to snarl already around my lips. Before my scowl occurs I can detect feelings around my eyes and brow. Before I rise and storm about, I feel my heart beating more heavily and my blood flowing more quickly.

(b′) Before I weep, I feel a rush—of what? water? blood?—

behind my eyes. Before I slump in melancholy, I feel the muscles of my face, shoulders, and back begin to relax.

(c′) Before I stride boldy in, head high, back straight, I feel the muscles of these parts beginning to stiffen.

(d′) Before I rush to my friend in a compassionate embrace, I feel the beginnings of the muscle relaxation that such an embrace—that is, one with true feeling in it—requires.

I feel the feelings described in (a′) through (d′) as "parts"—in particular, the "early" or "beginning" parts—of the overt acts that manifest my anger, melancholy, boldness, or compassion. But the same sorts of feelings—of subtle muscle tightenings and relaxations, of fluids flowing or beginning to flow, of temperature risings or fallings—may be present whether or not they are followed by overt actions manifesting the pertinent emotion or mood. And just as it is in or through such feelings that we feel our own anger, melancholy, boldness, or compassion before we express it, it is, I am claiming, in and and through such feelings that we feel our own anger, melancholy, boldness, or compassion even when we do not express it.[36] This claim, incidentally, provides one kind of explanation of why we can feel emotions, moods, feelings, and sentiments in various parts of our bodies and, indeed, throughout our bodies: different expressive acts require different muscles and physiological conditions. Moreover, most emotions, moods, and so forth may be expressed in complex acts or series of acts involving the whole body.

Even if my claim above is true, however, it will not do to attribute the qualities of angriness, sadness, boldness, or compassion in arousals like (a) through (d) to *incipient acts* of our own.[37] For only in some cases does our sense of muscle movements, temperature changes, and fluid flows betoken *actual* acts in their incipience—namely, in those cases in which we go on to manifest our moods, emotions, and so forth in overt actions. I therefore introduce the term "act-beginning." The term does not imply that there is an act of which that to which it refers is the beginning, but neither does it imply the contradictory. I propose, then, that in arousals, the mood, emotion, feeling, or sentiment that is felt be construed as a quality of various act-beginnings in the person "aroused." The concept of an act-beginning will play an important role in the analyses of expansion experiences other than arousals.

14. *Arousals and Motions of the Soul*

Arousal experiences confront us with a problem of the one-and-many. We feel our anger, melancholy, boldness, or compassion—successively or simultaneously—in many ways and in many "parts" within us. And yet, in a given arousal experience, it is clearly the "same" anger, melancholy, boldness, or compassion that we feel. In terms of my analytic construal of arousals, the latter consist of many experiences of the "same" quality possessed by different "objects," that is, different act-beginnings.[38] But the problem here is a problem only because the various manifestations of the "same" quality in a single arousal are so various as to raise the question of *how* they can be seen as the same at all. Why do I feel that same emotional quality (which I call my anger) in the merest beginning of the pull of my facial muscles, the incipient rise (of blood?) up to my scalp, the commotion in my throat and thorax, the agitation spreading through my limbs? The question is no less insistent with respect to arousals of melancholy, of boldness, of compassion, or of anything else.

Let us not misconstrue the problem. The problem is not why I *call* all of these various inner manifestations by the same

61

name, say, "anger," or "melancholy." *That* is a problem in linguistics, say, or in the philosophy of language. The problem I am trying to identify logically precedes the linguistic problem. It is the problem of what is *included in the phenomenon* that presents itself as a candidate for some linguistic labeling or other. The problem is analogous to the problem of why I treat my views of the wine glass on my desk from different perspectives—even very different perspectives, such as from underneath, through the glass top of the desk—as examples of seeing that wine glass. The answer seems to have little directly to do with my linguistic expertise regarding the phrase "wine glass." For the same problem arises with respect to objects whose names (in any language) I do not know. Similarly, the one-and-many problem remains in arousal experiences even if, as frequently happens, there is no standard name for my mood, emotion, or sentiment and even if I do not know, moreover, how to describe it (to your or my satisfaction) in nonstandard terms.

Assuming the problem is adequately clear, I turn now to the solution. We might initially hope that we could solve the problem by some "principle of association"; that is, we might look, in all arousal experiences, for some unambiguously unitary element with which all manifestations of the aroused emotion, mood, sentiment, or feeling are associated in some specific way. And we might find such a solution if, for example, for each arousable emotion, mood, sentiment, or feeling there were a simple "core" element, a simple feeling or sensation, say, that we could identify as the very emotion E itself, or the very mood M itself. But there seems (to me) and has seemed (to many) to be nothing like that.

Suppose, however, we were to suggest the more sophisticated notion that the variety of inner manifestations are all related to some *cause* of the arousal itself, whether that cause be some objective circumstance or some thought of our own. The hypothesis would then be that, conscious of the cause, we associate the various manifestations of the aroused emotion, mood, sentiment, or feeling with that cause as its effects and hence perceive them as manifesting the "same" quality. There are probably many arguments—complex and subtle ones— against this hypothesis. But I think one simple one makes pursuing any of the others pointless. Whereas many emotions, moods, sentiments, and other arousable feelings have, when aroused in us, definite and clearly recognized causes, others simply have not. This is especially true, of course, for moods, since they typically have no *objects*. They may therefore arise in us without an accompanying thought of an object and hence without a cause recognizable to ourselves. I turn then to my own solution to the one-and-many problem in arousal experiences.

There are characteristic metaphors we reach for to describe our arousals: anger may *surge* through me or *burn* through me; melancholy may *seep* into me and finally *overwhelm* me, or it may invade me like a poisonous *mist*; *waves* of compassion may *wash over me*; a feeling of boldness may gradually *fill* me. Figures of water dominate, but they are mixed with figures of fire and air. The generic metaphor is that in an arousal the mood, emotion, feeling, or sentiment *spreads* in me, through me, or over me. Analysis of the idea of liquid, gaseous, or pyric spread yields four factors the presence of which in arousals is corroborated by our "raw" experience of arousals. Call these factors "motion," "increase," "continuity," and "self-generation."

"Motion" indicates the dynamic character of the arousal experience—the experience we have of things moving in us. But, more specifically, it indicates the experience we have that the particular emotion, mood, feeling, or sentiment being aroused is itself moving. Perhaps it is the—explicit or implicit—sense we have in an arousal of bodily fluids, organs, and muscles literally moving that, in part, *gives rise* to this other experienced motion, but I do not want to confuse the two. I use the term "motion" to refer to the experience of the aroused emotion, mood, or sentiment *itself* moving through us.[39] This factor is experienced by me preanalytically as the emotion, mood, or sentiment itself seeming to move through me as from one "part" of me to another. In terms of my analysis of these experiences into *qualities* experienced in various act-beginnings, however, this "motion" becomes one of a quality proceeding "within" me from one "object" to another, for example, from one act-beginning "located" around my jaw muscles to another "located" around my tear glands. Furthermore, as the scare quotes around "motion," "parts," and "location" indicate, some of the ordinary *spatial* connotations of these terms do not apply. In particular, these "parts" and "locations" are such *in our experience*; they may or may not correspond to any parts of, or locations in, our bodies. As far as our experience of them is concerned, therefore, they are not identifiable in terms of geometrical coordinates. Similarly, the "motion" essential to arousal is not describable in geometrical terms. Nor is it, or any of its properties, arithmetically measurable. We might wonder whether there *exists* any "motion" of such a sort. As with other matters concerning the metaphysics of qualities, however, I choose to remain for the present agnostic on the answer to this question. For it is irrelevant to my point. Whether anything answers *in reality* to the sort of "motion" we experience in arousals does not affect (what I take to be) the *fact* that such "motion" is a salient feature of such experiences.

The second factor—"increase"—derives from and qualifies the first. We can, in fact, "read it off" the generic metaphor of "spread." The "motion" experienced in an arousal is not simply of a quality *"moving"* from "object" to "object" but of a quality *"spreading"* from "object" to "object." There is thus, as in the "spreading" of water, fire, or mist, the sense of "covering more territory," the sense that within a defined space there is *more* of that which is moving. Thus in arousals (a) through (d) above, we feel progressively more angry, more melancholy, bolder, and more compassionate.

The third factor in our experience of arousals is the "continuity" of its peculiar kind of "motion." When things like fluids, fires, and gases spread, they so do, not necessarily *evenly*, with respect to speed or degree of saturation, but nevertheless with both spatial and temporal continuity. Spatially there are no "gaps," and temporally there are no complete halts. The spread is typically from place to contiguous place. This is true also of the emotion, mood, sentiment, or feeling in an arousal. Whatever the *cause* of this feature of arousals may be, the experiential fact is that the "spread" of emotion or mood through us proceeds "without gaps." My anger or sadness does not seem to me to "jump around" in me from one distant part of me directly to another, nor does it appear to overtake me in "lurchy" steps. It is this fact of our experience, I take it, that makes metaphors of fluid motion so apt in describing our arousals.

The fourth important factor in arousal experiences is "self-generation." Whatever in a given arousal is in "motion" seems to us to be the immediate source of its being in motion. Once the anger or melancholy is "in motion" it seems to *propel itself* through us, and it seems in need of nothing other than itself to spread. This fact, too, seems to justify the metaphor of fluid, gaseous, or pyric spread. As we experience them spreading, water, mist, and fire often seem to move *of themselves.* Of course, this is not always so. Sometimes we also experience the wind blowing the fire or the mists, the brooms or shovels moving the water. But more often we do *not* see such agencies, and then the experience is of fire begetting fire, wet here making wet there, misty air producing more misty air. It makes no difference to such experiences *as such* that we know that there *must* be other agencies at work than mere fire, water, and mist in producing *more* of the same. The experience is that these things *spread themselves*. Just so, our experience in an arousal of anger is that one "part" of us catches anger from another "part" until we are completely "burnt up." In an arousal of sadness, the melancholy in one "part" of us seems to seep into the next "part" and so on until we are saturated with it.

My claim is that the four factors just described can solve the one-and-many problem manifested in arousals. In particular, they are especially well suited to explain how we experience all the (ostensibly) various qualities manifested in an arousal as *the same quality*. First, the factor of "motion" accentuates, of course, the *diversity* of manifestations of the aroused emotion or mood. But, since the "motion" is experienced as "continuous," the *unity* of that which is in "motion" is thereby emphasized. More particularly, the fourth factor—the experience that what is in "motion" generates itself in that very "motion"—would tend to make us see not merely a unity but indeed an identity among the various stages of the thing in motion. But the "thing" in motion is precisely the emotion or mood considered as a quality, and the various stages of the "motion" are the various instantiations of the quality in succeeding act-beginnings throughout the course of an arousal. Finally, the second factor I identified was that the aroused "thing" *increases* by virtue of its "motion," but that this "motion" itself is not determinable in geometrical or numerical terms. Thus the "increase" that we experience in an arousal cannot be a quantitative increase. Such an increase, therefore, is eminently suited to the sort of thing that is being increased in an arousal. For the emotions, moods, feelings, or sentiments in arousal experiences can be construed precisely as qualities, and it is a defining feature of qualities that they are subject to increase or decrease by degrees that are not numerically determinable. What more plausible cause, then, of seeing qualities—which are by nature things of nonquantitative degree—as *the same quality* than the experience of seeing them as the subject of a continuous self-generating "expansion" that is *also* not quantitatively describable?

15. *Preparations*

"Preparations" are like arousals in that they are experienced internally and are accompanied by little or no externally detectable action of our own. Furthermore, they typically are, though they need not be, preludes to manifesting a corresponding quality in our own external acts. Now, although these "corresponding qualities" *may be* qualities of emotion or mood, they may also be purely qualities of movement—gracefulness, delicacy, firmness, and so forth. Such experiences characteristically occur in contexts of play, of drama, of theater, or of pretense. But they may also occur in circumstances when it is important to summon one's resources to act in such a way that one's whole body manifests a certain quality. Thus too, preparations differ from arousals in that one may quite deliberately have them; they do not, generally speaking, simply wash over us. A preparation, then, is precisely the result of this summoning up of a certain quality within us, characteristically with a view to preparing ourselves to act with that quality permeating our total behavior. Thus:

(a) The dance instructor is trying to get us to move with a large sweeping quality (after all, the music *is* Strauss), and I'm not getting it, mostly because I'm still having trouble remembering the sequence of steps. But last time I was almost there, and I think now that I've got the concept at least. As my turn comes up, I try to think the sweeping quality into my muscles before I go out onto the floor. I feel it in my neck and shoulders, let the feeling flow into my arms, press it through my torso into my legs—so that when I actually have to *do* the dance, some "momentum," as it were, from the quality I feel inside me will carry over into my actual movement.

(b) Or imagine a situation, say hearing a prowler in the house at night, in which it is crucial that if you move at all, you do so very lightly. Even before you move, you "gather that lightness together," as it were, within yourself. You feel the lightness first perhaps in your fingertips and feet, but from there it travels up your limbs to shoulder and abdomen, and at last you feel it in your chest.

How can this happen? We can feel such qualities "within" us and without moving our bodies (or at least without moving them very much) in an externally detectable way, it seems to me, because of very subtle impulses that we sense successively "in" various of our muscles.[40] And these impulses feel, at least, precisely like impulses to move with those muscles in specific ways, ways that will *manifest* the qualities that we experience as "within" us. Even more explicitly in preparations than in arousals, then, we experience certain qualities within us as attached to act-beginnings. And the "movement" of the qualities within us, then, can be easily interpreted as the progressive instantiation of more and more act-beginnings "located" in various parts of the body.

A problem of the one-and-many arises in preparations just as in arousals. For in preparations we feel a single quality in the whole sweep of the experience through our bodies. And yet if we consider each "part" of that sweep, it seems impossible to see how the same quality could be in all of them: the feel of the rise of the head and neck, say, is different from the lifting feel in the shoulders, as well as from the falling feel through the torso and through the thighs; the tingle of lightness in the fingers seems not the same as the lifting feel of the shoulders, the "breathy" feel in the chest, or the buoyant feel in the thighs. How then can a sweeping quality or lightness of movement be felt in all of these act-beginnings?

We might be inclined to explain it thus: In preparations, far more clearly than in arousals, the internally felt qualities are easier to "read" in the experiences themselves as qualities of act-beginnings. That is, in feeling the lightness in ourselves *before* we move lightly, it really seems to us as if we *were* moving lightly, but "to ourselves," as it were—something like talking to ourselves, without uttering sounds or moving our lips. Thus we can read all of these "inner" motions as having the *same* quality because we read them easily as act-beginnings which, if they develop into complete acts, will have precisely that quality. We borrow, as it were, the quality from the complete acts and read it into the act-beginnings.

But this explanation will not do. For it assumes, falsely, that there is no comparable problem of the one-and-many in *completed* acts exhibiting the "same" quality. Indeed, as I indicated earlier in introducing the basic issue of sameness of quality, the problem appears even in the area of human behavior that is clearly external and unambiguously qualified. The kind of behavior that can be seen as exhibiting any single quality—a sweeping quality, lightness, even anger or melancholy—can be enormously varied. And that is true not only between different cultures, or persons, or for the same person at different times, but between different aspects of the same person at (more or less) the same time. The root of the difficulty is nothing less (or more) than that the human organism is itself complex. A face differs greatly in size, shape, and relative position on the body from a torso or a finger and is neurophysiologically wired into the organism much differently. A person therefore acts differently with each part of his body even when the *same* quality is present in those acts. It is only because we are so familiar with this fact that it may seem unproblematical to us. I turn then to my own solution to the one-and-many problem in preparations. Not surprisingly, it is like the one I offered for arousals.

Preparations, unlike arousals, have not called forth from the vulgar linguistic consciousness standard metaphorical descriptions—probably because they are neither as common nor as important in our mental lives. Nevertheless, liquid or atmospheric metaphors seem as suited to preparations as to arousals. We let the feeling of passion—trying it out, as it were—surge through us. We feel the sense of delicacy or gentleness waft through us. This suggests that the same four factors I distinguished in arousal experiences can be located here as well: "motion," "increase," "continuity," and "self-generation."

The "motion" that I have in mind, in preparations as in arousals, is the sense we have that the quality we feel in us is itself moving through us. I again distinguish such "motion" from two others that occur in preparations: (1) the sense that "parts" of us—perhaps muscles, breath, fluids—are moving, even if so subtly as to be unnoticeable to others; and (2) the sense that our feeling or experience of the moving quality is itself moving. The first of these may or may not *cause* our sense that the quality is itself moving; in either case, the two experiences of motion are distinct. The second of these I shall make use of later in this study. Moreover, the motion that we attribute to qualities in preparations, though experienced by us as "in" our bodies and moving "through" them, is not describable in geometrical or numerical terms.

The factor of "increase" too applies to preparations as I have defined them. In the examples, the sense is of lightness that I feel progressively throughout *more* of my body, and hence of a greater degree of these qualities that I am progressively aware of. It should be noted, however, that neither "increase" nor "motion" need be present in preparations. I freely acknowledge that in some cases of feeling a certain quality "within" myself in preparation for *acting* with that quality, I might feel it throughout my body *all at once*; there might then be no sense of the quality spreading to all of my "parts" and no "motion" and no increase of degree. What I want to focus on, however, is precisely those preparations in which qualities are felt as *spreading through us*. While artificial, this move is nevertheless justified by my larger purpose of isolating a diverse class of expansion experiences, of which preparations are a subclass. And, as will become increasingly clear, "motion" and "increase" must be features of all expansion experiences. Yet this theoretical tactic is not a distortion of experiential facts, only a *selection* of facts. For ultimately all I want to show, by means of the phenomena of preparations, is that it is *possible* for the kinds of qualities we experience in them to be experienced as spreading through us. I do not claim that these qualities are never experienced otherwise. But then neither do I claim that the emotions, moods, and sentiments that we experience in arousals are experienced *only* in experiences of that form.

"Continuity" too characterizes preparations. Although we can often deliberately start, stop, or continue a preparation, we cannot make the feeling of a quality within us arbitrarily "jump around the body." If the feeling starts in one place, to spread throughout the body it must pass "through" intervening "parts." In some cases, as in feelings of lightness, the feeling can "start" in the fingers and then occur in the feet (act-beginnings of touching and walking, I would say). The feeling may, of course, remain only in these areas, but then there would be no preparation, as defined. If the feeling is to be felt *throughout* the body, it will then "proceed" from the fingers, the feet, or both to other parts of the body. In some cases, as in feeling a sweeping quality, the quality may be felt "more" in some parts than in others, but that is surely because sweeping qualities, unlike lightness, require a pronounced rhythm in the body that accentuates certain parts of the body. Sweeping qualities in the body by their very nature require a "heavy" or "pulling" sense in some "places" and a "light" or "rising" sense elsewhere. The heavy moments will therefore be more pronounced, but not to the obliteration of the "lighter" moments. Indeed, if we could not "read" these "lighter" moments in our preparations, they would not then be experiences *of a sweeping quality*.

We should remind ourselves at this point that "continuity," in both preparations and arousals, is the *experience* of a quality passing from "part" to "part" through *all the intervening* "parts." If we want to analyze this experience in much more detail, the experience seems to crumble in our hands. That occurs, I take it, because "parts" and "intervening," like "motion" and "increase," seem in these experiences to be spatial and yet seem not to yield to precise spatial analysis, in particular to a geometrical one. What I am claiming, then, is that in arousals, preparations, and a few other expansion experiences that I shall note, it seems to us that qualities pass through all the intervening parts in moving from one part to another. Experiences precisely of this kind of "continuity" confirm this claim. What confirms, or could confirm, our experiences of such continuity, I have no idea. But these questions are not relevant to my present project.

Finally, "self-generation" too is a factor in preparations. This is so even though often if not always the preparation experience is initiated by us quite deliberately. Once a quality is in "motion" in us, it seems to take its own course. What control over that course we have seems limited to (1) halting it and beginning it again *at the same "place"* if we like, (2) pressing the feeling deliberately into a "part" we select, and (3) deliberately *allowing* it to continue. Yet these features of control seem analogous to damming, rechanneling, and removing obstacles to a flow. Apart from these controls, the quality itself seems to generate its own increase through the body. In a preparation experience, there is no sense that we must, or do—like an occasionalist's deity—intervene at each moment to make the experience continue.

Having argued that these four factors are present in preparations as well as arousals, I now claim that they are as well suited to explain the unity in the former as in the latter, and for the same reasons. It may seem, however, that there is a better explanation of this unity in the case of preparation experiences. Preparations are experiences that we have, often deliberately and (arguably at least) always intentionally, to prepare ourselves for the manifestation in outward behavior of some particular quality. Consequently, we might suppose, all of the "parts" of such experiences are seen by us as exhibiting the "same" quality simply because we *intend* them as experiences precisely of that particular quality. And it makes no difference to this point whether the quality is *described* adequately or not. I may, after all, intend this quality that I feel surging through myself as nothing but *that quality there* (that the instructor has just been demonstrating).

To this hypothesis we may raise the following objection: In preparations I intend the overall quality of the experience either to match particular quality Q or to fall under the quality-concept Q-ness. But so to intend is already to see the whole experience as having a single quality. Thus the intention, far from explaining the relevant unity-in-variety, *presupposes* precisely that unity.

In response to such an objection, however, we might entertain a second hypothesis: My intention in preparation experiences is neither to match a quality nor to bring about a quality that falls under a quality-concept. My intention, rather, is precisely that this experience, prior to its having an overall quality, manifest a single quality that either matches Q or falls under the quality-concept Q-ness. Now, such a suggestion, of course, assumes that we can, simply by our intentions in initiating and controlling our preparation experiences, bring about in an experience a quality that it does not already possess. And yet that suggestion runs counter to our experience vis-à-vis preparations. For, after all, if we could experience such qualities simply by intending to, we could learn to move with certain qualities much more readily than we do. As it is, only when we virtually have that quality already in our muscles, as it were, can we give ourselves preparation experiences. Good intentions alone, alas, do not suffice.

More seriously, however, even an intention that *this* experience manifest a single quality already presupposes an identification of *this* experience as a *single* experience. Whence comes this experience of unity? Note, now, that my explanation of how the four factors solve the one-and-many problem in arousals and preparations also explains how each one of such experiences can be seen as a single experience. They are single precisely in virtue of exhibiting a single quality in all of their "parts." That is, the second "intentional" hypothesis requires a *prior* explanation of unity, but such an explanation is already provided by the four factors. And since the four factors can also provide a solution to the one-and-many problem, the second "intentional" hypothesis becomes completely unnecessary. I therefore propose we dismiss it and accept the four factors of "motion," "increase," "continuity," and "self-generation" as the phenomena most eminently suited to explain why we see the diverse "parts" of a preparation experience as manifesting the "same" quality.

16. *Expressions*

Arousals and preparations are, by definition, truncated experiences. For in the typical case, both arousal experiences and preparation experiences immediately precede the manifestation of their respective qualities in our outward behavior. Of such behavior, of course, we also have experience; we have in fact both "internal" or kinaesthetic experience of it and, frequently if not always, external experience of it. That is to say, we have bodily sensations of our own expressive behavior, but we also can, and often do, experience our own expressive behavior by means of the "external" senses of sight, touch, and hearing. Now, the experience we have of a quality that consists of either an arousal or a preparation immediately followed by an experience of its respective quality in our own expressive behavior as manifested in our whole body, or a large part of it, is a case of what I shall call an "expression" or an "expression experience." An expression experience I define as an experience of any quality, experienceable in an arousal or a preparation, insofar as it is first felt as solely within a person, then felt as affecting her external behavior, and finally experienced as fully manifested in behavior that engages a large part of her body.

The problem of the one-and-many becomes even more severe in expressions than it is in arousals and preparations. For here, not only is the same quality experienced in a wide variety of complete and incomplete actions,[41] but at least some of these sometimes are experienced in a wide variety of modalities. The fact that a single expression experience may consist of kinaesthetic, visual, auditory, and tactile experiences, through all of which we experience the same quality, raises the problem of the one-and-many in an especially poignant way. The solution I offer to this problem is by now familiar. Expressions too, I claim, contain the four factors of "motion," "increase," "continuity," and "self-generation," and these factors are peculiarly well suited to solving the one-and-many problem posed by expression experiences. The second part of the claim I shall take as established by earlier arguments, once the first part of the claim is made good. I shall therefore briefly argue that the four factors indeed occur in expression experiences.

There is no question that an expression experience is an experience of motion; it is an experience of parts of our own body in motion. But that very fact may hinder our realization that expressions are also experiences of "motion." The first step in this realization is to see that besides an experience of our body in motion, an expression is also an experience of parts of our body *coming to be* in motion, and coming to be in motion in a particular way—angrily, sadly, compassionately, gently, lightly, delicately, sweepingly, gracefully. Moreover, in an expression experience that particular way of being in motion is felt as the result or effect of something "inside us." In some cases, it is experienced as the effect of some inner state like a sentiment, emotion, or mood; in other cases, it is experienced as the result of the momentum of some internal experience. Thus quite distinct from the sense of my body in motion is the sense, in an expression, of the quality of that motion itself proceeding from what is "inside me." And what is "inside me," moreover, is felt—as my descriptions of arousals and preparations make clear—not only as a quality but as a quality in "motion." Thus when we act in such a way as to manifest a sentiment, emotion, or mood we have the sense of what is "inside" coming "out." And thus too when we deliberately try to feel a certain quality "inside us" as a preparation to manifesting that quality in our external behaviour, we hope that that interiorly felt quality will "come out" in our bodily movements. And when the preparation is successful, that is precisely what the experience is: an experience of the quality inside coming out.

Furthermore, the "motion" of coming out seems, in both kinds of cases, clearly to be a kind of "self-generation." It is the *anger* or the *melancholy* of our inner feelings that seems to produce the anger or melancholy of our shout, our tears, our stride; it is the quality of our innerly felt motion that colors our very actions. In other words, the experience is something like a self-transference of the quality from the inside to the outside. And yet it is not experienced as a "transference" that requires or implies a spatial or temporal "gap." There is no sense of the "inner motion" stopping and *then* "starting up" again on the "outside." There is a felt "continuity" in this "motion" of "coming out," in this "self-transference" of qualities. Indeed, the experienced continuity of this transference from inside to outside is no different from the continuity of the quality's "progress" "inside us," or from the felt continuity of our own wholly *external* action. The "motion" through us, from within us to the outside and through our outer actions, is experienced by us as being all of a piece.

But where in this experience of a "continuous," "self-generating" "motion" is there a sense of *"increase"*? Several metaphors seem especially apt in describing expression experiences: sometimes they seem like explosions, sometimes like unfoldings, sometimes like blossomings, or growths. In all of these figures, the sense of something smaller getting bigger is important—something "opening out" from a smaller center. This figurative sense of increase can, moreover, be construed fairly straightforwardly. There are, in an expression, simply more "objects" that are progressively qualified by the same quality: first a small, scarcely felt act-beginning, then full-blown acts and movements, and more and more of them.

17. *Penetrations of the External World*

By imagining an arousal or a preparation leading into behavior that *exhibits* the same qualities figuring in the arousal or preparation, we can conceive of the sort of expansion experience I call an expression. In this section I want to add three new kinds of experiences to my catalogue of expansion experiences. The three differ significantly from one another, but they share a common feature. Let us imagine the "motion" of an arousal, a preparation, or an expression "continuing" on and "generating" the "same" quality in one or more nonhuman "objects" of the experiencer's external world. The problem of the one-and-many in such experiences becomes thereby even more acute.

My claim is, again, that this problem is solved by the same four factors in these experiences that I isolated earlier in arousals, preparations, and expressions. In this exposition, however, my main concern is to give a diverse array of examples of these new expansion experiences; I shall not argue in detail that the four factors are present in them, assuming that by now such argument will be sufficiently obvious to the reader.

(a) Imagine reading a letter with wonderful good news. As the message sinks in, you feel the joy spread over you and break out as you leap up with joy, dance about, snatch up your nearby shirt, and wave it exuberantly in the air. Your friend sees the joyous dance of the shirt as it flaps in the breeze (as *you* do also, of course) and comes running over to join you.

But suppose other news. You are walking the edge of your property and notice that the row of saplings you had planted has been maliciously mowed down. "That crazy neighbor," you think. "He's at it again." The anger steams through you and out as you stomp and swear, pick up a cut branch, and thrash the air and the neighboring bushes (your Hellespont), the fierce motions of the branch and the angry rhythms whipping the air and thwacking the underbrush echoing your own anger back to you.

Now suppose that, having felt a sweeping movement within yourself in preparation, you launch into the movement itself. You have "got it." Your movement has the quality it is supposed to have, and you know that, in part, because you can *see* parts of your costume flowing with precisely the sweeping movement *it* is supposed to have as it swirls around with you.

The experiences these three examples illustrate I call "extensions" or "extension experiences." In each a quality we experience within ourselves or in our own behavior is also experienced in a "dead" object—the shirt, the stick, the costume. Because they are moved by us as we manifest a certain quality, these objects take on that quality as if they were a kind of extension of our bodies.

(b) Sometimes when our bodies move with some quality, the movement leaves a "mark" or "trail" in the world that seems to us to take on that quality. In the experience of making the "mark" it can seem to us as if the quality we experience in ourselves were communicating itself to that small piece of the world. Such experiences I call "markings." Do a dance on the beach, and as your arm or hand or foot touches and sweeps over the sand, the grace that you feel within you and the grace of your movements (if you have it) *can* leave a graceful track in the sand. Or dance with sparklers in your hands, as you did as a child, in the Fourth of July night, and your graceful movements, which you can feel but may not be able to see, will leave their graceful swirls burnt for a brief moment onto the dark. Or notice yourself at work on your doodle pad during a faculty meeting when an especially foolish colleague is holding forth. You feel, as always, the agitation begin deep inside you and grow outward from there, affecting your scribbling hand, which, as it moves with *its* agitation, is leaving its trail of agitated lines and marks all over the page.

(c) A third form of expansion experience I shall call, for reasons that will be obvious, "empathies" or "empathetic experiences." These involve perceiving "objects" in the world as "in tune" with qualities we experience as being in or of ourselves. More specifically, we perceive these "objects" as having the *same* qualities we experience in ourselves. And more specifically still, we perceive ourselves as perceiving the qualities in those "objects" *because* of the qualities in ourselves. That is, in empathetic experiences we perceive qualities that we experience in ourselves or as belonging to ourselves as "coming out," as it were, and "coloring" our perception of "objects" in the world in the same "hue."

Imagine awaking to the usual glories of a spring day in Laguna Beach with the sun clear, the sea blue, and the birds twittering happily in the trees. But suppose then that you receive a call informing you that your credit card has been stolen and dozens of purchases charged to your account. As the news sinks in, confused agitation swamps you, and as your mood changes, so does the landscape. The wonderful spring day takes on some of the painful agitation of your own state of mind. Where before there had been benign sunlight, now you see the trees riddled with a combination of harsh sunlight and nervous black shadows; the serene blue of the sea is now ignored in favor of the restless motion of the waves; the sweet chattering of the birds becomes a tuneless nattering, like static on a phone line.

Or suppose that you decide to walk down to the beach on a somewhat stormy night to mull over the day's disturbing events. The faculty meeting is on your mind, because of the remark a colleague made to you which has unaccountably unsettled you. You finally untangle your reaction and realize the colleague's remark was in fact simply an insult, and anger wells up in you. As your blood races and your heart pounds, they seem to receive an echo in the smashing of the waves on the rocks below, and in your imagination the motion of the waves beating the stone seems to be your own anger magnified a hundred times and reflected back to you.

Perhaps then (if there is no one around) you even rant, Lear-like, at the heavens and curse your foe, finally getting your feeling out. Recovering, you feel a return of a certain sense of well-being, realizing that the colleague is, after all, a fool, and his petty insult of no real consequence. As a certain serenity settles over you the thrashing of the waves recedes from your consciousness and you feel yourself drawn to the full, distant, constant roar of the sea playing like a ground bass under the particular smashings and splashings of particular waves. And that dull and distant roar takes on in your experience the quality of serenity that you have settled into.

Suppose that the person who was supposed to call in the morning fails to do so. The morning had appeared bright and shining, and the leaves of the weeping willow just outside the study window had reflected back the joy of the sun. But as the morning wanes, so does your joyful expectancy; it turns slowly to melancholy. At the stroke of noon your whole body slumps; you feel your mouth and eyes turn down, and as your head falls, and with it your glance, they seem to you to duplicate the "fall" of the willow branches, which your eye "reads" as the melancholy of the willow.

But you can be in control of yourself, you say; you need not give in to this melancholy. Where is your pride? Your determination not to be so dependent on others? As your lecture to yourself continues, you sense a feeling of pride take hold, vanquishing the melancholy. You feel your chest expand, your shoulders rise, your back stiffen at the base of the spine and the feeling ripple upwards to your neck. As your head rises, and your glance with it, you catch sight of the tall, straight Canary Island pine in the middle distance standing out in the landscape. And your rising glance catches it and seems to rise with it, finding in the tree the very pride you feel in your bones.

I issue two caveats about interpreting what I say about empathetic experiences. First, in my conception, "empathy" refers to *experiences* we have in which qualities, emotional or otherwise, that we feel within ourselves or sense in our behavior influence our perception of external "objects" with those very qualities. I do not intend "empathy" as a theoretical term for an *explanation* of *why* we perceive qualities of ourselves in external "objects."[42]

Second, I do not allege that *every* time we perceive an external "object" as having an emotional or other "anthropomorphic" quality, we perceive that "object" as a part of an empathetic experience. I am not even claiming that whenever we feel a quality within ourselves and sense it as manifested in our behavior *and at the same time* perceive that quality in an external "object," we are having an empathetic experience. Empathy occurs only when that quality in us or in our behavior is *experienced as* coloring our perception. We must experience the quality in ourselves being projected, as it were, onto "objects" in the world. Only then do we get the sense of "motion," "increase," "continuity," and "self-generation" that I claim occurs in all expansion experiences.

18. *Influences*

In this section I describe and illustrate a kind of expansion experience I call "influence." There are two main sorts: our influencing others and others' influencing us. To understand the first sort, imagine either a preparation or an arousal leading on immediately to an expression experience and the expression experience continuing in the presence of another person in such a way that the quality you experience in yourself is experienced (by you) as generating that very quality "spreading" in the other. We may also call such complex experiences "experiences of influence."

Experiences of influence again escalate the severity of the problem of the one-and-many. For now, in addition to the vast array of different experiences we have of a "single" quality within ourselves and in our own behavior, we have the vast array of different experiences of such a quality in others. In my introduction to the general problem of the one-and-many with respect to qualities I already suggested the dimensions of this problem. The simplest of emotional qualities, such as sadness, or of qualities of sentiment, such as compassion, can "show" in ourselves or in others in many diverse ways: in the expression of our eyes, the gestures of our hands or arms, the manner in which we walk, the "set" of our heads, our necks and shoulders, our torsos. And take "purely behavioral" qualities of the simplest and most banal sorts—gracefulness, say. Prima facie, what does the grace of a movement using all our limbs and our whole body have in common with the grace of each individual part—the grace of our neck or head position, of the movement of the arch of our feet, of even one finger, of the opening of an eye? As in other expansion experiences, I want to claim, the problem of the one-and-many in experiences of influence is solved by the four factors of "motion," "continuity," "increase," and "self-generation." In the following, however, I shall not attempt to spell out these factors, but merely try to recall examples of experiences of influences and to suggest the diversity of such experiences.

(a) Your sixteen-year-old daughter calls with the news that Matisse the kitten has fallen from the second-floor balcony into the tangled garden below and she *knows*, of course, that Matisse is dead, though she can't see a mangled body below. You try, as you listen, to resist the panic over the phone, and as you feel your own determined calm spread through you and express itself in your measured tones and calm advice, you sense at virtually the same time your own calm "taking over" the girl on the phone, as she gradually cools her panic and finally begins to *tell you calmly* the reasonable steps she should take to investigate the "disaster."

(b) Imagine you drag yourself in to tell your friend that the packet with *all four* of the copies of your recently completed manuscript was left on the bus and is not recoverable. You know, of course, that he knows just how great a loss this is—how many months, even years, you had worked on the thing, what high hopes you'd had for it. Knowing this, you also know that he will sympathize with you, and he does. As you, in the doldrums, tell your sad story, you find him becoming as sad as you are.[43]

(c) Frequently, pedagogical contexts give rise to experiences of influence. Thus I might teach a dance, say a Balkan folk dance, to a friend by teaching him the steps and their sequence until he has them down. But he still might not be doing them with the right qualities in his movements. I describe these qualities and demonstrate them, to no avail. Finally, I take his hands and dance *with* him in a tight line of dancers. That way, wedging him between myself and another experienced dancer and exaggerating my own movements, I force him to feel in his own body the qualities in the bodies of the surrounding dancers and almost force his body to move with the quality of ours. He thus gradually picks up the movement quality, not well the first time perhaps. But by the second or third time I can feel the rhythms and pulses of my own body affecting his. This technique can work with couple dances, too, like polkas and waltzes.

(d) Finally, consider Jason, who at sixteen months is old enough to torture the kitten but also old enough to learn some compassion. So the next time Jason holds up the kitten by her tail, you do not scold him. Instead, you pick up the animal and comfort her with exaggerated motions, expressions, and sounds of compassion and concern. You do this in front of Jason, of course, but, better, you do it with the child in your

85

arms. You surround the child with your own body so that he can feel the soothing qualities in you as you stroke the cat, as you coo tenderly *to* the cat but *in* the child's ear, as you take Jason's hand in your own, gently and tenderly, and *with it* stroke the kitten, gently and tenderly. In so doing you can feel certain qualities in your own behavior take hold in Jason too, as he relaxes and begins gently to stroke kitty on his own and to coo "poor kitty" in *her* ear.

The second main sort of "influence" or "experience of influence" is, as it were, the reverse of the first. To understand, put yourself in the place of the *recipient* of the influence in examples (a) through (c) above. (It will not work, at least for me, with respect to [d] because of Jason's youth; my imagination, or memory, does not reach back that far.) In such reversals, we imagine the *other's* calm, or sadness, or style of movement gradually infecting *ourselves*. The experience "starts" with our experience of a certain quality in a person, in her face, voice, demeanor, or motions, and proceeds to experiences of that quality both felt within ourselves and experienced in our own acts. The sequence of the latter is not important. What is important is that we feel that quality gradually "take hold" of us and "spread through" us, whether as a mere felt quality or as a quality of our external behavior or both. It is also important that we experience the quality as *proceeding from* the other *to* ourselves. We thus experience "motion," from the other to us, as well as "through" us. We experience the quality "increasing," because not only do two persons share it, but it is "increasing" throughout ourselves, being experienced in more and more "parts" of our bodies or aspects of our external behavior. The factor of "continuity" too is experienced, for the experience is one of the direct and "ungapped" affecting of one person by another as well as of the "flow" of the quality through us, which is very much like the "flow" in an arousal or preparation. And, finally, there is the experience of "self-generation," for the experience of influence is very much the experience of the quality of the other "directly" producing the quality in us. There is no sense in an experience of influence that first there is a quality *there* (in the other), which then, by some agency such as, for example, some deliberate activity of my own or some manipulations of the other, gets transported into me.[44]

19. *Penetrations from the External World*

Just as, in the second variety of influence, we can experience the qualities of other persons generating precisely those qualities in us, either in our external behavior or as felt "within us," so, too, we may have experiences in which qualities that we perceive in things and events of the nonhuman world seem to "penetrate" us, so that we feel those very qualities within ourselves, sometimes even to the point of feeling them and perceiving them in our own more or less external behavior. I call such experiences "penetrations," or "penetration experiences," and I shall be concerned here not so much to analyze them as to exemplify them in their great variety. I hope that, by now, it will be plain to the reader how to proceed in the analysis of them. I emphasize here, as I did in speaking of influences, that a penetration experience is *not* simply an awareness that I have been affected by some quality of an external thing, and not simply an awareness that I have been affected in such a way that I feel that "same" quality in myself, in my act-beginnings or in my external acts. It is, more particularly, the experience that that quality in the thing there is *generating itself* in me. Thus:

(a) I am suddenly struck by the delicacy of the new leafing

of a tree in spring, and concentrating on that delicacy produces feelings in my fingertips as if I were about to touch, with corresponding delicacy, those tender leaves, or as if I had just made that delicate effect by some delicate touch of mine, and the leaves had just left my fingers. As I continue to savor the experience, the sense of delicacy moves up my arms and from there spreads throughout my body.

(b) Running my eye over the soft smoothness of a newly sanded plank, I feel the smoothness there, as it were, in my fingers, as if I were running them smoothly over that smoothness, and the smoothness in my fingers seems to travel to my arm and shoulder in a kind of bodily fantasy of making or remaking that smoothness in the board.

(c) Walking around a bend in the garden, I come upon the sight of an unusually elegant specimen of *Eucalyptus citriodora*, and it *makes* me, or so it seems to me, want to pose, to move in a similarly elegant way, as if in a dance with it, so that I feel the little beginnings of such elegant postures in myself, and then, when no one is looking, actually *break out* into some imitative stance or step.

(d) Walking down to the shore on a wintry evening, I encounter a more agitated sea than I had expected, and, surrounded by that turbulence for some time, I feel it churn up in myself an emotional turmoil of no particular cast, a generalized agitation in which a dozen disturbing recollections and fantasies, along with their corresponding inchoate emotions, roil within me with no more coherence than the sea itself seems to me, at the moment, to possess.

(e) Hiking the walls of Yosemite Valley, I come to a view of El Capitan and am struck anew by what seems to me the boldness of that monolith, as if it were, indeed, striding into the valley like an explorer captain. And it seems to send through me those sensations of standing, or striding, boldly, sensations of my head going up, of my back stiffening, of my chest expanding, as if El Capitan's boldness had suddenly, through my eyes, "invaded" my body and made me, if not bold, at least to some, however faint, degree bold-*feeling*.

That penetrations occur when we see or hear works of art is surely too obvious to need argument. These, or experiences like them, are very common: hearing the optimism in almost any one of Haydn's symphonies and feeling it spread through you; listening to even the happiest of Berlioz and gradually feeling its melancholy sift through you; watching the exuberant dancing and feeling the exuberance spread from the persons on stage to your own limbs, to produce a barely concealed, or unconcealed, itch to join in the exuberant movement; hearing the pensiveness in the Brahms clarinet quintet and discovering its pensiveness stealing over yourself; reveling in the elegant balletic figures of Tintoretto and feeling yourself begin to "feel like" standing with similar elegance; following the deftness of Zurbarán's brushwork and beginning to feel in your own fingers unexpressed motions of what seems to you to be deftness, even though your fingers are not even capable of that special Zurbaranesque deftness; feeling deep within yourself the motion, postures, and swellings of self-respect that Sydney Carton exhibits as he steps to the guillotine.

It is not difficult to see that experiences such as these are plentiful in our intercourse with the arts; it may be difficult to keep in mind, however, the modesty of my claims here about these experiences. First, I do not claim that every time we feel like or act like some work of art, or some aspect of it, with respect to a given quality, we can say we have had a penetration experience. A penetration requires specifically that we experience being affected by an external quality and, even more specifically, that we experience that quality producing "itself" in our feelings or overt behavior. Second, I do not claim that every response to a work of art, even a response of mood, emotion, or sentiment, is, or even is significantly like, a penetration. Some responses, though quite "emotional," are more like *reactions* to a quality in the work, which may then be or involve quite different qualities in ourselves from those that are in the work—such as our disgust or anger at the sadness of a character in a drama. Third, I am here making no claim whatsoever about the *aesthetic relevance or importance* of penetrations experienced with respect to qualities of works of art. Nor do I claim that such experiences are, in general, appropriate (or inappropriate) to works of art, desirable (or undesirable) experiences to have, significant (or insignificant), or subtle and sensitive (or coarse and banal). My reluctance to make such wholesale claims is not due simply to a sheer lack of interest in what we may call the "ethics of artistic intercourse." Rather, it seems to me obvious that some penetrations might be aesthetically relevant and others irrelevant; some appropriate, others not; some desirable, other less so; some significant, subtle, or sensitive and others the very opposite. Being "penetrated" by its qualities is, for better or worse, simply one quotidian kind of experience in our congress with art.

I mention one further caveat in interpreting penetrations, whether they involve qualities in art or qualities in natural objects. In keeping with the general metaphysical agnosticism I am trying to maintain in this study, penetration experiences are to be understood as metaphysically neutral in the following way. When we feel "penetrated" by some quality in an object, a work of art, or some feature of a work of art, such as a character in a novel, we do not necessarily feel (though we may so feel) that that quality is truly attributable to us, nor is that

90

quality necessarily (though it may be) truly attributable to us. Thus in hearing a melancholy piece of music, we may experience the melancholy of that music invading us and seeping through us, without our either being (really) melancholy or experiencing ourselves as (really) melancholy. On the other hand, we may experience that melancholy seeping into us in such a way that we then experience ourselves as *really* being melancholy, or in such a way that we truly become melancholy. It seems to me that all of these possibilities, and many more combinations and gradations of them, are possible as a result of, or in conjunction with, a penetration experience of melancholy. I thus want to disengage the notion of a penetration experience from (and I hope transcend) a set of issues that have exercised philosophers who concern themselves with emotional responses to art—namely, whether we become "truly" melancholy, become melancholy only "in imagination," take on a "semblance" of melancholy, or what.[45] I want to disengage the idea of penetration experiences from such attempts to put our "responses" to qualities in art into metaphysical pigeonholes because, first, the notion of a penetration is consistent with any possible answer to these metaphysical questions, and second, there is no single answer to these questions which will truly describe all cases of "responding" to qualities in art that fall under the concept "penetration experience." That is to say, sometimes we will have a penetration experience of melancholy and really become sad; sometimes we will have such an experience and have "mere" feelings of sadness; sometimes we will have a penetration experience of melancholy and recollect a former instance of our melancholy; sometimes we will pull a melancholy face and move in a melancholy way without *being* melancholy; and so on. The possibilities are practically endless, but the notion of penetration experiences is consistent with all of them.

20. *The Directions of Expansion*

Thus far I have argued that it is possible to have expansion experiences with respect to qualities that fall into two classes: (1) qualities of emotion, mood, feeling, or sentiment; and (2) qualities that can describe human motion, movement, or behavior but do not fall within the first class. I now point out a feature of all the expansion experiences I have described, namely, their "directionality." By this I mean that the perceived movement of the experienced quality in an expansion experience seems to proceed *from* "somewhere" *to* "somewhere else."[46] Thus in arousals and preparations we experience qualities moving "through" our own bodies. But in expressions we experience qualities moving "through" our own bodies and "into" the external action of our bodies. Then, in extensions, markings, and empathies, we experience a quality "moving" from our actions to some element of the world other than ourselves. In some cases of influence, we feel qualities proceeding from ourselves to other persons in the world; in other cases of influence, we experience qualities proceeding from other persons in the world into ourselves. In penetrations, again, we experience qualities proceeding from nonhuman elements of the external world into and even through ourselves. I do not intend to give a thorough analysis of the "logic" of such directionality, but I do want to offer two important observations about it. First, the expansion experiences described thus far manifest, together, three fundamental "directions": (a) "through" ourselves, (b) "from" ourselves "to" elements in the external world, and (c) "from" elements in the external world "to" ourselves. Second, as I have tried to show by my selection of examples, qualities of two kinds—qualities of emotion, mood, and sentiment and qualities of human movement—may figure in expansion experiences that, together, exemplify all three of these directions.

With these observations as background, I hereby make the following claim, which I take to be an important claim about qualities and a fundamental proposition in the philosophy of love and beauty: *Every quality, as and insofar as it appears in the experience of a human being, may appear in expansion experiences that, together, exemplify all three of the "directions" described above.* I intend the "as and insofar as" qualifier in this statement to leave open the following possibilities, in accordance with the metaphysical agnosticism assumed in this study: (1) that there may be ("exist") qualities that either do not or cannot appear in the experience of some, all, or any human beings (or indeed of any sentient beings whatsoever); and (2) that some or all qualities that do appear in the experience of human beings may (a) have properties that do not appear in those experiences and (b) be *known* to have such properties by sentient beings who do not or even cannot experience those qualities. In short, my claim is solely about conditions of the experience of qualities.

But how can I argue that this claim is true? The best kind of argument would be, of course, a deductive one based upon some essential characteristic of qualities. I cannot at present offer such an argument. After a few sections, however, I shall offer some *general considerations* based upon such an essential characteristic—namely, the "degree" feature of qualities—that make my general claim plausible. To make such general considerations themselves plausible, however, I shall continue to pursue the strategy of reminding the reader, by hypothetical examples, of expansion experiences that "move" in *all three "di-*

rections" and that are experiences of *qualities of all kinds*. Thus far in my presentation of expansion experiences, the experiences I have defined and the examples of them I have chosen exemplify this strategy with respect to two important kinds of qualities, namely, qualities of emotion, mood, and sentiment and qualities of human movement. In the following three sections, I shall do the same for three more classes of qualities. I am assuming that these five classes exhaust the world of qualities of the reader and myself or, at least, that any other qualities in that world resemble qualities of one or more of these kinds with respect to the sorts of expansion experiences they yield. I place no theoretical importance on this classification of qualities; I see it merely as a heuristic tool. Thus I shall not be concerned with precise definitions of each class, nor with whether each of my examples is *properly* classified. My point will be to try to persuade the reader not only that expansion experiences are possible throughout the vast range of qualities, but that the "tridimensionality" of such experiences also obtains across that range.[47]

But my present claim is stronger. It is that *all* the qualities in our worlds can figure in expansion experiences that exemplify all three "directions." To argue this claim I need a fivefold classification of qualities that cuts across the four categories introduced in Section 9. Since categories 3 and 4 are derivatives of categories 1 and 2, I begin by dividing qualities in the first two categories into four classes: (i) qualities of emotion, mood, and sentiment; (ii) qualities of movement; (iii) moral qualities; and (iv) mental qualities. That done, only some qualities that describe "objects" of the nonhuman world remain. These I lump together under the rubric "qualities of *claritas*" and argue that, superficial appearances to the contrary, they too can figure in expansion experiences in all three directions.

94

Once again, in the expositions and analyses that follow, I shall not argue that the expansion experiences I shall describe embody the four factors that I take to be essential to expansion experiences. Rather I shall assume that they do so and that after my earlier analyses of expansion experiences, the reader is able to confirm (or disconfirm) that assumption for herself.

21. *The Expansion of Moral Qualities*

Examples of moral qualities are the following: generosity, compassion, benevolence, honesty, justice, dutifulness, responsibility, truthfulness, courage. Finding expansion experiences with respect to such qualities would seem, prima facie, to be impossible. After all, such qualities are attributable primarily to persons and to them, it seems, primarily on the basis of kinds of actions they perform. And while such moral actions usually involve some bodily movements, they would not seem to involve necessarily movements of a certain "character." That is to say, they would not seem to require characteristic movements that mark them as, say, honest or generous. Thus we would not initially be tempted to describe the "unity" of the variety of honest or generous acts in anything like the same terms in which we would describe the unity of anger or gracefulness. We would look for such unity instead in the kinds of *circumstances* in which the moral action is performed. Thus, a compassionate act requires that the object of one's compassion be in distress; a dutiful act presupposes that one is under some particular obligation.

I do not intend to deny these obvious facts about moral qualities and the differences between the latter and qualities of emotion, mood, or bodily movement. Nevertheless, to make my case that expansion experiences with respect to moral qualities are possible, I shall argue that certain kinds of *feelings* are systematically joined to moral qualities that we possess. With no originality at all, I call these feelings "moral sentiments." Moral sentiments have "natural expressions" in our behavior, and thus they can give a character to the *movements* that we perform in accomplishing moral acts. Consequently, there may be act-beginnings associated with such behavior into which we may "read" that character even when we do not act externally. And such act-beginnings as experienced *with that character* constitute the internally felt aspect of moral sentiments. Furthermore these moral sentiments can be so associated in our experience with moral qualities that we can take experience of the former as experience of the latter. Then, since moral sentiments, being kinds of *feelings*, are experienceable by us in expansion experiences, *moral qualities* too are so experienceable. To make this argument persuasive, I shall have to show that there are such moral sentiments. And to do that, I shall try to describe some kinds of moral sentiments in such a way as to reveal their "natural" connection, in our experience, with certain moral qualities. As the following descriptions will reveal, moral sentiments are characteristically described in terms of *acts*, or more precisely, in terms of *inclinations* to act in certain ways. And it is precisely such acts that reveal the relationship to certain moral qualities.

(a) *Moral sentiments associated with courage.* These are feelings of resisting fear, of calming oneself before one's own imminent panic, of steeling oneself against possible harm to oneself, of girding oneself against pain or loss. And they are, more microscopically, feelings of hardening oneself physically, of stiffening, of tightening one's muscles.

(b) *Moral sentiments associated with compassion, benevolence, or generosity.* These may be feelings of sympathy for another, inclinations to weep for and embrace or comfort another, feelings of that slight expansion in the chest described in the cliché "my heart went out to him."

(c) *Moral sentiments associated with honesty or truthfulness.* These may be feelings of innocence or guilelessness, of disclosing or unmasking ourselves, of opening up, feelings of our bodies inclining to "blossom" outward, to expand, to loosen, to relax its muscles, feelings of the brow beginning to clear, of the face beginning to lift up and outward, of the palms inclining to stretch out and upward.

(d) *Moral sentiments associated with responsibility, dutifulness, or justice.* These are feelings of pulling oneself up, of straightening, of stiffening, of hardening the muscles, of steeling the glance, of jutting the jaw, of puffing out the chest, of putting the head back; feelings, too, of stifling feelings, of hardening oneself specifically against emotion.

I take it to be obvious that moral sentiments as just described can indeed figure in expansion experiences. Expressions are perhaps the commonest kind of expansion experience in which moral sentiments "within us" are "read" by us as experiences of our own dutifulness, honesty, compassion, or courage as we *act* in ways that seem to us dutiful, honest, compassionate, or courageous. Influences, too, both to others and from others, are common experiences with respect to moral qualities. But arousals, especially with respect to such qualities as compassion and generosity, are also easy to imagine. With respect to qualities like honesty and dutifulness, we are more likely to have the experiences I have called "preparations," for we characteristically "set our mind" to act with virtues like these. With respect to courage, I can imagine experiencing both arousals and preparations; we can be aroused to courage, as it were, spontaneously, but we can also set our minds to act courageously, as we can "gather up" our courage. I emphasize, further, that I do not take the moral sentiments described in (a) through (d) to exhaust the possibilities; I mean them only as kinds of examples, though of course salient ones.

I caution the reader against misinterpreting my claims about moral sentiments. First of all, I do not claim that *every* time we perform an act to which some moral quality is truly attributable (that is, every time we do the honest thing, the benevolent thing, the generous thing, and so forth), we feel within us moral sentiments or experience such moral sentiments being expressed in our actions. Nor am I claiming that we *always* feel such sentiments *before* we act virtuously. It is enough for my purposes that such things happen only some of the time. Second, I am of course not claiming that when we do experience moral sentiments or their natural expressions before or in acting, such experiences are reliable indicators that we are *in fact* acting virtuously. This is no more likely than that we are always in fact moving gracefully when we experience ourselves as moving gracefully. Finally, I am not suggesting that for us to act *truly* honestly, compassionately, or dutifully (that is, for us not only to do the honest, compassionate, or dutiful thing, but to act in such a way as truly to exhibit our *virtue* of honesty, compassion, or dutifulness), we must have or show in our outward behavior some moral sentiment. But I am not denying that suggestion either. I intend my position to be agnostic on this point.

22. *The Expansion of Mental Qualities*

I divide what I call "mental qualities" into three subclasses. Let us consider the primary "objects" to which qualities in the first two classes belong to be human acts. There are thus

98

"flashy" qualities, like brilliance, wittiness, insightfulness, cleverness, clarity, imaginativeness, shrewdness, and inventiveness. And, second, there are "sober" qualities, like prudence, efficiency, soundness (as of judgments), sensibleness, reasonableness, rationality, and wisdom. Obviously, qualities of these groups can also belong to persons themselves and to their "products," like arguments, books, advice, statements, or theories. Qualities in the third class I call "derivative mental qualities." Qualities in this group might belong to acts and persons, but let us consider them here as belonging primarily to "products" of sentient beings or to what we might see as "products" of sentient beings (as, for example, a living organism might be seen as the product of an intelligent being). This third group includes such qualities as being coordinated, being composed, being organized, being integrated, and being systematic, as well as harmony, simplicity, and complexity. I call this group "derivative mental qualities" because, for the purposes of my present argument, I shall restrict the group to include only those instances of qualities like the ones mentioned that *can also be adverbially described in terms of qualities belonging to the first two groups.* Reflection will disclose that few instances of such qualities are thereby excluded from the third subclass of mental qualities. What I hope to achieve by this rather artificial maneuver is the insight that many, if not most, instances of the qualities belonging to the "derivative" group are (or are easily seen by us as) specific instances of qualities of the other two groups.

My strategy now will be to point out (1) that there can be kinds of feelings in us when we act and our actions manifest either "flashy" or "sober" mental qualities; (2) that such feelings are at least part of what we "read" as experiences of those mental qualities in our own acts; and (3) that such feelings, like other feelings, including moral sentiments, are experienced by us in expansion experiences exemplifying all three "directions."

Mental qualities are chiefly, but not exclusively, manifested in verbal behavior: statements, judgments, discourses—utterances of various sorts. Let us ask now what *characteristic demeanor* accompanies utterances that manifest various mental qualities. Though I think it unlikely that we could describe a characteristic demeanor associated with each distinct mental quality (corresponding, say, to distinct words for mental qualities), it is much easier to describe the characteristic demeanor associated with the first two *classes* of mental qualities distinguished earlier.[48] Behavior associated with "flashy" mental qualities includes speedier speech; animated, even excited movements of the face, hands, and possibly (in Sicilians) the whole body; flashing, brightening glances and other eye movements; raised spirits; raised voices; smiles; and sometimes even laughter. Indeed, it is precisely such demeanor that motivates some of the standard metaphors surrounding this kind of mental quality; people who manifest such qualities show "quickness" of mind or wit. "Brilliance" or "flashiness" or "clarity" themselves not only signify light "opening our eyes," thus accounting for the wide-eyed, alert look, but also suggest the quickness of rhythms of the appearing light—as does "scintillating."

Now, we may of course feel this demeanor in ourselves when we manifest "flashy" mental qualities in our utterances. But we can also feel the act-beginnings of such demeanor in ourselves, even when we do not act out such behavior or have not verbally expressed anything that manifests some mental quality. In such cases we feel the mental qualities within us as we can feel anger within us. We may do so when, for example, we merely think to ourselves ideas that "exhibit" such qualities, or before, and as, we prepare to come out with some utterance that will manifest such qualities. We may also do so when we apprehend such qualities in the utterances of others; we may simply sympathetically feel those qualities in ourselves, or we may actually be stimulated by the other's qualities not only to *think* in a way that reflects those qualities but eventually also to *speak* and *act* in ways that manifest them. The latter sort of "influence" may, of course, work in the other direction too, as when our manifested mental qualities stimulate others to manifest them as well—as in, say, a good philosophical discussion.

But the demeanor associated with "sober" mental qualities is in a different range. This behavior typically is slow, deliberate, heavier, careful; the face is graver, the voice is lower as well as slower, the head is lowered, the chin seeks the chest. Thus it is precisely this *style* of behavior that characterizes *persons* whom we describe in terms of mental qualities of the "sober" type. It needs no prolonged discussion to see that behavior of this sort can be experienced in act-beginnings within ourselves and thus can count for us as experiencing some corresponding mental quality "in" ourselves even when there is no such quality being manifested in our behavior. Also, like the feelings associated with mental qualities of the "flashy" sort, such feelings can be ingredient in expansion experiences in all three "directions."

My presentation of the feelings associated with mental qualities may raise the following question. Given that one of my ultimate points, in fashioning the concept of an expansion experience, is to show how such experiences can account for our experiencing apparently different qualities as the *same* quality, how is such a purpose consistent with my argument here that the same (sorts of) behavior and, hence, *feelings* can be associated with different mental qualities, that is, all those in the "flashy" group, or all those in the "sober" group? My answer is fairly simple: Expansion experiences, like "feelings," can be described in many different ways; description of them as being "of" some quality or other is only one kind of description applicable to them. Expansion experiences "of" different qualities may nevertheless *share* another kind of description. Indeed, if that were not so, there could be no descriptions true of expansion experiences *in general*. Perhaps more to the present point, however, there may be descriptions *shared* by the feelings involved in expansion experiences of such different emotions as anger, joy, and fear—such as the feeling of a rapidly beating pulse. Moreover, it is perfectly consistent with my concept of expansion experiences that at some levels of description, at which true descriptions are presently unavailable—for example, the neurophysiological or the metaphysical—all expansion experiences may turn out to be exactly the same. And such descriptions may be consistent with my concept of expansion experiences even if they imply, as they might, that there exists only one quality.

23. Claritas *and Expansion*

Some of the kinds of qualities considered thus far may seem to belong primarily to human beings and their acts: qualities of emotion, mood, feeling, or sentiment, qualities of movement, and moral and mental qualities. My argument for the possibility of expansion experiences with respect to these qualities, therefore, has proceeded from the possibility of our experiencing them when they apply to ourselves. But there are some qualities that seem at least prima facie to apply exclusively to "objects" other than ourselves and specifically to nonhuman "objects." Such qualities might seem to provide counterexamples to my general thesis about qualities and expansion experiences.

I do not refer here to qualities—such as the delicacy of foliage, the smoothness of a tree trunk, the boldness of El Capitan—which, though they are experienced primarily as belonging to nonhuman "objects," are nevertheless clearly experienced as "anthropomorphic." The very terms we ordinarily use to describe such qualities already relate such qualities to the feelings, emotions, or movements of human beings. There is thus no real mystery as to how my thesis applies to such qualities. But there are other qualities that, at least at first, may seem not only to apply to nonhuman "objects" outside ourselves, but also to be in no way "anthropomorphic." They may thus seem to apply exclusively to such "objects" and thereby to block any attempt to find expansion experiences of them. I refer here to certain qualities of light and, by extension, of color—qualities like lustrousness, clarity, brilliance, radiance. Unlike softness, warmth, and subtlety, these qualities seem to belong to light qua light; they seem not to borrow any character from the human. I refer also to qualities of *sound* that, significantly, are ordinarily described in terms of "light": brilliance, clarity, radiance, and so forth. And there are qualities of taste and smell that take their very names, not from anything human, but precisely from the objects that characteristically *yield* such tastes and smells—qualities like the piney smell of pine woods, the winesap taste of a winesap apple, the almond taste of fresh almonds, the gingery smell of fresh ginger. These qualities are *characteristic* tastes and smells of *natural* things.[49] This whole class of qualities I shall call "qualities of *claritas*."[50]

My argument for the possibility of expansion experiences

with respect to qualities of *claritas* has three (not necessarily sequential) parts. I shall argue, first, that there are feelings in us that characteristically, though not unfailingly, occur in the perception of qualities of *claritas*. Implicit in my description of these feelings will be the point that they figure in expansion experiences of all three "directions." Finally, I shall argue that in these feelings the qualities of *claritas* that we perceive outside ourselves are indeed felt to be in ourselves and in our actions as well.

I first take up qualities of light. My argument here depends upon noting the peculiar metaphorical structure of terms ordinarily used to describe these qualities. These metaphors I take to reflect our perhaps unobvious but not unusual experience of such qualities. "Brightness" can denote *feelings* in us of alertness and sensitivity as well as a look, especially of our faces: alert, expressive, wide-eyed. And, of course, my experience of having such a look on my face often includes my feelings of being alert, of movement that plays, or is about to play, on my face, of my eyes opening wider, or seeming to. "Clarity" too describes a quality of our perception. When we experience ourselves as seeing clearly, we experience our sense of sight as alert, our eyes as attentive and, frequently, filled with light, opened up precisely because of the clarity of the light that we are seeing or that is allowing us to see clearly. Lustre we may see in lighted objects, but it may also appear on our faces, again, as brightness of eyes and alertness of expression.[51] Note, too, that a synonym for "brightness," "lustrousness," and even "clarity" of color is "vividness." But "vividness" is precisely "liveliness," which in turn can describe our faces when they are bright-eyed, alert and expressive. And the *feelings* associated with such faces are precisely feelings of (our own) liveliness. Such considerations show that, contrary to first impressions, even "nonanthropomorphic" qualities of light—those pertaining to it most essentially *as* light—are at root anthropomorphic.

But what can convince us that, apart from these linguistic facts, the qualities we perceive in objects and those we feel in ourselves in perceiving those qualities are experientially "the same"? The following consideration will not, cannot do that job, but it may lower our resistance to allowing that we may in fact experience them as the same. Note that, other things being equal, vividness of color depends upon there being relatively *more light* on the colored object. When we perceive such vividness, therefore, there is literally more light entering our eyes. More light entering our eyes allows us, generally speaking and of course within limits, to *see* more vividly and clearly. Moreover, the more light that there is on an object and that thereby is reflected off the object and into our eyes, the more wide-eyed[52] and alert we become, both because we can see better and because there is more to see.

I could analyze brilliance and clarity of *sound* in much the same way, allowing for the obvious difference that we cannot literally "open" our ears (we perk them up). I shall not offer such an analysis, however. I note merely that sound waves from objects literally enter our ears, just as light literally enters our eyes. I turn now to characteristic smells and tastes, which require a slightly different analysis. Observe first that both the feelings associated with brilliance of color and those associated with brilliance of sound typically occur when there is a *high degree* of brilliance in the perceived color or sound. The same is true of characteristic tastes and smells. For in an object that yields a taste or smell of a high degree, the perceived quality is experienced, as well as often described, as especially "potent." And the very potency of the taste or smell seems, in the expe-

rience of it, to consist in part in its impact on the corresponding *sense*. This "impact" is sometimes even experienced as literal impact, as when we feel our sense react in physical ways to
the received qualities. Such felt impact is, of course, the experiential register of the fact that some physical matter from the
smelt or tasted object is literally touching our sense organs.
And the latter, in turn, is the direct analogue of light entering
the eyes or sound waves hitting the ear in the perception of
visual or auditory brilliance. The reason, I take it, that such
impact registers more clearly and obviously in the perception
of characteristic smells and tastes of a high degree is that there
is in some way *more* of such literal impact.

But in the case of characteristic smell and taste qualities,
such impact is "read" precisely as *potency in the receiving senses*.
Thus just as a high degree of a characteristic taste or smell in
an "object" betokens a robustness or vigor or potency of that
taste or smell, our tasting and smelling of those robust and
vigorous qualities are experienced by us, in part, as the robustness and vigor of our own sense capacities. Moreover, just as
visual and tonal brilliance work "through" us to make us more
visually and auditorily alert—wide-eyed and "wide-eared"—
so too olfactory and gustatory potency work "through" us to
invigorate our sensitivity to tastes and smells. Our senses can
thus become sharpened and more avid. Hence, presumably,
the description of characteristic tastes and smells of *edible* objects as "appetizing."

Even if all of the above is convincing, there is still one missing link. I have presented considerations suggesting how there
can be expansion experiences in which qualities of an external
object "penetrate" us to produce experiences of those very qualities—kinds of clarity or vigor—in us and in our perceptual
actions and facial expressions. Such experiences, however, do

not yet show how these "actions" of our own influence or otherwise affect, *in any experience of ours*, the external world. In other words, I have not yet shown how there can be expansion experiences of qualities of *claritas* directed *from ourselves to the outer world*. I fill the gap thus: The sense of the clarity or vigor of our senses "moving through us"[53] also "moves" to those parts of us *expressing* the clarity or vigor of our sense. From there, these qualities appear to move, via these experiences I call "empathies," to the external world. There we see, hear, taste, or smell, as projections of our own clarity or potency of sense, clarity of light or tone and potency of smell or taste. It is a fact, I think, that the vivification of sense organs that can occur in the perception of qualities of *claritas* leads naturally and frequently to the *further* perception of them in the same object or in ones close by. This is just a natural effect, I think, of the avidity of the senses brought about by their heightened potency. That fact, together with the affinity that we already are inclined to perceive between these qualities and our sense perception (for reasons, linguistic and physical, that I have described), may easily lead us to see those *additional* or *further* instances of a given quality of *claritas* as *projections* of our own brilliance, clarity, potency, vigor, or robustness. Hence the closing of the "tridirectional" figure.

24. *Nights of Love*

Mention of closing a figure recalls an implication, suggested from the very beginning of my exposition of expansion experiences, of the multidirectionality of those experiences. With a little imagination we can see that instances of all the kinds of expansion experiences characterized earlier can occur in such a way that they are joined together, as it were, to make a longer composite expansion experience. Thus an arousal or a preparation can lead to an empathy, extension, marking, or influence in the external world, which can, in turn, lead to an influence from the world back to us, or to penetrations by elements of the already influenced or penetrated world, which may then progress to more arousals or preparations, and so on. Moreover, these "leadings to" and "progressions" might be continuous, making of the whole experience a single expansion experience. Indeed, it should be clear that when we have an expansion experience of any one of the types distinguished earlier, it is often continuously joined in this way to others of other types. My earlier categorization of expansion experiences was (deliberately) somewhat artificial in comparison with the more seamlessly continuous *reality* of such experiences.

Now, because of this "joinability" and because (as I shall now assume) for all qualities there can be expansion experiences exemplifying all three "directions," it is abstractly possible for us to have, for all the qualities we experience, composite expansion experiences each of which includes components exemplifying all three directions. To say that such composite experiences are possible, is, notice, not to say either (1) how many different *kinds* of component experiences they may have, (2) *which* kinds of component experiences they may have, or (3) what the *sequence* of these components must be.

In this respect expansion experiences are somewhat like visual experiences of three-dimensional objects. We know we can have visual experiences of an object *from* continually changing perspectives. Furthermore, we know we can have such experiences from *different* perspectives. We also know that whether or not we have actually had experiences that connect continuously our actual continuously changing visual experiences of the object, we *could*, in principle, have (or at least could have had) such longer continuous experiences of the object. We further know that the given object could, in principle, be experienced by us from all possible visual perspectives and, moreover, that all of these possible visual experiences could in principle be linked in a continuous experience moving, as it were, literally *all around* the object. Nevertheless, we also know that the bare possibility of such a "complete" visual experience puts only minimal constraints on the sequence of such an experience; it certainly does not preclude either *repeating* experiences or backtracking. The only requirement of such an experience is that all possible visual perspectives be included in the overall continuous experience at least once, at some "point" in the overall experience. Similarly, the only requirement I am placing on possible composite expansion experiences of this kind is that all three directions be exemplified somehow, at some "point" in each of them.

I want now to introduce the idea of a *fourth* "direction" with respect to expansion experiences. In addition to the "movement" of qualities "through" ourselves, "from" ourselves "into" the external world, and "from" the external world "into" ourselves, we also experience the "movement" of qualities "through" the external world. This fourth "direction" is exemplified in experiences that are not true expansion experiences. In particular, the "movement" of the experienced quality in the fourth "direction" is not felt within us, as is the "movement" in expansion experiences exemplifying the other three "directions." Consequently there is also no experience of continuity or of self-generation in these experiences. Rather, there is an experience of increase of a quality in the external world, either within a single "object" or as an accumulation across many "objects." And we then *project*, on the basis of our own genuine expansion experiences of those qualities, the other

109

factors onto the experience of increase of quality and imagine a full-fledged expansion experience occurring there in the external world. For these reasons we can think of experiences in this fourth direction as "derived expansion experiences." We may, for example, see a person grow apparently angrier and angrier until he is in a towering rage and see that growth as an outward manifestation of an arousal-cum-expressing *in him*. Or we may see the calm or the irritation of one person spread, apparently, to others with whom she is interacting. Or we may observe the joyousness of a spring day apparently communicate itself to people around us. Or the melancholy of a sonata apparently "come off" onto the expressions of listeners. Or the brightness of the colors in a room gradually brighten the faces of those who enter it. Or the robustness and vigor of a smell or flavor increase before our eyes the robustness and vigor, apparently, of the *senses* of smell and taste in a dog or cat (the human beings I know being usually too discreet to allow their own olfactory or gustatory avidity to show in similar situations).

Now, it is not essential that composite expansion experiences exemplify this fourth direction. But it is possible for constituent expansion experiences in the other three directions to be connected to other constituents in those directions via an experience in this fourth direction. I take such composite experiences exemplifying all four directions, in whatever sequence, to be genuine composite expansion experiences exemplifying all three of the essential directions. That is, the addition of an experience of the fourth direction, though not itself an expansion experience, will nevertheless allow an experience made up of genuine expansion experiences to count as a single expansion experience as long as the "seams," as it were, *appear* (to the experiencer, of course) to make of the whole an

110

experience of continuous, self-generated movement of an increasing quality.

I have already stressed that experienced qualities need not always be experienced in expansion experiences. Nevertheless, I make the following claim: *For any experiencing human being S and for any quality Q_s that S has ever experienced, it is possible for S to imagine having an expansion experience of Q_s, of whatever "shape," "length," and complexity, that includes as component experiences expansion experiences exemplifying the three "essential" directions, possibly connected by experiences exemplifying the fourth direction.*

My argument for this claim is as follows: We can in principle, under some conditions or other, call up in memory any experience we have had. Such a memory experience is a form of imagining that experience; it is a memory image of the experience. Since this is universally true, there would seem to be no reason to suppose it would not hold for any possible experience of ours. Then, since (1) for any S and for any quality Q_s that S has experienced, expansion experiences of Q_s exemplifying all three essential "directions" are possible, and (2) because of the "joinability" of expansion experiences, *composite* expansion experiences of Q_s are also possible, it follows that there is no reason to suppose that S cannot imagine having such a composite expansion experience.

Now, although this argument for imaginability depends upon the possibility of memory images, I do not want to restrict my italicized claim above merely to this sort of imaginability. In other words, my claim is that if it is possible for S to have an experience, it is possible for S, *under some conditions or other*, to *imagine* having that experience. Thus generalizing the conditions under which the imagining can take place allows for obvious differences in imaginative power among human beings. For some, having had an experience is necessary and sufficient to allow them to imagine it. For others, having had the experience is necessary, but hardly sufficient; they may need all sorts of coaching, memory jogging, and so forth. For yet others—and I presume that most of my readers will fall into this category—the mere unrealized possibility of having a given (described) experience will be sufficient to enable them to imagine such an experience. Then, too, for some people, knowing or believing that they can have an experience, or knowing or believing that they can imagine having an experience, may be sufficient to enable them to *imagine* having the experience. But I want to deny that for all S, S can imagine having an experience only if S knows or believes he can have the experience or knows or believes he can imagine having the experience. Such a denial means, among other things, I take it, that being convinced of what I say in this book is not necessary to the having or imagining of experiences described in this book.

I want to remain emphatically agnostic on certain philosophical questions about what enables us to imagine having such experiences. It may well be, for example, that our past experiences of Q, imbedded and not imbedded in expansion experiences, together with our past expansion experiences of all kinds of other qualities, or some combination of all of these, is what enables us to imagine having a composite expansion experience of Q without actually having had such a composite expansion experience. On the other hand, it could be that the "multidirectionality" of expansion experiences with respect to *all* the qualities in our "world" constitutes something like a "form of intuition" that applies to any possible experience of quality. That is, it may be that such "multidirectionality," together with the connectability of the directions, either is or indicates some kind of "pure form of qualitative space" that is a precondition of the possibility of any experience of quality whatsoever. Finally, of course, there may be other possible explanations of how we are able to imagine composite and "complete" expansion experiences of the sort I have described. My claim is neutral with respect to all such explanations.[54]

It is time to give an example of imagining having such a composite and complete expansion experience. Imagine a night of love in which, we can suppose, one quality dominates the lovemaking to the exclusion of others. We can choose among many: tenderness, gentleness, delicacy, languor, enthusiasm, joviality, roughness, power. But imagine in this case that sensuality rules the night. Imagine then the following:

It's late and he's not in yet. One of those nights in August with Mexican weather that never gets cool. The sultry air clings to your body like a kiss you feel all over you as you walk to the record shelf. Inevitably, it seems, your glance lingers on Ravel's *Scheherazade*. As the sensual music mates with the sultry atmosphere, he comes in, his thin wet shirt clinging to his torso like lips, his mouth heavy, his eyelids low, clearly affected by the Mexican air and now by the Ravel that greets him. The sensual feelings that by now are coursing through you take your arms and you move to slip his shirt off. His torso responds to your touch, and the sensuality that meets your sensual touch there travels up to his lips and from there to yours, to your tongue, throat, nipples, groin, and you feel your legs melt with it. These waves of feeling somehow carry you to the satin sheets, which, warm tonight, participate in your caresses, enveloping you both in qualities of touch that are renewed with each of your movements. These movements of love themselves are like perpetual exchanges of sensuality between yourself and him, as the qualities continually move over your bodies and through your bodies, igniting the same perpetually in the other. Even the room seems to participate in your embrace as the dim light softly touches your eyes and then languidly focuses, as it were, on the giant pink anthurium on the bed table, with its veins seemingly engorged by the shadows, its protuberance offering itself to you both. You see its sensual gesture, as it were, with your mouth; and your tongue moves slightly as if to respond, while through the open window the jasmine insinuates its scent through you; and in the distance the heavy beating of the surf against the shore comes to you as the rhythm of a slow, sensuous copulation, repeating your own, or as the pulses of an infinite, cosmic orgasm invading you to your secretest parts . . .

And so it can go on, as we know, for hours. I have concocted this fantasy as a reminder that the experienced "interpenetrations," with respect to a single quality, of an experiencing self and a complex world—consisting of other persons, natural "objects," works of art, sights, sounds, odors, and the very atmosphere itself—can proceed in wave after wave of expansion experiences; that these experiences can be of virtually all the sorts distinguished earlier and can, further, occur simultaneously or in many different orders of succession; but that all can seem to lead from and into others, to make up what seems a continuous experience of a quality in "motion" in four "directions" of qualitative "space." I have difficulty finding in my own experience any actual contexts, other than making love, in which such a long and varied composite expansion experience ordinarily might occur; I suspect others may have similar difficulty. Nevertheless, the example should illustrate the *kinds* of fantasies that *imagining* composite expansion experiences involves.

114

I want to use the description of a night of love, indeed, as a paradigm of all composite expansion experiences exemplifying the three "essential" directions of qualitative space. And I shall now introduce a technical term for such experiences, in honor of that paradigm. Were the night of love described above an *actual experience* it would be, according to this new nomenclature, a *Night of Love*. Since it was not an actual one, but only an imagined one, it is a *Fantasy of a Night of Love*. The claims I have argued for in the present section, then, are these:

(I) For any experiencing human subject S and for any quality Q_s in S's world, it is possible for S to experience a Night of Love with respect to Q_s; and

(II) for any experiencing human subject S and for any quality Q_s in S's world, S can have a Fantasy of a Night of Love with respect to Q_s.

I am prepared now, finally, to offer an account of why experienced qualities that seem the same to an experiencing human subject do so. *For any experiencing human subject S, any qualities distinctly experienced by S that seem to S to be the same quality seem so because S can have a Fantasy of a Night of Love in which those distinct experiences figure as components.* My argument for this claim has the following structure. First, what I take to be two important consequences of the claim are true, namely: (1) if S's distinct experiences of qualities can figure in S's Fantasy of a Night of Love, then the qualities so distinctly experienced do seem to S to be the same; and (2) if qualities distinctly experienced by S seem to S to be the same, then S can Fantasize a Night of Love in which those distinct experiences of qualities figure as components. The truth of (1) and (2) of course does not imply the truth of my explanation claim. If, however, to the truth of (1) and (2) we add the fact that, as I argued earlier, the characteristics of expansion experiences, of which Nights of Love and Fantasies of Nights of Love are special cases, are *peculiarly well suited* to explain *sameness of quality*, and further observe that *S*'s experience of sameness of quality in a variety of "objects" does not seem powerful enough by itself to explain *S*'s ability to put all these experiences together into a Fantasy of a single Night of Love, then all of these facts together, while not strictly implying the above explanation claim, *are themselves reasonably and, indeed, best accounted for by taking the explanation claim to be true.*

Now, the truth of (1) above simply follows from the nature of Nights of Love as expansion experiences. Expansion experiences are special kinds of experiences in which the "same" quality is experienced in a certain way. The truth of (2), however, is based on "empirical" evidence, namely, the introspective experience of quality-experiencing subjects. To test it we can try to imagine having a single expansion experience incorporating the distinct experiences of qualities that seem the same to us. If we can imagine such an experience, that is confirmation of (2).[55] It is also confirmation of (2) if we fail to be able to imagine having a single such expansion experience with respect to qualities that do not seem the same to us.

REPRODUCTION

25. *Love and Reproduction*

I am ready to construct a theory of enjoyment, or Love, as I am calling it. Recall from Section 5 that this requires us to discover some activity at the core of Love in which the Lover desires to engage indefinitely. As a step toward that discovery, then, I now introduce the notion of "producing" an experience of a quality. A basic element in this concept is that the subject that "produces" such an experience can "produce" it only in himself; that is, one subject cannot "produce" an experience of a quality in another subject. Second, the notion of "producing" is not a process concept. By this I mean in part that there is no such production without what is produced. This in turn means two things: (1) there is no "act" of producing if the experience produced is not forthcoming; and (2) consequently a subject is not engaged in producing an experience for any time, no matter how brief, until the experience itself occurs. Producing an experience of some quality Q is not merely having an experience of Q. But insofar as a subject S is producing an experience of Q, S has an experience of Q.

To produce an experience of Q is to have an experience of Q *by doing* something else under certain conditions. What the "something else" is can vary enormously depending upon, chiefly, the nature of Q and the modality of the experience. You can see the delicacy of a leaf by opening your eyes (under the right conditions) or by paying close attention to it; you can hear the sensuousness of the Ravel song by listening to it on the stereo; you can feel the subtlety of the colors of the sunset "in" the tips of your fingers by imagining yourself painting that sunset; you can feel the gentleness of the spring air by

119

gardening in it, the richness of the earth by running it through your hands.

But the "certain conditions" under which S produces an experience of Q *by doing* something else are that S must do the something else *in order to* have the experience of Q. Thus I may have an experience of a quality without producing it. If I am idly lying on my back watching the sky and a gracefully soaring hawk comes into view, I may see the grace in the hawk's flight, but not by having done anything *in order to* see it; I did not know it was going to be there *to see*. Even if I see the sensuous-looking fur on the woman in the lobby, I may not do anything in order to feel the fur; but if she happens to push past me and the fur happens to touch my hand, I may well feel its sensuousness without nevertheless having *produced* that experience. Qualities of emotion and mood, at least when the emotions and moods first come over us, are often perceived by us without our having produced the experiences. In later stages of the mood or emotion, of course, we may indeed produce experiences of their qualities by, say, dwelling on the insult or the depressing news, or simply by *allowing* the emotion or mood to invade us.[56]

I now introduce the notion of *reproducing* an experience of a quality. To reproduce an experience is not to produce it again or to repeat it, nor is it to duplicate it. Rather, it is to produce one or more other experiences, different (and possibly *very* different) from the reproduced experience *as* experience, but like the reproduced experience in *being of the same quality*. Moreover, to count as reproduction, the production of an experience of Q must be done by S *in order to* have another experience or other experiences of Q.

With one more preparatory step I shall be able to state necessary and sufficient conditions of the Love of experiencing qualities. The step is to disambiguate "experiencing a quality." As I argued in Section 6, my enjoyment, or Love, of any activity of mine is reducible to the Love of my experiences of one or more qualities involved in that activity. One can say, then, that a theory of Love must be a theory of the Love of *the experience* of qualities. Furthermore, as I mentioned earlier, a demand on such a theory is that it find an *activity* in terms of which to understand this Love of the experience of qualities. This activity will be, in fact, the "activity" of reproduction just defined.[57] Reproduction, however, is defined in terms of *experiences*. A problem surfaces, in other words, in the nominalization of the term "experiencing." When we have experienced something we can then be said either to have had experience of that thing or to have had experiences of that thing. Generally speaking (and felicities of language aside) it does not matter which of these nominalizations we choose. There are reasons, however, for thinking that a theory of the Love of experiencing qualities must be first a theory of the experience of qualities and only derivatively a theory of the experiences of qualities. But since one component of the explanans in my theory will be described in terms of experiences of qualities, there is a problem of bridging the gap between that explanans and what is in the explanandum described in terms of the collective noun "experience." As steps toward bridging the gap I shall first say something about how experiences are individuated. Then, on the basis of that, I shall explain why "experiencing" in the explanandum must be nominalized collectively.

I do not want to develop here a full-scale theory of the individuation of experiences. I shall say only as much as I need for my purposes. Any experience, collectively speaking, of a subject S that is, according to S, (1) *of* what falls under a single description and (2) temporally continuous I shall call *an* expe-

rience. Second, anything that seems to S to be a temporal seg-
ment, of whatever duration, of such an experience I shall also
call *an* experience. Thus my temporally unbroken visual experience of the telephone on my desk is *an* experience of mine. If
it lasts a while, such an experience is also constituted by several
"shorter" experiences of the telephone some of which "overlap"
one another in various ways. Similarly, any expansion experience that I have of a quality counts as *an* experience, whether
it comes to me in one modality or several, since the expansion
experience is in all of its moments both *of* what (according to
me) falls under the same description and temporally continuous. And if it is "long enough," such an expansion experience
too is constituted by several temporally "shorter" experiences
of that very quality.

Now, how do these points bear upon the fact that when we
are enjoying (Loving) some activity, what we are enjoying
(Loving) is the experience of some qualities involved in that
activity? Suppose it is gardening yesterday that I enjoyed. Part
of what I enjoyed, let us say, was the feel of the richness of the
earth that I experienced while gardening. But if my enjoyment
yesterday was typical (and I was really gardening!), I was definitely not feeling the richness of the earth during each moment
I was gardening. Rather, it was every now and then, with
longer or shorter temporal gaps between, that I actually felt
the richness of the earth during the whole stint of gardening.
Probably, too, every now and then I would let my fingers linger over the earth, savoring its richness. It is all of these experiences that I label with the collective noun phrase "my experience of the rich-feeling earth." Yet it is also clear that we can
analyze the collective "experience" in terms of "experiences."
The collective experience of a subject S on a given occasion or
during a more or less definite period of time of a quality in S's

world—$Exp_s(Q_s)$—may be either (1) identical with *an* experience of Q_s, which may or may not have constituent experiences of Q_s, or (2) a class of experiences of Q_s, some, all, or none of which may have constituent experiences of Q_s. A "part" of $Exp_s(Q_s)$ I hereby define as an experience of Q_s that is either (1) a constituent of $Exp_s(Q_s)$, (2) a member of $Exp_s(Q_s)$, (3) a constituent of a member of $Exp_s(Q_s)$, or (4) a constituent of a constituent of $Exp_s(Q_s)$.

I am at last ready to state the New Theory of Love. I state it in terms of four propositions (I–IV). For the present, think of the term "Love" and its cognates as simply other terms for "enjoy" and its corresponding cognates. Although these terms are not strictly coextensive, every case of enjoyment is (or so I claim) a case of Love. We shall see later what else, besides enjoyment, the New Theory of Love comprehends. I intend propositions I–III together to state necessary and sufficient conditions for any experiencing (human) subject S to enjoy her (collective) experience on a given occasion or during a more or less definite period of time of any quality of her world Q_s—$Exp_s(Q_s)$. And I intend proposition IV to state a necessary condition for any experiencing (human) subject S to enjoy any complex activity, state, condition, or object that involves S in experiencing a quality or qualities but is not identical with such experiencing ($CASCO$).

(I) For any S, any Q_s, and any $Exp_s(Q_s)$, if S is Loving[58] $Exp_s(Q_s)$, then there is some part or parts of $Exp_s(Q_s)$ that S is reproducing such that what S so produces are themselves part(s) of $Exp_s(Q_s)$.

Or, less technically and more roughly, if anyone is enjoying an experience of a quality, then she is "reproducing" that experience, and her own "reproductions" become part of the total experience she is enjoying.

Recall now that the motive for finding an activity such as reproduction was to provide what can simultaneously and continuously both arouse and satisfy a desire. Accordingly, let us build this factor into another necessary condition:

(II) For any S, any Q_s, and any $Exp_s(Q_s)$, S is Loving $Exp_s(Q_s)$ only if S's reproducing part(s) of $Exp_s(Q_s)$ both arouses and satisfies S's desire so to reproduce.

Or, less technically, a person is enjoying an experience of a quality only if he is "reproducing" it (as in [I] above) and if such "reproducing" both stimulates and at the same time satisfies precisely a desire in him so to "reproduce" the experience.

We shall have to investigate, of course, just *how* a desire to reproduce can be *aroused* by such reproduction itself. Nevertheless, the necessary conditions stated in (I) and (II) may also be affirmed as jointly sufficient conditions, yielding together a theoretical definition of Love, when the object of Love is the experience of some quality of the experiencer's world:

(III) For any S, any Q_s, and any $Exp_s(Q_s)$, if S is reproducing a part or parts of $Exp_s(Q_s)$ such that what S so produces are themselves part(s) of $Exp_s(Q_s)$, and if such reproducing both arouses and satisfies S's desire so to reproduce, then S is Loving $Exp_s(Q_s)$.

Or, less technically, if a person is "reproducing" an experience of a quality (as in [I] above) and is doing so in such a way as to both stimulate and satisfy a desire in herself so to "reproduce" that experience (as in [II] above), then that person is enjoying that experience.

Furthermore, on the basis of the reduction principle de-

124

scribed in Section 6, we can arrive at the following statement of necessary conditions of Loving, when the object of Love is some complex activity, state, condition, or object that is not an experience of a quality:

(IV) For any S and for any "object" $CASCO_s$, if S is Loving $CASCO_s$, then there is some $Exp_s(Q_s)$ involved in $CASCO_s$ that S is Loving. ("Involved" here covers all those relations, brought to light by the reduction technique, standing between any $CASCO_s$ and the experiences of S with respect to which S is enjoying that $CASCO_s$.)

Or, less technically, if a person is enjoying any sort of "object" whatsoever *other than* an experience of a quality—such as an abstract or concrete object or a complex activity, state, or condition of his own—then that person is enjoying at least one experience (of his own) of a quality, which experience is somehow "involved" in his relationship to that enjoyed "object."

In the following sections I shall elaborate, explain, and justify various aspects of (I)–(IV), which jointly constitute the New Theory of Love (NTL).

26. Some Observations about Love and Reproduction

While NTL encompasses necessary and sufficient conditions for anyone's enjoyment of his own experience of qualities, it offers only necessary conditions for his enjoyment of all other kinds of "objects." In this regard NTL parallels the New Theory of Beauty (NTB). NTB lays down necessary and sufficient conditions for the beauty of qualities, but only necessary conditions for the beauty of "objects" other than qualities. The reasons are analogous in the two cases. A given "object" may have one or more beautiful features, but will also almost always have features that are not beautiful. Thus whether the presence of beautiful features (qualities) in an "object" makes the "object" itself beautiful is a matter of whether the beauty outweighs the nonbeauty. NTB offers no theory of how to carry out such "weighing." I doubt very much that a perspicuous theory for such a weighing can be produced, but whether it can is, as far as NTB is concerned, an open question. Similarly, most enjoyable "objects" have a combination of enjoyable and unenjoyable aspects. Even the most enjoyable of things present a mixture of pleasures and pains. On a hike, for example, I may be enjoying the freshness of the air, but may be annoyed by the voracious insects. Or I may enjoy the serenity and clarity of the sky but curse the tangled underbrush. Whether I enjoy the hike, on the whole, depends upon how I weigh these good and bad points. For such a weighing, too, NTL offers no help, and I doubt that a theory of such a weighing is possible. Even so, however, since according to NTL *all* the enjoyment we have is either already the enjoyment of our experience of qualities or reducible to such, nothing is lost in theoretical power. For of the enjoyment of our experience of qualities NTL does offer both necessary and sufficient conditions. Thus, just as no beauty that we experience escapes NTB, no enjoyment we have escapes NTL.

A second thing to notice about NTL is the logic of the notion of "reproduction" and, in particular, how it meets the demands on a theory of enjoyment developed in Section 5. One of those demands is that the theory describe an activity R such that one has, in enjoyment, an "intrinsic desire" to *continue* doing R. In the above statement of NTL, that activity R is reproduction. NTL incorporates an intrinsic desire for R by specifying (in proposition II) that S's reproducing a part of his enjoyable experience both arouses and satisfies S's desire so to reproduce. Just how such arousal takes place I have yet to describe. But for the present I want to focus on how the notion of reproduction satisfies the demand that R be desired to *continue*.

Superficially, reproduction does not meet this demand, because the notion of continuing does not explicitly figure in NTL. The reasons that it does not are as follows. Continuing to do R presupposes the present doing of R, but at any given moment of enjoying some "object" $CASCO$, I may *not* be experiencing the quality Q that is precisely what I am enjoying *about* $CASCO$. Hence I am not at that moment reproducing an experience of Q. In other words, a consequence of my reducing the enjoyment of some $CASCO$ to the enjoyment of the qualities involved in it is that the continuity in the enjoyment of $CASCO$ "drops out" in the theoretical analysis of that enjoyment. But the notion of reproduction retains the idea of "going on" with something *without* presupposing continuity in the experience of qualities. At the same time, reproduction is compatible with such continuity. Thus my reproductions of my experience of a quality in any case of enjoyment may or may not be experienced by me as continuous with what they are reproductions of. The "going on" element in "continuity" is captured in the "re-" of "reproduction," which I define as the production "of another one."

Of course, a striking feature of NTL is that in producing an activity R as an essential feature of any case of enjoyment, including cases of enjoying any $CASCO$, it has *not* produced in R what might have prima facie been expected. For it would appear initially that in my enjoyment of, say, an instance of cooking, hiking, or dancing, what both arouses and satisfies my desire to "keep on" is just that stint of cooking, hiking, or dancing. Now, NTL does not imply that it is *false* that in my enjoyment of a hike, say, it may be the hiking itself that arouses my desire to go on hiking. But via its reduction of enjoyment to the enjoyment of the experiences of qualities, NTL insists that this sort of arousal (the hiking arousing the desire to hike) is complex and derivative, that it must be analyzed into more basic components. For NTL implies that since not everything about an enjoyable hike is enjoyable, it can only be the enjoyable aspects of the hiking that arouse the desire to keep on hiking. But since those aspects are precisely enjoyable experiences of qualities, and those enjoyable experiences arouse the desire to reproduce them, and since, in a case of hiking, continuing to hike is an obvious *way* to reproduce them, the desire to keep on hiking is aroused. But notice that in this story, the hiking becomes a *means* of reproducing what is more immediately enjoyed, namely, the experiences of qualities. NTL thus implies that though in enjoying any complex activity, state, or condition we usually do want to continue in that activity, state, or condition, it is only "for the sake" of the enjoyable experiences that it affords. It is not "for its own sake."

Thus not only does NTL reinterpret an enjoyable complex activity, state, or condition as a *means* for the reproduction of the primarily enjoyable experiences of qualities, but it opens up the possibility that remaining in that activity, state, or condition is not the sole means of such reproduction. And, indeed, that implication accords with certain ordinary facts about enjoyment. Thus when we enjoy hearing a concert, we may be enjoying, among a vast number of things, hearing a certain elegance in the performing style of the artists. In so hearing and enjoying, we produce more experiences of that elegance by—of course—continuing to sit there and listen to the music, but also by "relaxing" and allowing that sense of elegance to "expand through" us however it will; or, if we play one of the instruments, by imagining playing with such finesse and elegance; or, if we do not play, by imagining the elegant playing as elegantly drawn lines on a page, or as elegant body movements of our own. Or if we are enjoying dancing, we may enjoy hearing and feeling the heavy sexuality of the music. And so we may do a variety of things to produce those experiences further, such as continuing to dance, letting the raunchiness "sink into" our bodies, imagining ourselves as sexy as the music sounds to us, recalling from the past images and contexts of our own heavy sexuality, or observing the raunchiness of the other dancers on the floor.

Now, the first of these examples at least may raise some protests along these lines: insofar as I let my imagination "wander" in listening to a concert, so that I imagine myself playing music, or drawing, or dancing, I am to that extent simply not *enjoying the concert* any longer; there are limits to what can count as "enjoying the concert," and insofar as NTL does not respect those limits, it is incorrect or otherwise defective.[59] My response has two parts. First, such an objection may come from an impulse to try to find the "proper" aesthetic response to art. Insofar as those moved by such an impulse are concerned with enjoyment at all, they are seeking what I would call a *normative* theory of enjoyment—a theory of how one *ought to* enjoy things, especially high art. (Thus the same persons who might object to my description of enjoying the concert would probably consider my description of enjoying dancing beyond the aesthetic pale altogether.) NTL remains, by contrast, resolutely nonnormative. Thus, as there are, in fact or in possibility, persons who can enjoy concerts in the way described, NTL simply *accounts* for that fact without attempting a judgment of propriety or impropriety.

But, second, NTL has no dispute with anyone who alleges that the above description is not a description of enjoying *the concert* or *the music*. For NTL establishes only a necessary condition for the enjoyment of complex activites like listening to a concert. It thus does not claim to be a complete theory of enjoyment *of such activities*; it claims to establish neither *sufficient* conditions for such enjoyment nor *all* necessary conditions. As far as NTL is concerned, there may well be some (even nonnormative) theory of enjoying concerts, compatible with NTL, according to which some of the above descriptions would not be part of enjoying the concert. Such a theory might maintain, for example, that for enjoyment to be (genuinely) *of the concert*, the qualities enjoyed must be restricted in a certain way, or that the *means of reproducing* qualities must be restricted in a certain way. NTL claims only that whatever the outcome of such a theory, the means of reproduction described above will still be elements of enjoying the certain elegance that the performers of the music exhibit. NTL claims further that if the concert is genuinely enjoyed, on whatever theory, there must be *some* qualities the enjoyer enjoys experiencing and, moreover, that the enjoyer must reproduce the experience of them *in some way*. Just as NTB is a general theory only of beautiful qualities, not of beautiful "objects," NTL is a general theory only of enjoyable experiences of qualities, not of all enjoyable "objects."

Thus from the point of view of NTL the enjoyable complex activity, state, or condition becomes simply a means of reproducing enjoyable experiences involved in, but not necessarily only in, that activity, state, or condition. This theoretical reinterpretation of enjoyable "objects" suggests an explanation of

130

why, when we are enjoying some complex activity, state, or condition, we are universally *pleased that* we are in that activity, state, or condition. Recall from Section 5 that such an explanation is required of an adequate theory of enjoyment. The explanation NTL offers is simply that we are pleased that we are in an activity, state, or condition because our being in that activity, state, or condition satisfies a desire to be in that activity, state, or condition. And we have such a desire precisely because to remain in that activity, state, or condition is an obvious and reliable means of reproducing many enjoyable experiences of qualities. But of course, according to NTL, being so pleased does not *constitute* our enjoyment of that complex activity, state, or condition. For, on this reading, we are pleased that we are in an activity, state, or condition only because we are enjoying (something about) it; we are not enjoying it because we are pleased that we are in it.[60]

There is one further observation I want to make about NTL. It is an explanation of why, according to NTL, the *experience reproduced* in a case of enjoyment must itself be a "part" of the enjoyed experience. For it is by this means that NTL seeks to augment the notion of "reproduction" so that it captures a necessary element in the notion of *continuing* to do R. Whereas one can continue to do only what one is already doing, one can of course reproduce any experience that one can recall. This feature of the concept of reproduction has advantages that I have already discussed. But unless the experience being enjoyed and the experience being reproduced are explicitly linked, as in NTL, the possibility will remain open of the reproduced experience occurring *before*, even well before, a current case of enjoyment. But a basic intuition behind NTL is precisely that, in enjoying a thing, I want more of *that very thing* and hence reproduce *it*.

131

Now, in blocking the possibility of my reproducing in enjoyment some (relatively distant) past experience, NTL does not deny the possibility of cases such as (1) enjoying in memory an experience from the past and (2) reproducing an experience from the past because it was enjoyable. NTL interprets case 1 as follows: in remembering a quality from one's past, one *ipso facto* has a present experience of it, since remembering is a mode of experience; thus in enjoying the remembered quality, one reproduces the present (memory) experience of it. Case 2 does not even count as a case of enjoyment, according to NTL, unless the reproduction of the past experience is itself reproduced. After all, I may return to the scene of some great past enjoyment precisely to experience those once enjoyed qualities again, but find my soul, twenty years older, dead to them now.

27. *Some Corroborating Experiences*

In this section and the next I discuss (1) certain kinds of cases of enjoyment and how NTL comprehends them and (2) certain kinds of *descriptions* of enjoyment and how NTL interprets them. These discussions are intended to show not only how NTL applies to a variety of cases of enjoyment, but also how NTL is consonant with some common ways of describing enjoyment, as well as how NTL "accounts for" both those cases and those descriptions.

A characteristic way of enjoying something, especially a simple quality, is to "savor" it. Savoring, of course, is most at home in the world of taste. Thus if I savor the taste of a wine, I let it linger in my mouth, but not in a static way. I allow it to come into contact with more of my taste-sensitive parts; I pay more attention to its taste as, in the course of my swallowing it, it passes over my taste-sensitive parts. But we can enjoy visual and tactile qualities in a similar way. We can run our hands back and forth over the fur, or the sanded board, or the waxed surface. Or we can return our glance over and over again to the gorgeous color, or run our eyes up and down the graceful lines of a chair. It is, I take it, obvious how such "reperceivings" of qualities can count as cases of "reproduction" in the technical sense of NTL.

Closely related to "savoring" are the characteristic moves we make to increase our perceptual access to something we are enjoying. Thus, when the stunning legs stride past us on the beach, we sit up to prolong the view, or to see more clearly. Or we move closer to, or around, what we enjoy looking at, again to see it more clearly, from more points of view, or simply longer. Sometimes when we see something enjoyable to look at whose enjoyed qualities are also tactile, we move to touch it, to pick up and stroke the gnarled driftwood or the smooth rock, to run our hands over the graceful lines of the vase, even up and down the muscled legs. We move to engage our sense of touch even, as in museums, when we know we may not complete such a move. Such cases of enjoyment, again, show clearly the kinds of phenomena that the concept of "reproduction" applies to.

Sometimes we think of enjoying a thing as "feeling it deeply." This is often true of our enjoyment of art. Thus I may feel the tactile qualities of a sculpture very deeply. And though I am forbidden to touch it, and do not, the urge to touch, even to embrace it with my whole body, may be very strong. And this urge may signal itself to me precisely by kinaesthetic feelings throughout my body, by my feeling throughout my body "almost as if" I were embracing it. Or I may feel the exuberance of the dancers "down to my toes." Or experience, as I read of Sydney Carton's self-sacrifice, feelings of self-esteem swell in my own breast. Or feel in my own eyes and face and "heart," as I hear Purcell's "Lament," the desperate melancholy of Dido's final moments. Such cases of enjoyment as "deeply feeling" a quality are, of course, varieties of what I call "expansion experiences." And such experiences may, of course, *simply* "flow into" or "over" me. But I may also, when I find myself having such experiences, *allow* such experiences to invade me, deliberately not put a halt to them. Even more, I may—perhaps because of my expectations about the particular work of art, or because of certain social conventions of appreciating art I have adopted—*encourage* such deep feelings. Such "allowings" and "encouragings" are, of course, instances of "reproduction."

Occasionally a contrast between enjoying and not enjoying a thing becomes an "issue" for us. The issue is often whether we want to, should, or can learn to enjoy what we do not now enjoy or have not enjoyed. I may find riding a high and steep roller coaster frightening, though some people aver it to be enjoyable. I may resolve to try to enjoy such rides. I realize that if I am afraid, I tend to tense up, probably as a natural way of preparing myself for impending disaster. So I resolve to relax and try to enjoy the experience. If I am successful, I train myself to cease resisting the swooping and diving sensations in my innards. I learn, instead, to "go with" those sensations; I allow myself to feel those very qualities of the motion of my body throughout my body. In a similar way, I may learn to overcome the minor unpleasantness of the ride (and the stop) of an elevator by deliberately "imitating" in a global way the qualities of the motion my body takes on in an elevator ride and thus come to enjoy such rides. What such enjoyment involves is thus accentuating the qualities felt by feeling them in more "places" and more "fully" and more "lingeringly" than before. Again, such "imitatings," "accentuatings," and "allowings to feel" are cases of what NTL describes as "reproduction."

In the *Nicomachean Ethics* Aristotle says that pleasure, or at least one sort of pleasure, *is* an "activity" (1153a8–16). I do not claim to know what Aristotle meant by this, and here is not the place to try to find out. But we are free to suppose that Aristotle meant by such pleasure what I am calling "enjoyment." Prima facie, this is not an unreasonable assumption, for according to both Aristotle and NTL such pleasure not only "arises from" such complex activities as, for example, thinking and learning, but *is* an activity. What that activity is, Aristotle does not say. NTL says it is "reproduction." Aristotle does say of the activity that he has in mind, however, that it is "unimpeded." Whether the reproduction that, according to NTL, is a case of enjoyment fits the description "unimpeded" I do not know, for Aristotle gives us little to go on in interpreting this term. I bring up the term in this context only because a natural interpretation of "unimpeded" is "uninhibited." And if we look at some cases of being uninhibited in the enjoyment of a thing, we find more interpretations and applications of the concept of reproduction.

Suppose that I enjoy some qualities of a given performance by reproducing those qualities in certain expansion experiences of mine, but that those enjoyed qualities are reproduced only in my own "act-beginnings." But suppose some fellow spectators refuse to inhibit their own enjoyment in accordance with late bourgeois conventions of spectatorship. Suppose they refuse to stop their "reproduction" before it affects their external actions. Suppose, further, that they quite deliberately act out their enjoyment. Then I may find, depending on what I am spectator *to*, people dancing in the lobby during intermission or standing during a concert and dancing in place, or small boys playing mock baseball behind the bleachers during a baseball game and imagining, I can assume, within themselves the cleverness, grace, or power they are witnessing in the real game. Or I may find actual weeping over the loss, on the stage, of love and fortune. Now, these sorts of uninhibited behavior occur. And my point is that, not only can they constitute cases of enjoyment, but they can exemplify the concept of reproduction. For if we make in such cases the reasonable assumption that these overt acts of the spectators are accompanied by those spectators' *experiences* of the relevant qualities in their own acts, those experiences can easily be inferred to be "reproductions" of experiences of those very qualities exhibited on the stage or in the field.

Some readers may balk at my describing a case of weeping over sadness on the stage, screen, or radio as enjoyment. I do not mean to describe every such case as a case of enjoyment, only such as conform to NTL. There are possible cases that do not. My "sympathetic" response to sadness in a *character*, say, can be a case of enjoyment. A fictional disaster which reminds me of a disaster of my own may not be a case of enjoyment; it may just be a case of my being saddened. But, of course, NTL does not imply that every case of my being saddened, any more than every case of my being made joyous, is a case of enjoyment. In fact, there is no more reason to balk at the possibility of my enjoying the sadness on the stage than at the possibility of my enjoying my own sadness, a possibility that NTL also countenances.

But if the latter is true, the hypothetical balker may retort, there is even more reason to question this consequence of NTL. I have several responses. First, one must cleanse one's mind of the Disneyland conception of enjoyment, according to which enjoyment is unrelieved "fun." Such a conception would make it impossible to acknowledge any serious or sober activity as enjoyable. But since Aristotle's time we have been reminding ourselves that many activities that are not pure fun are in fact enjoyable. Of course sadness is not merely *not fun*; it is worse than merely serious or sober: there is real *unpleasantness* connected with sadness. But again we must distinguish between the unpleasantness, the disappointment or frustration, caused by what also causes us to be sad, and the sadness itself. And we must further distinguish such unpleasantness from the "pleasure" of enjoyment. The unpleasantness is, to adapt an earlier term, a kind of "propositional unpleasantness"; it is the result of some desire of mine *not* being satisfied. Even if to enjoy the sadness that results from such an unpleasantness is to experience some form of pleasure, it is not necessarily to deny the existence of, counteract, or ameliorate *that* unpleasantness. Indeed, were it to do so, in terms of NTL it could hardly count as enjoyment at all, for its effect would be to *diminish* my sadness.

But quite apart from these possibilities and distinctions, the balker might retort, do we in fact *enjoy* our own sadness? I think so. And it is precisely when we give way to it, when we do not inhibit its expression, that we enjoy it. Quite apart from any commitment to NTL, I could understand what a psychotherapist, say, or a good friend might mean if she told me, in a time of my grief, to enjoy my sadness. She would mean to live it through (which is not the same as "living through it"), to feel it to its "bottom." She would mean not only to allow myself to feel it deeply within myself but also to experience it in my overt behavior. How such things relate to "reproduction" is, I trust, clear.

But the skeptical balker might still object. By what right is such activity included under the concept "enjoyment"?

Where, in other words, is the *pleasure* in such activity? My response again depends partially upon the point that not all pleasures are "fun," and some of the best are far from it. In the case of enjoying my sadness, or the sadness of a character in a movie, the pleasure is, among other things, the pleasure of release, the pleasure of being free from inhibiting feelings or behavior. It may be not unlike the pleasure, therefore, of *literal* purgation. And it may be just this similarity that led Aristotle to use the medical metaphor of "catharsis" to describe similar phenomena in the *Poetics*. For the enjoyment of my own grief, or that of a sympathetic character in fiction, usually feels very much like "unbinding" myself. Admittedly, it does not seem right to call such feelings "pleasures," or even "pleasant." A more colloquial, and accurate, description, which is still very much to the present point, is that it "feels good" so to "unbind myself."

28. *Further Corroborations*

There are yet more connections between enjoyment and uninhibited behavior. Generally speaking, we think of a person as enjoying a given activity if his performance thereof is more expansive, less restrained than if he were not enjoying it. A person really enjoying an activity does it "all out"; he "gets into it." These phrases connote the special enthusiasm, verve, intensity, or involvement that enjoyment brings to an activity. The question for NTL, of course, is how, if at all, the latter kinds of "uninhibited" activity are interpretable in terms of the key theoretical notion of "reproduction." The connection, I believe, runs along the following lines. To look uninhibitedly at a beautiful body, say, is to look at it longer, or examine it more carefully, or look at it more intently than when one *simply* looks at it. Similarly, if I enjoy looking (on an occasion) at that body, I probably look at it longer, more intently, more carefully than I would if I did not enjoy looking at it. And the latter sorts of looking behavior are precisely *means* of reproducing visual experiences of that body. So too, if I am uninhibitedly listening to Strauss waltzes, I may sway to the music, move my hands as if conducting it, and even hum along. Such behavior can count as signs of my enjoying listening to the waltzes. But such behavior is also the means of reproducing experiences of certain qualities. The movements of my body and of my vocal cords are the more than incipient, but less than overt, acts in which I can *feel*, say, the grace, or the drama, or the flamboyance that I enjoy *hearing* in the music. Then again, I may be enjoying playing a game of volleyball, enjoying precisely the competitiveness, the aggressiveness, the energy of that particular game, and my enjoyment may show in the uninhibited way I play. In such a case, my playing will exhibit a *great deal* of competitiveness, aggressiveness, and energy. And that will be just because I am "reproducing" the experiences of (my own) competitiveness, aggressiveness, and energy by behaving *very* competitively, aggressively, and energetically. For the more aspects of my behavior that show such qualities, the more experiences of such qualities I shall have, the more uninhibited my playing will be, and the more I shall (according to NTL) enjoy playing the game. I am not arguing here that all enjoyed activities are uninhibitedly pursued activities. I am only trying to show how, insofar as enjoyed activities are truly described as uninhibited activities, such uninhibitedness may be interpreted in terms of "reproduction."

There are many cases of my enjoying doing a thing that it would be inappropriate to describe as uninhibited. The very enjoyable playing of a subtle, refined, intellectual piece on the piano, the enjoyable reading of a scientific article, or the enjoyable playing of a game of chess is not likely to be called "uninhibited." Nevertheless, important features we noticed in cases of uninhibited enjoyment can appear also in these kinds of cases, and such features, too, are interpretable in terms of "reproduction." In particular, it can be a manifestation of my enjoyment of an activity—that is, of certain qualities of an activity—that precisely those qualities are "magnified" in my performance of the activity. If in writing a paper I am really enjoying constructing arguments for my points, and in particular if I am enjoying the subtlety of distinctions or the carefulness needed to thread my way exegetically through a text, then I will characteristically expand upon these distinctions and multiply them or begin to pick my way with even more care and finesse through the textual labyrinth. Thus we say of an author whose writings are replete with subtle distinctions that she "enjoys" making such distinctions. Or sometimes I can even so enjoy my own industriousness or energy in cleaning the house that one task done leads me to undertake another and yet another unpremeditated chore; my own (enjoyed) energy feeds itself, and the industry I exhibit in one activity shows up in the others. Or suppose that, planning to spend a short time relaxing before writing another few pages, I start to enjoy the calm of that pace so much that I not only prolong my period of relaxation, but expand it to include lying on a comfortable chair with pillows and drinks in the warm sunshine. Thus the calm, even languor, of the relaxed pace of my mental activity becomes a quality of my whole posture, attitude, and manner. In such cases, the enjoyed qualities in my own actions become, as I enjoy them, qualities of more and more of my actions. And as a consequence, I exhibit greater degrees of those qualities, just as, in the volleyball example, I exhibit, because of my uninhibited playing, greater degrees of competitiveness, aggressiveness, and energy. But since the "magnitude" of the relevant qualities is, in both cases, a function of those qualities being exhibited by a large number of different kinds of acts of mine over a lengthening period of time, it should be obvious how such acts are construable, given the (I take it) unexceptionable assumption of my own consciousness, as *means of reproducing* experiences of the respective qualities.

Of course, according to the New Theory of Beauty, if the qualities I exhibit in my actions add up, in a given case, to my exhibiting a *high degree* of such qualities, then I *ipso facto* exhibit *beauty* with respect to those qualities. Some of the preceding examples of enjoyment, therefore, suggest that my acting beautifully with respect to certain qualities may be, on the one hand, a means of reproducing experiences of those qualities and, on the other, a result of reproducing such experiences. Or it may be both at once. In such cases, then, my own beautiful actions could be, not only the object of my own enjoyment, but both its means and its result as well. In conjunction with NTB, NTL is able to account well for this interesting kind of case. But I want to stress that such cases of beautiful performance are only special cases of enjoyment. There is no necessary connection between our enjoying a thing and that thing either being beautiful or being taken by us to be beautiful. There is, nevertheless, a peculiar relation between enjoyment and beauty, of which the above cases are only special examples. In the following I want to show how NTL, again in conjunction with NTB, can account for that peculiar relation.

I take the following propositions to be true: (1) beauty in an "object" is neither necessary to the enjoyment of the "object" nor the only thing about an "object" that is enjoyable; and (2) even when it is apprehended, the beauty of an "object" is not always enjoyed. The grounds for believing these propositions are simply that there are obvious counterexamples to their negations. Furthermore, not only is NTL consistent with these two propositions, but it can "explain" them as well. NTL explains (1) by the supposition that all that a person needs to enjoy any "object" is to experience some quality *of whatever degree* involved in that "object." It explains (2) by the requirement that to enjoy the experience of some quality in any "object," I must *reproduce* that experience. There is a third proposition, related to the above two, that *seems* to be as indisputable even though the *grounds* of our believing it—pretheoretically, as it were—are extremely obscure. That is the proposition that beauty in any "object" *ipso facto* makes that "object" more enjoyable, though not, in every case, enjoyed. NTL provides an explanation of why the latter proposition should be so, an explanation that can also serve as grounds for believing it.

According to NTB, beauty is a high degree of a quality in an "object." But in most, if not all, cases of beauty that we experience, we can divide that experience in imagination into "parts" each of which is itself an experience of an "object" that is a part of the experienced beautiful "object." Moreover, each of these partial "objects" possesses the very quality possessed by the beautiful "object," but may not possess it in a high degree. Furthermore, we can so divide the experience of beauty that each part of the beautiful "object" possesses a *minimally* experienceable degree of the relevant beautiful quality. Thus, for example, my experience of the extreme smoothness of the polished tabletop I can imagine as consisting of experiences of tabletop segments that are recognizably, if not necessarily beautifully, smooth, in such a way that the experience of the complete tabletop is an experience of a beautifully smooth tabletop. I can imagine similar divisions of my experience of the

142

beautiful feathery quality of the tree outside my window, of the beautiful calm of the sea, or of the beautiful clarity of Helen's skin. Or I can imagine my experience of my own high energy during the volleyball game as divided into experiences of my own energetic actions or even movements during the game, no one of which may count for me as beautifully energetic, but all of which add up to an experience of my being, over the whole game, beautifully energetic. I believe that most experiences of beauty can be thus divided into experiences of "increments" of beauty; only some experiences of qualities of "claritas" would appear to elude such a division.

The possibility of this sort of division suggests how experiences of beautiful qualities that are so divisible *lend themselves*, in a way that other experiences of qualities do not, to reproduction, and hence to enjoyment. First, divisible experiences can be initially experienced, or reexperienced, *serially*, and even if such a serial experience is not a reproduction because it is not produced *in order to* reexperience a quality, it nevertheless has the serial *form* of reproduction. A similar argument can be made that expansion experiences that are not reproductions may nevertheless *lend themselves* to reproduction simply because they present the (serial) form of reproduction. More than simply possibly presenting the serial form of reproduction, however, such divisible experiences present more *opportunities* for reproduction than nondivisible experiences. Such experiences present a variety of possibilities for *reexperiencing* the quality in a "natural" way, that is, by varying the focus, or "objects," of each experience. By the very variety of their parts, in other words, experiences of beauty can provide, as it were, "tracks" for reproduction. A similar point can be made about the non-reproductive expansion experiences mentioned above; they too can provide suggestive "tracks," or possibilities for reproduction. Finally, in experiences of beauty there is, again because of their divisibility, simply *more* to reproduce than in other experiences of qualities. Again, a related point can be made about nonreproductive expansion experiences. NTL can thus explain why, generally speaking, beauty is more enjoyable than nonbeauty. And it can thus also explain, as a kind of corollary, why the experiences of qualities, whether beautiful or not, that are parts of spontaneous expansion experiences are in general more enjoyable than "simple" experiences of qualities.

But there is yet another, quite different, connection between enjoyment and beauty that "falls out" quite unexpectedly as a consequence of NTL. It is a surprising consequence, for it seems, to me at least, not to be anticipated by pretheoretical intuition. And yet it also seems to me to harbor profound implications, though I have only the dimmest notions at present what they might be. My brief remarks on how experiences are individuated imply that as a quality seems to us to "increase" in an expansion experience, the experience itself adds "parts," which are themselves experiences of the same quality as possessed by different "objects." Similarly, as we reproduce experiences of a quality we produce for ourselves additional experiences of that quality. Now, even without extensively analyzing the notion of "consciousness," we can reasonably infer that insofar as one has an experience of a quality, one is aware or conscious of that quality, even if one is not thereby self-reflectively or *self*-consciously aware either of the quality or of one's experience thereof. But from this it also seems to follow that the *more* experiences one has of a quality during a period which is "connected" in our experience in the way that reproductive experience is, the "greater," generally speaking, one's awareness of that quality is. That is to say, my being aware of a given quality Q seems itself to be a property of qualitative degree.

And a high degree of that property would seem to be a function of the greater "number" of experiences constituent of it.[61] But if that is so, then the more one reproduces, and hence enjoys, an experience of Q, the more aware of Q I am. I do not mean to imply here that degree of enjoyment is dependent *entirely* on degree of "consciousness." I want to imply only that the latter is a very important factor. But if that is so, then we can infer that, in general, to enjoy a thing is to increase one's consciousness of it, and to enjoy a thing very much is to have a high degree of awareness of that thing. But this in turn implies that the enjoyment we take in a thing at least moves us towards, and sometimes consists in, a state in which *we are beautiful*. This consequence presents a striking contrast to the most hedonistic theory of beauty that I know of, that of George Santayana. As is well known, Santayana, identifies beauty with pleasure of a certain kind, namely, pleasure that is "objectified."[62] What Santayana means by this is controversial. But its meaning is not important to my point, which is simply that in this radically hedonistic view, beauty is a *form of pleasure*. But NTB and NTL together have as a consequence, to the contrary, that pleasure—or at least pleasure that is constituted by enjoyment—is, or approaches, a *form of beauty*.

29. The Love of Virtue

Since it applies to all qualities, NTL applies to moral qualities as well. But this raises several questions. First, what are characteristic cases in which moral qualities are "reproduced"? Second, what does the term "Love" mean when applied to the reproduction of moral qualities? Can "Love" in such cases mean "enjoy"? If not, what does it mean? Does "Love" always mean the same thing when applied to cases of the reproduction of moral qualities? In this section and the next two I shall try to answer these questions. In doing so I hope not only to illuminate a range of cases of reproduction, and discover some surprising ones, but to come closer, as well, to determining what, after all, NTL is a theory *of*.

Imagine the following three situations in which you end up taking what is, by hypothesis, the morally correct action.

(a) On a lonely road at night you spy a motorist whose car has broken down and who clearly needs help. Your initial feeling is sympathy for his plight, but you do not immediately resolve to pull over and offer help. You wonder whether someone behind you might stop, but you see no one. You suddenly resent the fact that you are the only available help. You feel annoyed by this because you are tired and in a hurry to get home. You do pull over begrudgingly, and as you stop you have mixed feelings—resentment, irritation, and a new burst of sympathy—as it becomes obvious to you that the fellow has been waiting for some time and is very glad to see you.

(b) Imagine again spying a motorist who appears to be in distress, but this time on a well-traveled road at a "safe" time of day. Immediately you feel what you have come to call your "standard moral tug"—the feeling that you are morally bound to do something for this person. But you restrain your impulse to stop because you've lately come to mistrust those feelings. After all, you reason, you do not *know* the motorist is in trouble; and if he is, there are plenty of other cars on the road who might stop to help. Do I, you think, always have to play "savior"? Are not my all-too-ready feelings of obligation merely a disguise for a desire to be always "in charge" of a problematic situation? And so you accelerate past, glance over, and notice that the motorist does not really seem to be in trouble at all. Nevertheless, your "moral tug" proving too strong for your

146

second thought, you stop on a dime, back up, and discover that some help was truly needed.

(c) Suppose, coming out of the store reflecting on the change you received, you suddenly realize you have gotten back ten dollars too much. Without a thought you wheel back to return the money. But after a step or two you hesitate, thinking that "no one" will ever know, that although the clerk will be responsible for making up the difference, he will never see you again to accuse you, even if he remembers you and connects you with the error. But after some milliseconds of wavering, in which you begin to feel some compassion for the poor salesclerk, your initial sense of honesty returns in a flood, and as you feel the growing mask of deceit you were weaving for yourself crumble, you freely step back to return the ten dollars.

But now imagine the above situations *without* the hesitations and waverings, the hemmings and hawings. Imagine, instead, that you "go with" your initial feelings, allowing them free play in you and, especially, allowing them to freely "spill over" into your behavior. Thus in situation (a) not only does your compassion impel you to stop, but you allow this quality of compassion to be clearly perceptible in what you say to the motorist and how you say it and in how you go about helping him. Without patronizing the motorist, you give him appropriate emotional as well as material support, listening sympathetically to his tale, and so forth. In situation (b), your demeanor is "stiffer," since the moral sentiment involved is a "harder" one, but there is no apology for your action, or any begrudging it, in the way you sound, or look, or move. Your act is "freely" done, but out of a sense of obligation, and your words and actions, as you proceed to help the motorist, show that. In situation (c), since it is, by hypothesis, an unrestrained sense of honesty that is "behind" your action, that same open-

147

ness is visible and audible in your face and demeanor as you return the change. There is no tautness or sense of reserve in your manner, for in this case there is no consciousness of, and hence no shame about, an inclination *not* to return the money.

Now, the first set of cases illustrates what it might be to perform morally correct actions unaccompanied—from initial feeling to completed act—by any reproduction of the initial experience of your own moral quality. The second, modified set of cases illustrates the performance of the "same" morally correct actions, but with the addition of the kind of reproduction specified in NTL. I take the latter cases to exemplify clearly virtuous actions. They exemplify the virtues of compassion, moral responsibility, and honesty. I also believe they exemplify these virtues more clearly and obviously than do the corresponding acts in the first set of cases. I do not claim that the acts in the first set are *not* virtuous acts, but for all their (*ex hypothesi*) moral correctness and for all the fact that *some* appropriate moral sentiment is involved in them, the acts in the first set are nevertheless less admirable and less "morally worthy" than those in the second set. This says *something* interesting, I take it, about morally correct acts that are describable in terms of NTL. But *what?*

And what does NTL say about those "morally more admirable" acts that fall under it? In particular, does NTL say that the agents in the second set of cases, in contrast to the agents in the first set, are *enjoying* anything? For if we interpret the term "Love" in NTL as "enjoyment," it would follow that the latter agents are *enjoying* their own moral qualities and the acts that exhibit them. Are they? The vulgar answer, offered by those who speak from the most "ready-made" of intuitions, is: Clearly not. The most considered and imaginative answer, on the other hand, will be: Possibly so. There will likely be few shouts of: Definitely yes! One reason for the vulgar answer is the "Disneyland conception" of enjoyment as "unrelieved fun." And morality is, after all, always serious, often difficult, and sometimes downright unpleasant business. But the shortcomings of the Disneyland conception I have already indicated. Many things are enjoyed besides the frivolous and the jocular. Philosophy is serious yet can be enjoyed. Mountain climbing is difficult and yet enjoyed. Marathon running can be in some respects downright unpleasant and still be enjoyed.

Despite such considerations, however, it admittedly still sounds somewhat peculiar to speak of enjoying (our own) moral acts or moral qualities. An important reason for this is that for most people the term "enjoyment" suggests a self-centered concern for the agent's own pleasure that is at least inappropriate for genuinely virtuous action, if it does not actually conflict with it. Such concerns, however, seem to me to be confused in one or both of two ways. First, the complaint may be confusing the agent's enjoyment of virtuous action with his self-satisfaction in, or self-congratulation for, acting virtuously. But neither the second set of cases above nor anything about NTL justifies the latter. Pleasures of self-satisfaction or self-congratulation, while logically compatible with virtuous action that involves "reproduction" of moral qualities, are neither identical with it nor its necessary accompaniment. Such pleasure, moreover, unlike enjoyment, is purely propositional pleasure. One is pleased by, and congratulates oneself for, (what one takes to be) *the fact that* one is acting virtuously.

Second, the complaint may mistakenly assume that if an agent truly enjoys her "virtuous" action, then her *motive* for acting must be morally inappropriate, and hence such action *cannot* be virtuous at all. This assumption does have some plausibility. For if the actions in the second set of cases above do

149

indeed fall under the concept of "reproduction," then the agents in those cases must be taking overt action *in order to* reproduce their experience of their own moral qualities. But in those cases the virtue of the actions lay precisely in acting to help the distressed motorist, to do the moral thing, or to be honest. Thus to interpret actions according to NTL seems, *eo ipso*, to attribute *non*moral motives to the agent.

The solution to the problem this poses for NTL is this: There are many ways of reproducing moral qualities. Not all of them involve actually doing the morally correct thing or even acting overtly at all. When one actually performs a morally correct action one may well be doing it in order to produce thereby an experience of one's own moral quality. But one may also choose a particular way of producing such an experience precisely because it is also the morally correct (and virtuous) action. In other words, although the concept of reproduction specifies why the reproducer reproduces, it does not determine why any *particular* means of reproduction is chosen, thus leaving it open that a person might do a thing to help the stranded motorist, to do the responsible thing, to do the honest thing.

In the above I have tried to argue against some (hypothetical) reasons why the enjoyment of moral qualities in virtuous actions is not possible. But my arguments, even if convincing, can produce only the conclusion that it is possible to enjoy such acts. They do not show that such acts are ever *properly described* as "enjoyed." But I think no convincing arguments will ever yield the latter conclusion if the considerations I have adduced so far are insufficient. Any lingering fastidiousness about describing some morally correct and virtuous acts as "enjoyed" must surely have its source in the affective connotations of "enjoy." There may be some sentiment that, no matter what the "logic" of "enjoy" may allow, the emotional aura of the term is such that to speak of enjoyment in connection with virtue is somehow to trivialize the latter, or at least not to accord it its proper dignity. From this point of view, then, the problem is to find a word for the reproduction of moral qualities in morally correct and virtuous action that is more dignified than "enjoy," but related to it.

Fortunately, NTL suggests that word. It is "love" (not "Love").[63] In the immediately following I shall make a case for describing the agents in the second set of cases as "loving virtue." I start by trying to describe persons who can appropriately be said to be, not on this or that occasion only, but *generally speaking*, "lovers of virtue." Suppose, then, that the agents in those cases characteristically or always act morally correctly and virtuously. And further suppose that when they act virtuously they characteristically act in the same unhesitant, unwavering, undoubting style, that they always act "out of" their moral qualities and freely exhibit them in their moral acts. Suppose further that as a natural extension of the above such persons actively search out situations in which opportunities abound for the realization in action of the moral qualities in which they excel and that, furthermore, these persons more or less zealously—but gracefully and not strenuously—take advantage of such opportunities. Thus the courageous and just person joins armies of liberation, the compassionate or benevolent person founds charitable institutions in slums, the honest person becomes a leader in journalism or a reformer in the business world. In terms of NTL, these hypothetical persons seek out means for frequent and easy (because accessible) means of "reproduction" in themselves of experiences of their own moral qualities, and these means are precisely virtuous actions. They also regularly *use* just those means to reproduce experiences of those moral qualities. Finally, let us suppose that in their ordinary traffic with others such persons—quite naturally and spontaneously—characteristically manifest those very moral qualities in actions that are supererogatory. That is, they exhibit such qualities—again with a sort of natural effervescence—in actions that are not morally required, but which nevertheless show how deep-seated their moral qualities are, how they spread, as it were, to neighboring areas of their lives. I am thinking here about a more than ordinary thoughtfulness and kindness in even small matters, a remarkable openness and frankness of feeling and thought, a courage in minor matters of manners or business. If ever the term "lover of virtue" has a use, I submit, it is to describe such paradigms.

Of course, to say of such persons that they love virtue is to attribute a certain disposition to them. It is analogous to saying of a person that she enjoys, generally speaking, mountain climbing. And just as the person who so enjoys mountain climbing can, on an occasion, be enjoying climbing a mountain, so the person who in general loves (a particular) virtue can, on an occasion on which she is acting morally correctly and virtuously, be both exercising that virtue and manifesting her "love" of that virtue. Even though there is no *idiomatic* continuous present tense describing this manifestation of her "love," we know perfectly well how to make one up. The "lover of virtue" who is both exercising her virtue and manifesting her (dispositional) love of virtue is "loving" that virtue, or even "engaged in loving" that virtue. Just as there are both "dispositional" and "occurrent" kinds of enjoyment, there are "dispositional" and "occurrent" kinds of love, regardless of whether the English language marks the fact by giving both "enjoyment" and "love" continuous present tenses.

My case is made. A consequence is that, in addition to comprehending all cases of ordinary occurrent enjoyment, NTL also comprehends all manifestations of the (dispositional) love of virtue. It thus comes as no surprise to me that the only contexts in which I can recall seeing the term "lover of virtue" or its cognates used, namely, in (translations of) the works of Plato and Aristotle, are also contexts in which the connections between pleasure and virtue are assumed, asserted, and argued for.[64]

30. *Moral Self-Indulgence*

My aim in the previous section was to isolate the concept and phenomena of loving virtue *as an "occurrence."* For NTL comprehends directly such phenomena, which we can call "occurrent love," but not "dispositional love." Just so, NTL directly comprehends "occurrent enjoyment," but not "dispositional enjoyment."[65] But for expository purposes I found it more suitable first to introduce the phenomena of dispositional love of virtue. I want now to emphasize, however, that the dispositional love of virtue and the occurrent love of virtue are not necessarily linked. For just as it may happen, on an occasion, that I enjoy gardening without it being true, generally speaking, that I enjoy gardening, it may happen on some occasion that a morally correct act of mine is a part of my *occurrent* love of (some particular) virtue without it being true that I, generally speaking, love (that particular) virtue and *a fortiori* without it being true that I am, generally speaking, a lover of virtue (of that particular one or of virtue in general).

Having thus detached the occurrent love of virtue from the dispositional love of virtue, I now want to separate the occurrent love of virtue, on the one hand, from morally correct and virtuous action, on the other. In the three cases of occurrent love of virtue considered in the previous section the action involved is, by hypothesis, morally correct and virtuous. But what makes NTL relevant to these cases is the hypothesis that before, during, and after the acts the agents are experiencing their own moral qualities—compassion, moral responsibility, and honesty. Yet it is axiomatic to NTL that the experience of any quality in an "object" is independent of whether that "object" actually possesses the quality. Hence an agent might experience moral qualities in himself before, during, and after some act even if he or his act does not in fact possess those qualities—even if, in other words, neither he nor his act is in that instance either morally correct or virtuous. A person might even experience himself as having moral qualities when in fact he takes no moral action whatsoever. Moreover, in such cases the respective experiences of moral qualities might be "reproduced" in accordance with the conditions NTL places on occurrent "Love."

In the following I discuss a progression of cases in which persons' experiences of their own moral qualities are "reproduced" in accordance with the conditions NTL places on occurrent "Love." The progression begins with cases of the occurrent love of virtue that are also, though somewhat problematically, cases of morally correct or virtuous action. Next come cases of the occurrent love of virtue that are more and more problematically cases of morally correct or virtuous action, followed by cases that are more and more problematically cases of the occurrent love of virtue as well as problematically (or not at all) cases of morally correct or virtuous action. The progression concludes with cases of reproducing experiences of moral qualities that are neither cases of the occurrent love of virtue nor cases of morally correct or virtuous action. I also show how cases of "reproduction" that are not cases of the occurrent love of virtue may nevertheless be described in ways that relate them to love and enjoyment. My aim in this discussion is, first, to show the great range of cases of Loving moral qualities and, second, to give some additional interpretations and applications of the technical term "Love."

(a) It is possible, I take it, for a person who is both benevolent and just, on the whole, nevertheless to have "more" of the former virtue than of the latter. In such a case, the person might have, say, much sensitivity and feeling and concern for the interests of others but a less well developed sensitivity for and interest in matters of justice. Such a person might, for example, characteristically go out of her way to be benevolent, but not to be just. She might, in short, be something of a "lover" of benevolence, but not of justice, without yet being in the slightest unjust. Now, it is reasonable to suppose that cases might arise in the life of such a person in which the morally correct thing for her to do can be both a matter of benevolence and a matter of justice. Let us even suppose that some persons—lovers of justice, for example—would judge it to be *solely* a matter of justice. But let us suppose that she completely ignores the questions of justice in the matter, that she gives them no thought and has no "sentiments" that she connects with justice. And, finally, let us suppose that she acts fully, naturally, freely, and feelingly out of benevolence—that before, during, and after her action she "reproduces" experiences of her own benevolence.

By hypothesis, such a person does the morally correct thing. She surely acts virtuously, for she exhibits in abundance the (appropriate) virtue of benevolence and acts out of that virtue. The only thing wrong with her action is the insufficient concern she shows for justice. It seems wrong to deny that such a case is a case of (occurrently) loving virtue, namely, the virtue of benevolence. It is, if anything, a case of loving that virtue

155

"too much," or perhaps of "blindly" loving that virtue, for the love obscures relevant considerations and resists being moderated by such considerations.

(b) But there may be cases in which an act is done solely out of a virtue, say, compassion, in such a way that the agent experiences that virtue and reproduces it in his actions, but the action is not morally correct. Suppose that the case is one in which, although compassion for the accused is *in order*, for he has been surrounded by miserable conditions and pressed by terrible circumstances, justice *clearly demands* that he be convicted. It is, furthermore, at least dubious that freeing the accused out of compassion is a virtuous action, even if it is clearly done "out of virtue." The question for NTL, though, is whether the agent in so freeing the accused is *loving* the virtue of compassion. Again, I think so; it seems to me to be a case, to adapt the tag, of "loving, not wisely, but too well."

(c) There are cases in which morally correct, or at least not morally incorrect, acts are done out of compassion, say, and appropriately so, but the compassion in its expression and effect is "overdone." There may, of course, be many *reasons* why the compassion is "overdone," but the effect is almost always sentimental or patronizing or both. Almost of necessity, such instances of compassion occur in situations in which the *needed*, that is, morally required, compassion is less than great. Now, even in such cases, it is possible for the requisite "reproduction" to take place.

Other virtues too can be "overdone" in feeling and expression. Insisting on being "just" or "dutiful" or "honest" about the smallest of matters comes under this rubric—even if the resultant action genuinely is just or dutiful or honest. What is "overdone" in such cases is simply the amount of feeling and the expression of it. *Small* acts of duty, honesty, or justice, as of compassion and other virtues, are acts which, undone, would not have great consequences either for others or for oneself. Though not morally required, perhaps, such acts ought to be done, and done "out of" their respective virtues. They are better if done, furthermore, out of the love of virtue. What seems to be "wrong" when such acts are "overdone," and the overdone feelings and expressions are genuine, is that there is *too much* "love" of the virtue. And yet the reason for the scare quotes around "love" is precisely that "love" seems an inaccurate description. In such cases, in fact, I want to use "enjoy," and say that the agents in such "overdone" acts are enjoying, not the virtues, but *themselves* too much. Such a description demeans them—properly, in my opinion—by suggesting a kind of self-indulgence.

(d) We can extend the notion of self-indulgence to other cases in which there is an excess of moral sentiment and expression, but *no* moral action in the strict sense. These are cases in which there are "outpourings" of sentiment with respect to some person, event, or situation at such a remove from the agent as to make *acting* on those sentiments impossible. I am thinking of reading in the newspaper, for instance, of some story which evokes compassion, or benevolence, or even sentiments of responsibility, duty, or justice. Even when such sentiments are appropriate to their object, of course, there is a limit to how much we should "reproduce" the experiences of the respective virtues in our feelings, demeanor, and behavior. After all, we cannot *do* anything about the situation. To continue to feel and express such moral feelings seems indeed self-indulgent, if not downright self-congratulatory. In such cases there would seem to be no occurrent love of virtue; the Love of virtue involved seems really to be a kind of *enjoyment* of ourselves.

(e) There are, finally, the most degenerate cases of the Love of virtue—those in which our own moral sentiments are reproduced within ourselves, in our demeanor and external expressions, as well as in the actions we *fantasize* ourselves performing, but *not* in actions we actually perform. In such cases, we might have well-honed moral instincts and appropriate sentiments. The actions we imagine ourselves performing might even be, if performed, morally correct. It need not be the case even that we *substitute* such imagined actions for the real thing. It may be that the person who so fantasizes also performs correctly and virtuously when the opportunity arises. Such fantasies thus do not obstruct moral action and cannot otherwise be morally faulted.

What then is "degenerate" about them? Nothing serious, I want to claim. It is just that their claim to be cases of *loving virtue* is spurious. But their claim to be cases of Loving virtue is not. For such cases seem to be somewhat peculiar, if harmless, cases of simply *enjoying oneself* with respect to one's real and imagined moral qualities. Such cases would seem to be, not simply examples of moral self-indulgence, but instances of a kind of moral masturbation. Love, after all, comes in many forms.

31. *Loving Others*

Thus far I have discussed the Love of moral qualities in ourselves. But we can also Love moral qualities in others. Some of these "others" exist in fiction or art; others are our friends and lovers.

Moral qualities in artistic contexts often belong to characters in literature and theatrical pieces. And when such characters are "sympathetic," we often "feel the same" as they. Still, it sounds a little odd to say that when we felt within ourselves the loving tenderness, the noble courage, or the self-sacrificing discipline of the heroine or hero, we were *enjoying* those qualities in the character. On the other hand, it does sound right to say that we enjoyed the novel (play, movie, opera, or whatever) in part precisely because we did have such feelings. Or to say that we enjoy, in general, works that allow that sort of sympathy. This discrepancy is easily bridged, I think, by the concept of "identification."

The complex conditions under which we "identify" with a character—either totally or in this or that situation—need not detain us here. So much seems true, however: identifying with a character is what we are doing when we feel his moral qualities (or some of his nonmoral qualities, for that matter) within ourselves in act-beginnings, when we weep with, tense up with, become indignant with the character, when we want to continue our exposure to the character's qualities by following them to the end of the story. In such ways we reproduce the experience of those qualities and therefore, according to NTL, Love those qualities. Such cases of Love are, I think, unambiguous cases of enjoyment. For we enjoy works that portray characters we find sympathetic in part because we enjoy identifying with those characters, and we enjoy identifying with them because we enjoy experiencing those (moral and other) qualities in fictional "others" as if they were our own or those of someone to whom we are close. *Why* we enjoy such identification is probably a long story, but one that NTL is not committed to telling.[66]

But moral and quasi-moral qualities are exhibited even in works that have no characters, like nontheatrical music. Or in nonfictional works like Montaigne's *Essays* or Marcus Aurelius's *Meditations*. Or in fictional works that have no characters sympathetic enough to identify with. Even works *with* such sympathetic characters may exhibit moral qualities along a different dimension. For the "point of view" of the artist or writer—represented by his or her "artistic acts" or complexes of them[67]—may embody such qualities. The Love of such qualities is often a straightforward case of enjoyment; sometimes it becomes a genuine kind of love. Thus we may enjoy reading Montaigne predominantly for his unflinching honesty or his ceaseless but calm irony. We may enjoy reading Aurelius for his noble courage, Tolstoi for his wise compassion, Dante or Dickens for their (very different kinds of) moral seriousness. Or we may enjoy listening to Beethoven for his nobility of spirit, to Haydn for his optimism, to Corelli for his gravity, to Toscanini's interpretive readings for their directness and self-effacing integrity. We may enjoy such qualities during a given reading or hearing, reproducing the experience of them by *continuing* to read or listen, to feel them within ourselves. Or we may enjoy returning again and again to these works precisely to reproduce in ourselves the experience of these beloved qualities.

For, indeed, our enjoyment of qualities in this dimension seems often to go beyond "mere" enjoyment. We may have or come to have such an affinity for certain authors or artists that we seek renewed contact with their work as we seek the company of dear friends. For, after all, such moral qualities are the qualities of real persons, not of overtly fictional ones.[68] And we may come to like these real persons, as we know them in their works, for the same sorts of reasons that we came to like the real persons who are our actual friends and lovers. For we often are attracted to our friends and lovers for their moral qualities, though obviously not only for such qualities. And when we are, it is for those qualities among others that we love them. Alternatively, we may speak of loving those qualities in them.

160

But what is it to love such qualities in our friends and lovers? And how, in particular, does such love exemplify the "reproduction" of Love? To love (dispositionally) a quality in a friend is, in large part, to want to be with that friend in contexts in which the quality is likely to be manifested, and, at best, manifested repeatedly or continuously through a period of time. Thus, you enjoy the company of a friend with great *joie de vivre* when you are at a party; you enjoy the company of a philosophically sensitive friend when you are working on a problem in philosophy; you seek out a friend with great moral sensitivity when you need advice on the breakup of a personal relationship. But you do not enjoy the company of these friends only when you need specific services that their qualities enable them to provide. You enjoy their company "in general," too, simply because, being who you are, you enjoy being near, conversing with, sharing experiences with persons with such *joie de vivre*, philosophical acumen, or moral sensitivity. Thus such activity *vis-à-vis* such friends not only *constitutes*, on specific occasions, your (occurrent) friendship with them, it is also a way of reproducing experiences of their beloved qualities.

But it is not the only way. Often we love friends for qualities that they have and that we also have, or want to have, or want to continue to possess, or want to possess to a greater degree than we now do. And we seek as friends persons with whom and by whom, in the exercise of our friendships, actions and impulses that exemplify those beloved qualities will be produced in ourselves. And, adding only the reasonable assumption that *consciousness* (experience) of these actions and impulses accompanies these actions and impulses, we can see the pursuit of this kind of friendship as another chief means of reproducing in ourselves experiences of those qualities—qualities now exemplified both by the beloved other and by ourselves in that friendly (Loving) relationship. Phaedrus in the *Symposium*

161

(178e) speaks, I take it, for this aspect of friendship—though not in a philosophically general way—when he imagines an army composed of lovers who would in battle inspire courage in one another beyond the natural endowments of each lover singly. And it is this phenomenon that Plato—somewhat more generally if not perfectly so—adapts in his model of love for those whose "souls are pregnant."[69]

The applications of NTL made in this section and the preceding four raise the question in a poignant way: What is NTL a theory *of*? Or, in other words, what does the technical term "Love" comprehend? It comprehends (I claim) all cases of what would ordinarily and straightforwardly be called "enjoyment" as well as much that can be called "enjoyment" in reasonably extended senses of the term. But it comprehends more than that, too. It comprehends some clear cases of love for others, as well as friendship for others. But it also encompasses somewhat unusual cases of love: love of virtues; love of books, and authors, and art; excessive loves and bizarre forms of "self"-love. When we reflect, amidst all these loves, that we colloquially, quite naturally, and—for all the dictionaries care—quite correctly speak of "loving" what we enjoy, we can come to think that NTL is, finally, a theory of love: "Love" means "love." Against this idea it is unconvincing to argue that the kinds of love NTL covers are too diverse to be "one thing." For after all, one mark of an interesting theory is that it shows unity among what the vulgar, or conventional, or traditional imagination finds diverse. Indeed it might be, for all we know, some dim intuition of a theory like NTL that accounts for the willingness of speakers of the language to spread the word "love" over so many different phenomena.

CLIMAXES

Thus far I have argued that NTL comprehends a variety of phenomena that are straightforwardly, or at least arguably, called "love." I have also argued that some clear and central cases of love—namely, the love we have for friends and lovers in virtue of certain of their moral and other personal qualities—are comprehended by NTL. From the latter arguments it is clear, I trust, how all cases of love or friendship for a human being— or any sentient being, for that matter—fall under NTL when what is loved *about* that being is one or more of its qualities and when such qualities can range from the most "physical" to the most "spiritual." I shall now argue that *all* cases of love for human beings—and, by extension, all cases of love modeled on the love of human beings for other human beings (such as love for puppies or for gods)—fall under NTL.[70] It is, after all, such love that (1) seems to most people to be the center of love and (2) may seem prima facie to be most recalcitrant to the analysis embodied in NTL. I shall argue, in particular, that all cases of love for human beings are reducible to kinds of love and enjoyment which are comprehended by NTL.

The reduction of cases of love for human beings works somewhat differently from the reduction of cases of enjoyment described earlier. For cases of love, the reduction must proceed in two stages. In stage I, we ask about each case of love, *What about the beloved does the lover love?* As in the reduction of the beauty of "objects" according to NTB, if the answer to the question is one or more qualities, we stop. If it is not, we continue applying the question until we get one or more qualities in answer. We may thus accumulate a list of qualities: intelligence, responsibility, wittiness, skillfulness (in tennis), muscularity (of forearms), sexiness, and so forth. Then, as in the reduction of the enjoyment of "objects" in Section 2, we ask, What activity with respect to each of these beloved qualities do we love or enjoy? Finally, of each such activity that is not a case of experiencing that quality we ask, What about that activity do we love or enjoy? Whenever an answer is given in terms of *experiencing* the quality, the reduction has proceeded far enough for NTL to engage the phenomenon. "Experience," of course, must be taken in the senses relevant to each quality; the ways one "experiences" another's intelligence or responsibility are different from the ways one experiences his muscularity or sexiness. I am claiming that NTL will account for *loving* (the experience of) a loved one's qualities in the same way that it accounts for *enjoying* (the experience of) the qualities involved in any "object."

I do not claim, however, that accounting thus for the love of a loved one's *qualities* will necessarily account for *all* of the love of that person. But sometimes it will. And in most instances of love, such love will account for a great deal of the love. Furthermore, we should not suppose that the love of qualities in a person, *as such*, is enough to mark the love of the person as, for example, erotic or nonerotic, superficial or deep, "merely friendship" or "true love." A love for another, insofar as it is a love of that person's qualities, can be any of the above.[71] Nevertheless, there are kinds of love, of friendship, or of mere "liking" for persons that do not reduce thus to the love or enjoyment of those persons' qualities. In order to capture this unreduced remainder, let us subject those cases of loving persons that are not (completely) reducible to loving qualities of those persons to a stage II reduction. In stage II we ask, *In loving that person, what do I love (or enjoy) doing, being, or having?* In order to clarify what this question means and how to apply it, let us consider three types of love that clearly do not *reduce* to the love or enjoyment of qualities. I call these types "tribal love," "serving love," and "acquisitive love."

Tribal love is exemplified chiefly by love between family members, but I take it to comprehend all love between persons insofar as they are interdependent, or take themselves to be interdependent, in ways like those in which family members are interdependent. I shall simply refer to all such interdependent groups as "tribes." Now, it may very frequently happen that tribe members' love for one another is in part *constituted* by their love for the *qualities* of the others. Nevertheless, there is a "core" to the love that is appropriate among tribe members to which love of their qualities is irrelevant. And that core is the love that is obligatory or that is felt by tribe members to be obligatory. Such obligatory love is the core of tribal love because there may obtain no other sort of love between two tribe members except that to which they are obliged by virtue of their respective positions in the tribe. Thus Cordelia may say, "I love your Majesty according to my bond, no more nor less." Furthermore, tribal love would appear to consist of acting according to certain obligations: the obligation of a father, say, to bestow care, concern, protection, and material support on a child, and the obligation of a child to behave gratefully and respectfully towards the father. In each of these cases, moreover, the love of the tribe member is obligated, not by the *actual love* of the other towards him, but simply by the tribal relationship to the other. Tribal love, in other words, may be independent, not only of whether the beloved has lovable qualities, but of whether the beloved returns the love.

Now, assuming that my analysis of tribal love is correct so far, a case of such love must consist, at its core, of more than simply acting *in accordance with* such obligations. For one could

167

so act simply out of fear of punishment or of some other un-desired consequence to oneself. The actions must be done "out of love." And what does that mean? It means, first of all, acting in recognition of the obligation so to act, but further, I sug-gest, it means acting *out of and with a show of some feeling*. What feeling? The feelings may vary from person to person and must vary with the nature of the obligation. But they must be "moral feelings"—what I earlier called "moral sentiments"—and these sentiments must be relevant to the nature of the spe-cific obligation. Thus a father may perform certain actions with respect to his children out of concern, benevolence, solicitude, affection, or responsibility. And a child may perform certain acts of filial love out of respect, gratitude, affection, or respon-sibility. Note that sentiments of affection, which we may or-dinarily think of as especially relevant to love, represent only one of several possible relevant kinds. Note, furthermore, that this requirement of sentiment does not preclude the "cold" expression of (genuine) love. For some of these sentiments—notably those of "responsibility"—belong to a class of rela-tively "cold" feelings. Thus a father who acts towards his chil-dren as a father should, but *only* out of and with a show of the sentiments of responsibility towards them, may very likely be seen as affectionless and lacking in warmth. I am maintaining, nevertheless, that he will not thereby be deficient in *paternal* love, a specific variety of tribal love.

I can now make the crucial connection between tribal love and NTL. For, as I argued above in Section 29, cases of acting out of and with a show of some moral sentiment are cases of Love, according to NTL. And if NTL can comprehend this necessary ingredient in tribal love, NTL can comprehend tribal love as well as it comprehends any case of loving a person in virtue of her qualities or any case of enjoyment.

I have not arrived at the above result, admittedly, by a straightforward application of a general reduction technique. For, to return to my description of stage II reduction, let us try now to apply the reduction question to tribal love: In loving S (a given member of my tribe), what do I love (or enjoy) doing, being, or having? If the reply is always, "I love (or enjoy) performing such and such (obligatory) actions," or "I love (or enjoy) being obliged to perform such and such actions," then stage II reduction would work to reduce tribal love to a kind of love directly comprehended by NTL. But stage II reduction does not effect this reduction in every case. The reason is simply this: even a person who agrees (1) that all cases of (occurrent) tribal love must exhibit some relevant feeling and come out of such feeling and (2) that such cases are cases of Love need not agree that they are cases of love or enjoyment *as pretheoretically understood*. Or, in other words, it is not only possible, but even likely, that a person with a good understanding of the ordinary uses of the English words "love" and "enjoy" would answer the stage II reduction question with "Nothing," even if such a person would affirm (1) and (2). The reason has, I believe, almost nothing to do with the reducibility of tribal love to Love. It has almost everything to do with ordinary conceptions of love and enjoyment.

I do not mean to suggest that it would be impossible or even unusual for someone, using only ordinary concepts of love and enjoyment, to affirm that she loved or enjoyed behaving towards her children or parents in a properly maternal or filial way. I think many tribe members do love or enjoy acting on their tribal obligations and would admit to it. But I also think it would not be uncommon to *deny* such love or enjoyment. It would not be uncommon, especially, among those tribal lovers whose love is dominated by feelings of duty or responsibility.

For it is, I think, simply a fact that, not only for such persons, but for all of us, duty and responsibility frequently conflict with some clear-cut and indubitable cases of our love and enjoyment. We are thus accustomed to think of such feelings never as exemplifying and always as opposing love and enjoyment. In my view, one of NTL's most significant consequences is that it suggests that such customary patterns of thinking may be wrong.[72]

Now, the implication of all this for NTL and tribal love is *not* that the former does not account for the latter. It is merely that the *argument* that NTL accounts for all the love in tribal love cannot rely solely on the stage II reduction question. Cases of tribal love that resist reduction via that question must be seen as falling under NTL simply because (1) a necessary condition of those cases of love does exemplify the theoretical notion of Love, and (2) in this respect such cases of love are like *all other* cases of love and enjoyment. I mean by this last statement that the number and variety of cases of love and enjoyment that NTL does comprehend is so great that this fact alone, signifying a certain power in NTL, should be enough to persuade those reluctant to *call* certain cases of tribal love "love" that their (after all, not universally shared) reluctance does not imply that such cases ought to count as counterexamples to NTL.

To make good clause 2 above, I must still argue that stage II reduction brings all cases of "acquisitive love" and "serving love" under NTL. And this is fairly easy to do. What I call "serving love" is love that consists in serving needs and desires of the beloved independently of any specific obligation to do so. Certain extreme forms of this kind of love can appear "saintly" because they are extremely giving to others and extremely heedless of the lover's own ostensible needs. Extreme forms of this sort of love may thus lead to "sacrifices" by the lover, even to the giving up of the lover's life in the service of the beloved. Since this sort of love, by my definition, exists independently of any specific *obligation* towards the beloved, it must—it seems to me—be motivated by some powerful *feeling* towards the beloved, such as benevolence, compassion, generosity, or (generalized) responsibility. (I do not intend this list to be exhaustive.) Now, the very notion of such love seems to guarantee that the actions that manifest it will both exhibit and come out of some such feeling. And, once again, such actions will thus exemplify Love.

Unlike tribal love, however, serving love *does* always yield an answer to the stage II reduction question. For the answer to the question "In loving S, what do I love (or enjoy) doing, being, or having?" is always something like "I love (or enjoy) serving S, or being of service to S, in such and such ways." Indeed, were not some such answer forthcoming, it is difficult to imagine how my relationship to S could reasonably be called "love." In stage II reduction we can then go on to ask what I love or enjoy in serving S. At this point my answers may be something like "I just love being responsible for him," or "I enjoy giving myself to her," or (of someone else) "In serving the poor, she exhibits an overwhelming love of the virtue of compassion (or of mercy)." But the further reduction question may also yield other answers too, such as "I love seeing the joy (the comfort) it gives him," or "I love the looks of bliss on their faces," or "I love the thought of his going on flourishing after I've gone (or done my deed)." Such answers, I take it, fall under NTL simply because they can be reduced to the enjoyment of (experiencing) qualities.

I believe, finally, that "acquisitive love" can easily be reduced, via stage II reduction, to straightforward cases of enjoyment. By "acquisitive love" I mean the love of a person insofar as that person is loved because he or the love for him satisfies some extrinsic desire or desires of the lover for what benefits the lover, or for what the lover believes will benefit himself, irrespective of whether it benefits the beloved or whether the beloved believes himself to be thereby benefited. Such love may be trivial or ignoble, sometimes to the point of leading some to deny it the description altogether. But it does occur, often mixed with other forms of love, sometimes in its pure form. I may like, love, or be the friend of another because he relieves my loneliness, because he is fun to have sex with, because his beauty gives me a reputation for sexual prowess, because his wealth enables him to give me many material things, because his apparent weakness allows me to see myself as dominant, because his dominance relieves me of the need to make important decisions, because he can father an intelligent child, because I have reason to believe he will give me a secure future, and so forth.[73]

It is obvious, I take it, how any of the above grounds of "love" can be used to answer the question "In loving him, what do I love (or enjoy) doing, being, or having?" Since, then, any of my states or conditions that my "acquisitive loves" bring about may be states or conditions that satisfy my extrinsic desires, it should not be surprising that they can be enjoyable to me. And when they are actually enjoyed, their enjoyment can be reduced, like the enjoyment of any of my other states or conditions, to the enjoyment of (the experience of) qualities.

33. Love and Sex

I have suggested in many ways how NTL applies to sexual love. But I want now to draw out explicitly some implications that

NTL has for such love. First, just as NTL applies primarily to *occasions* of enjoyment, NTL applies primarily to *occasions* of sexual love. And occasions of sexual love are, simply, incidents of "making love." The core of making love is body touching body, whether one person's body, two persons' bodies, or more are involved. Nevertheless, no touching at all need be involved in making love; if fantasizing is a part of almost all cases of making love, fantasizing without touching may occur in some cases of making love. Orgasm too need neither occur nor be desired by participants in sexual love. Finally, making love is far from a simple activity, and there are no modes of experience—in the technical sense in which I use that term—which cannot operate in sexual love.

The first question that sexual love poses for this study is, How is a reduction of it to proceed? For reduction purposes, we should not treat it, I believe, like the other kinds of love. For one thing, in sexual love there is often no person, not even a person's body, that is loved or being loved. This is as true when two people are making love as when one person is alone making love. But we cannot treat incidents of making love simply as cases of (occurrent) enjoyment either. The reason is simply that not all cases of making love, as defined, are enjoyed. I propose, then, that the proper way of understanding sexual love, as subject matter for NTL, is as occurrences of enjoying sexual love. Under such a description, it is clear, the proper reduction technique is to ask about an enjoyed occurrence of making love, What is (was) enjoyed about it? I think I can show that everything that is either loved or enjoyed in making love can thereby be reduced to enjoying (the experience of) some qualities.

In sexual love we can, of course, enjoy the "purely" physical qualities of another person: firmness (or softness) of flesh, smoothness of skin, voluptuousness (or leanness) of shapes, muscularity, musky odors and tastes, and textures felt only by the tongue. To listen to certain moralists, one might think that qualities like these are all we ever enjoy in sex.

But often in making love with another we can enjoy what we *love* about that other: gentleness, tenderness, vigor, robustness, sensitivity, passion, kindness, concern, joyfulness, high-spiritedness. Not only are such qualities easily experienceable in sex, but they are experienceable there in unique ways. Sometimes, indeed, there are qualities that a person reveals only in lovemaking. Of course, it is also true that frequently when some of the above kinds of qualities are enjoyed in sex, it seems as if they belong, not to one or the other of the partners, but to both at once or to the lovemaking itself. They are no less enjoyed for this. Indeed, the very fact that the qualities—sensuousness, joy, passion, and so forth—seem *shared* in the lovemaking could indicate, on the basis of NTL, that they are indeed enjoyed. For such "sharing" of a single quality over a period of mutual activity could be an example of mutual *reproduction* of that quality.

But not infrequently the qualities enjoyed in lovemaking are not qualities of the other, but qualities of ourselves, or qualities we can imagine, in virtue of the lovemaking, to be our own. Sometimes, for example, we can imagine ourselves to be sexy and sensual, or dominant, powerful, rough, strong, and even violent, or caring, giving, protecting, or delicate and fragile. Our *fantasies* of ourselves, no less than our fantasies of the other, during and because of sex are as varied as we are. But these enjoyed qualities *need* not be fantasies; they can be the reality of ourselves, even if it is a reality manifested only during lovemaking. But whether fantasy or reality, these qualities experienced as our own may be part of what (or even solely what) we enjoy in sex. It is, I take it, not an original point that the objects of our wildest erotic fantasies are often such less for their own qualities than for the qualities they allow us to imagine we possess, or allow us actually to possess (often for the shortest of moments, to be sure).

Someone will surely protest at this juncture that my claim to reduce the enjoyment of sexual love to the enjoyment of qualities—whether of the beloved, of myself, or of our mutual activity, and whether real or imagined—must surely founder upon the "obvious facts" that in sex (1) our erogenous parts are stimulated and (2) orgasm frequently occurs. Such occurrences, it may be alleged, are inherently enjoyable and, in any case, are not enjoyed in virtue of the experience of some qualities. I shall reply to this hypothetical objection by examining the two alleged facts separately.

First, stimulation of erogenous parts of the body takes place either by direct touch to those parts, by imagining those parts touched or touching something else, or by feelings "traveling through" the body to those parts from some other parts that are touched or imagined to be touched. Second, the imagined or actual touch that is thus erotically stimulating must be perceived by the stimulated person as having some quality. And, third, that quality must be enjoyable to that person. For we can obviously be touched in our erogenous parts quite "meaninglessly," that is, in ways that do not seem to add up to being touched *in some particular way*. This could happen quite by accident, if, say, a (small) container of (fairly small and fairly light) objects of diverse shapes, textures, and weights were to drop on an exposed erogenous part. Or we could deliberately touch an exposed erogenous part in a random variety of different ways in quick succession. In these two cases it is likely that no erotic stimulation would occur. The point is that in love-

175

making such touches normally neither occur nor are imagined as occurring as part of the erotic moment. Sexual touches not only *have* qualities, but must have qualities in order, precisely, to *be* sexually "stimulating." If they do not, they either are not perceived at all, are ignored as "noise," or completely disrupt the proceedings. But even if touchings or being touched must be perceived (or imagined) by a person as manifesting a quality in order to be sexually stimulating to that person, this is not enough to *guarantee* that the person will (1) find it pleasant and (2) enjoy it. Most people find some qualities, even when or especially when experienced directly by a sexually sensitive part of their bodies, *unpleasant*. These unpleasant qualities can vary tremendously from person to person. But if persons find a quality unpleasant, they are not likely to enjoy it, that is, savor it, linger over it, try to prolong the experience of it or find other ways to experience it, and so on. On the other hand, if they find the quality pleasant, they will try to enjoy it. But enjoying it usually involves engaging *more* of the body in apprehending that quality, or engaging it for a longer time, or over and over again. Enjoying a pleasant quality of touch—in imagination or reality, in a sexual or a nonsexual part—is precisely "stimulating" ourselves to experience that quality. Thus, being stimulated in our erogenous parts, far from explaining the enjoyability of making love independently of our experience of qualities, presupposes our "reproduction" of our experience of qualities, and hence presupposes enjoyment as NTL understands it.

Finally, I come to orgasms. The hypothetical objection claims, first, that orgasms are inherently enjoyable and, second, that therefore the presence of orgasm in lovemaking is at least one element determining its enjoyment that is independent of the experience of qualities. The first claim is wrong (1) in confusing pleasantness with enjoyability and (2) in implying that orgasms are inherently pleasant. It is *a fortiori* wrong in what it literally states. Against it, I claim that even when an orgasm is pleasant, it is not necessarily enjoyed. (I take "enjoyable" in the objection to mean "enjoyed," because otherwise it is trivial.) To enjoy an orgasm—even when it turns out, as most do, to be pleasant—you must prepare for it, must be in a frame of mind to receive it, to "go with it," to make the most of it. In this respect, orgasms are of course no different from other enjoyable things. The point is, I take it, elementary. But, furthermore, orgasms are not always pleasant, either in whole or in part. I cannot claim myself to have had *un*pleasant ones, but I can imagine that happening. I *know* there are orgasms that are neither pleasant nor unpleasant. They sometimes seem so "neutral" that one hardly notices them. This can happen, for example, when one is sick, or worried, or otherwise distracted.

But the chief interest in the hypothetical objection about orgasms is the implication that *when* they are pleasant and, indeed, when they are enjoyed, they contribute an element of enjoyment to lovemaking independent of the experience of qualities. I dispute this implied claim in two ways. First, sometimes orgasms are enjoyed because they are interpreted as signs of certain qualities in the sex partners. For example, if the phenomenon of "scoring" means anything to the one who scores other than what his friends later find out, it probably means much of the time that the person scoring—and orgasm is the ultimate moment here—is able in the orgasmic moment to see himself as powerful. Such an "interpretation" of the (male) orgasm is, of course, only partially supported by certain of its inherent features: thrusts, explosions, largeness. The rest of the interpretation comes from the surrounding society's supportive "reading" of the "score." But the latter fact is far from implying that the orgasm "itself" is not enjoyed and not enjoyed precisely for the quality of power it imparts (or seems to impart) to the owner of the orgasmic organ. This example is only one of many possible ones. Quite a different one is this: the (male) orgasm also supports a fantasy of the ejaculator as generous and giving (powerful in another way). Furthermore, it is not only the sex partner who *has* an orgasm who can enjoy it. What one might call the "recipient" of an orgasm might also enjoy it because it gives support to his fantasy of being generous and giving, or perhaps fragile and delicate, or even strong and powerful in his ability to provoke such a marvelous event. My point in these examples is simply this: sexual lovemaking is sometimes enjoyed for qualities it allows the participants to experience themselves as having. It therefore can hardly be denied that what is traditionally thought of as the essence of sex—the orgasm—is also enjoyed for those reasons.

But my second reply to the hypothetical objection from orgasms is that orgasms can be enjoyed (more innocently perhaps) *for their own qualities.* Orgasms, in fact, can bear many qualities and differ from one another tremendously with respect to their qualities. One need not be a connoisseur of orgasms to recognize qualities which are commonly enjoyed in them. Male orgasms, at least, have a structure that itself determines two such common qualities: the "rising" and the "falling" qualities. Some may perceive these as the "tensing" or "tightening" quality and the "releasing" or "relaxing" or "loosening" quality. There are also "pulsing" and "driving" qualities, "exploding" and "flowing" qualities.

Some may wonder why I add the term "quality" to the above participles. Why not describe an orgasm simply as "tensing" or "relaxing," "driving" or "exploding"? The response: What transforms an act of a certain kind into a quality in our experience is just the fact that these "acts," or rather aspects of their "texture," "shape" and "rhythm," can be felt in parts of the body other than the genitals. Specifically, these qualities of the orgasm can be communicated to, and felt in, other parts of the body when the orgasm is *enjoyed*. And it is precisely this sort of communication to other parts of the body that NTL calls "reproduction" and that constitutes therefore the enjoyment of the orgasm. An orgasm which is really enjoyed for itself and its own inherent qualities is indeed felt throughout the body. But this means more than simply that we feel pleasure throughout the body, although it does mean that. For in order to feel the orgasmic pleasure throughout the body, we must feel some quality (or qualities) of the orgasm throughout the body. And this phenomenon usually feels like *feeling in our whole body what we perceive the orgasm to be like*. If it feels like force to us, we will then feel that *kind* of force throughout our bodies; if it feels like overflowing to us, we will feel that kind of overflowing quality throughout ourselves. We can, of course, refuse to feel any of these things; we can for example simply "contain" the sensation of the orgasm where we think it belongs. Or we can refuse to apprehend it as having any qualities. But if we do, we will also eliminate opportunities to enjoy it.

34. *Loving Pain*

The New Theory of Love reveals to us a richly lovable world. It begins as an account of what we *in fact* love, which may be, depending upon who we are and our circumstances, a more or less meager portion of our world. But it ends by telling us what is "inherently" enjoyable and lovable in our worlds, namely, qualities, whether we have ever enjoyed or loved them all or not. Even though NTL cannot tell us each what and where those lovable qualities are in our worlds, we can easily see that our worlds are brimming over with qualities. If NTB revealed an enormous amount of beauty in our world(s), NTL reveals considerably more potential love and enjoyment. For, according to NTL, we may enjoy qualities that are present in an "object" to *any* degree, not just to a *high* degree. The theory, moreover, implicitly gives us broadly stated "directions" as to *how* actually to enjoy the treasure of lovables it has led us to.[74]

Just as there is no *sort* of "object" that cannot be beautiful, according to NTB, so there is no particular "object"—complex activity, condition, state, concrete or abstract object, or experience—that cannot be loved or enjoyed in some respects. Thus no matter how we in fact choose to compartmentalize our lives—and reserve our enjoyments and our loves for certain "objects" only—the potential for love and enjoyment is present in the most mundane and unlikely of things. But NTL penetrates even deeper still. For it implies that we can enjoy and love not only the banal and the ordinary, but the downright unpleasant and the positively painful as well.

Before I substantiate the last statement, let me first dispel the air of paradox hovering over it. Note that once divested of the Disneyland conception of enjoyment, we immediately see that nearly every enjoyable "object" involves something unpleasant, along with many things that are neither enjoyable nor unpleasant. Even a day at Disneyland brings to its most committed fans sweaty armpits, long lines, and an environment of compulsive tidiness and wholesomeness. Some of our most enjoyable activities, like mountain climbing, piano playing, and philosophizing, often involve, *during their enjoyment*, drudgery, discipline, anxiety, and sacrifice of other pleasures. These facts are what necessitate the "relocation," via the reduction technique, of the Lovability of complex activities, states, and conditions to the enjoyable experience of qualities. However much of what is negative or neutral a thing may involve, its enjoyed or loved aspects may outweigh them for us, and we may say that, on balance, we enjoy or love that thing. NTL, however, allows us to identify enjoyed and loved aspects of "objects" which do *not* outweigh for us the negative or neutral aspects. We therefore might say that we do *not* love or enjoy a certain "object" even though we love or enjoy some aspects of it. But we can go a step further. I may have found a hiking trip extremely unpleasant—because of the constant rain, the soaking wet socks and boots, the pneumonia I caught, the loss of my backpack, the flat tire coming home—and still admit to loving the (rather brief) experience of my first thunderstorm in the high Sierras. Or I may emerge from what has been a very unpleasant department meeting—full of ugly dissension, anxiety, frustration—and yet admit to enjoying the calm sanity and rationality of a single colleague at the meeting (the one who agreed with me). All of these implications of NTL seem unexceptional. They accord with our experience, and they do not entail the unpleasant proposition that unpleasant experiences are enjoyable precisely insofar as they are unpleasant.

A further consequence of NTL, however, may seem to press too far in this direction. For NTL entails not only that we may enjoy some aspects or parts of unpleasant and, by extension, painful experiences, but also that we may enjoy that very paradigm of unpleasantness—pain itself. The plain fact is that pains can differ a great deal from one another. They differ not only in "location" but in intensity and in quality. They may be sharp or dull, searing or throbbing, traveling or stationary. Some of these descriptions can indicate qualities. There are many qualities of pain that have no "standard" descriptions;

the social usefulness of such descriptions is, after all, rather small. Pains have qualities of shape, of size, and of movement; they have rhythms and periodicities that have qualitative aspects. These aspects are, moreover, genuine qualities—properties of qualitative degree that are not properties of defect, deficiency, or lack. The pain may, of course, indicate that there is something "wrong" with me. But it is not my pain itself that is "wrong" with me, much less the qualities of the pain. Indeed, experiencing the pain usually means that something is "right" with me: (1) I am still conscious, and (2) my nervous system is working appropriately. *A fortiori*, that I am able to experience the *qualities* of the pain means that something is very right with me; I am not so oppressed by the hurt of the pain that my faculties of discrimination are impaired. Finally, the qualities of a pain are not defects, deficiencies, or lacks *of the pain*. It is difficult, in fact, to understand how a pain *could* lack anything, or be defective or deficient in any way.

But can we *enjoy* the qualities of our pain? Yes, in the same way that we enjoy other qualities of pure experience, such as fantasies and memories and orgasmic feelings. We pay close attention to them; we try to retain them in our consciousness; we try not to ignore them, steel ourselves against them, forget them, or put them out of mind; if they are bodily experiences, we allow them to reverberate throughout our bodies. These are all means of "reproducing" the experience of them. Can we do this with all pains? Probably not, if the pain is too severe. Some people may not be able to do so with any pain at all. It is easiest to do with rather minor pain like toothaches, the pain in a runner's legs or lungs, or the irritations of a hair shirt. Why should we call this way of experiencing pain *enjoyment*? For one thing, it has the same "structure" as more easily and ordinarily recognized enjoyments. In other words, it conforms to the model of enjoyment embodied in NTL. But, furthermore, it *feels* like enjoyment, too, when we do the sorts of things listed above. Finally, however, so to experience pain is to make it hurt less; it has the same kind of distractive power that other forms of enjoyment have. It is like enjoying the balmy weather as I take the garbage out. The pleasantness of the one takes my mind off the stink of the other and the coffee grounds on my shoe. On this interpretation, therefore, enjoying pain does not entail enjoying the *hurt* of pain.[75]

But under what conditions, one might ask, would we ever want to enjoy pain? Mostly, for most of us, when we are already in pain and have no immediate prospect of getting out. Enjoying a pain is less fun, for most of us, than enjoying almost anything else, but it is more fun than having that pain without enjoying it.

35. *Loving Evil*

Closely related to the unpleasant and the painful is a set of phenomena that NTL might appear to exclude necessarily from the universe of Lovable things—namely, our experiences of properties of qualitative degree that are properties of defect, deficiency, or lack, or of the "appearance" of such. For NTL offers necessary and sufficient conditions for the enjoyment only of the experience of qualities that by their very definition exclude the aforementioned properties (which for convenience in this discussion I shall label "negative qualities"). Now, the latter exclusion raises some questions: Might there not be cases of enjoying experiences of negative qualities? And if there are, is NTL unable to account for them? My answer to the first question, which I shall presently justify, is yes. My answer to the second question is no. For it is possible to reduce cases of enjoying experiences of negative qualities to enjoyed experiences of qualities. In the following I shall illustrate not only the enjoyment of negative qualities, but the ways it can be reduced to the enjoyment of qualities.

Least problematic are cases of the enjoyment of negative properties that belong to nonhuman "objects" in the external world. Such enjoyment is fairly straightforwardly reducible to the enjoyment of qualities. Thus I may enjoy the rottenness of a tree because of the rough texture or the rich and subtle coloration it gives to the wood. I may enjoy the rustiness of a metal gate for the experience it affords of crustiness of texture and subtleties of color. I may keep dead tulips in the vase for weeks because I enjoy the softness and complexity the fadedness of their petals lends to the lavender color, or because I enjoy the baroque drama the dryness of the flowers gives to the forms of the petals and leaves. Such negative properties are easily enjoyed; often they simply exemplify the "flowers of evil" phenomenon I identified in *A New Theory of Beauty*.

Negative qualities of human movement and morally neutral action, whether of ourselves or of others, are similarly rather unproblematic. A person may adopt, more or less deliberately, in his manner, movement, or dress a certain inelegance or even clumsiness. Artists often do this as a conscious reaction against certain norms of grace or elegance. In some cases the very lack of elegance or clumsiness may be enjoyable for its boldness or audacity. Inelegance and clumsiness may be enjoyable for the solidity, earthiness, or primitive quality they lend to a person's movement, manner, style, or dress, or for the simplicity and directness they bring with them. But most cases of clumsiness and inelegance, like most cases of all negative properties of human movement, manner, style, or dress, are, I wager, simply not enjoyable. I am not arguing, after all, that all cases of negative qualities are enjoyable; I am only trying to illustrate how *some* of them *might be*.

Enjoying, or loving, negative emotional, moral, and mental qualities is more complex than enjoying the negative qualities hitherto discussed. The first problem is imagining any of them that could be convincingly described as "enjoyed" or "loved." But let us try. Imagine a person who is, on the whole, rather unfeeling, who admits to being unfeeling, and who, further, is not in the least chagrined by the fact. Imagine that he is, on the contrary, somewhat proud of this trait and that, without being a monster, he nevertheless seems readily to accept opportunities to display the trait. Such a person would appear to "enjoy" his own unfeelingness. What, we should ask—whether we are committed to NTL or not—might he enjoy about such a trait? Or suppose that I *love* such a person and love—as far as I or anyone else truthfully can tell—precisely his unfeelingness. What might I love *about* that quality? What indeed *could there be* to love about it? A possible answer: He and I might both perceive in his unfeeling behavior a certain kind of strength, a quality that resists the power of feeling and, in particular, its "softness." One might object that such love (or enjoyment) is misplaced, that there are many ways of demonstrating strength—even against "softness," against emotionality—without being unfeeling. One might even object that only someone who has no "true" strength might *believe* he has found it in such an inappropriate corner of life. Such objections are not unreasonable, but they do not damage my point. Persons may genuinely experience strength in their own unfeeling behavior and inclinations or in that of others. As it is experienced, such "strength" can seem no different from the strength that resists sentimentality and other inappropriate appeals to feeling. Indeed, the unfeeling person is especially good at resisting the latter; such resistance is part of his general pattern of unfeelingness. The fact that unfeeling behavior, unlike unsentimental behavior, is *deficient* behavior and calls for negative moral judgments is not a reason for concluding that there is *nothing* that is *not* deficient in the behavior, and certainly not a reason for concluding that the pattern of behavior and inclination is not *in some respects* enjoyable or lovable. There are, after all, many possibilities, in general, of enjoying a thing, even when that enjoyment is precisely the wrong thing to do (morally, legally, or practically) in the circumstances.

My point in the preceding paragraph is complex and needs expansion. First, a person might "see" in a defect or deficiency some positive quality. But such a "seeing," since it is a way of experiencing, need not be simply an *arbitrary mis*interpretation. It is an experience that interprets a pattern (of unfeelingness), first, on the basis of something that truly is "there"—the resistance to feeling—and, second, by omitting to take into the experience crucial *circumstances* that may make such resistance appropriate or not. In this analysis, the person who experiences unfeelingness as strength does not simply invent or "make up" something that is not "there" and substitute it for what *is* "there." Rather, he experiences a "part" of what *is* "there," fails to see the rest, and "reads" the part for the whole. Experiencing unfeelingness as strength is, on this analysis, not to have *illusory* experience; it is to have selectively *partial* or *limited* experience.[76]

The same sort of analysis can be applied to cases of loving, or enjoying, negative moral qualities, such as uncaringness, violence, and irresponsibility. For in the first one might find ingredients of strength or discipline; in the second, elements of energy and power; and in the third, some kind of freedom. And it is to the love or enjoyment of such qualities that we can reduce the love or enjoyment of the negative qualities. Once again, it is not to the point to say that to love negative qualities in such a way is to misapprehend those qualities. For it does not follow from such misapprehensions that the negative qualities are thereby not loved. It follows only that they are loved for some nonnegative elements of which they are, in part, composed.

Another sort of objection to the kind of reduction I am presenting is the following: Even if we agree that negative qualities in human beings can be partially composed of nonnegative ones, that it is these that are enjoyed or loved, and that NTL can account for this love or enjoyment, it does not follow that NTL thus accounts for the love or enjoyment of negative qualities. For this analysis—and hence NTL—is still unable to account for why a person might choose to love or enjoy just those qualities that are ingredient in negative qualities. And while it is not universally true that those who love or enjoy qualities ingredient in negative qualities love or enjoy those qualities only *insofar* as they are so ingredient, frequently they have a predilection for those qualities precisely insofar as they are so ingredient. In any case, it is just the love of such qualities *insofar as* they are ingredient in negative qualities that creates the "problem" of loving evil, and it is this problem that the above analysis cannot solve.

My first response to this kind of objection is that it places irrelevant demands upon a reductive analysis of love. The objection essentially requires NTL to explain or account for choices or patterns of choices in *reproductive acts*. According to NTL, in loving or enjoying some quality we reproduce the experience of it. Those who love the qualities that are ingredient in negative qualities reproduce the experience of them by acting in ways that exemplify those negative qualities or by being around persons who exemplify them. But NTL is designed to account for the reproductive behavior of loves only insofar as it reproduces experiences of the loved qualities. The many different ways of reproducing experiences of a given quality are of no particular concern to NTL. Why one reproduces one's beloved experiences of qualities and how and when one does, are, from the point of view of NTL, accidents of "history," broadly construed.

Another way of putting the above response is this: NTL does not claim to account for why a lover loves what he loves, only for what he loves in his loves. But here the hypothetical objector may exclaim: "That is precisely my objection! A lover of negative qualities in himself or others *surely* loves more than simply a few 'positive' elements that are ingredient in those negative qualities. There has to be more to an adequate analysis of the 'love of evil' than that!" And I agree; there is usually more. Saying what "more" there is constitutes my second response to the objection.

The "more" that is loved in loving negative qualities is neither complicated nor arcane. Just as we sometimes love qualities in ourselves or others not for themselves, but for what they bring us, so we can love negative qualities, not only for some positive elements ingredient in them, but for desirable consequences they may have for us. These consequences can in turn be or involve qualities of *ourselves* that we enjoy. I may, for example, love my own clumsiness, incompetence, imprudence, or helplessness simply, or in part, because of the help, comfort, and concern such traits bring me from others. And I may enjoy the latter for any number of qualities, depending upon how the particular help, comfort, and concern is manifested. Indeed, I may even enjoy the power (my own feeling of powerfulness) over others that my various ineptnesses bring me. Similarly, I may enjoy my own inelegance as a way of rejecting my mother's expectations of me, of thumbing my nose at the Establishment, of getting some attention. And I may love the latter for the sense of power, of control, of domination they give me. It should be obvious how the experience of similar kinds of qualities in myself can result from *any* of my own negative qualities.

But I may love negative qualities in *others* for positve qualities they bring out in myself. I may feel myself more competent, prudent, intelligent, elegant, or knowledgeable in the presence of the opposite in my friend; I may actually have to *be* more competent, prudent, or intelligent in the company of a friend who is none of these. In the company of a friend who is uncaring, irresponsible, or violent, I may be called upon to be (and hence to feel) compassionate, responsible, calm, and tranquil. And it may be precisely to enjoy these qualities in myself that I love my friend, whose negative moral qualities inspire them.

It is sometimes alleged by writers on love, and it seems to be a truth based on our own experience, that the love or enjoyment of negative qualities exists. It follows from NTL, however, that negative qualities are not enjoyable intrinsically or in themselves, for the only things so enjoyable are qualities. Nevertheless, as I have tried to show through examples, NTL is able to account for such love of negative qualities by reducing it to the love or enjoyment of qualities.

36. The Ethics of Love

The love of "evil"—of negative qualities in general—raises in a poignant way a series of questions, at least some of which philosophies of love have traditionally tried to answer: What or whom is it right to love? And under what conditions? Which loves are better, which worse? Which loves are more important, which less important? Which more worthwhile? More proper? More genuine? More sublime? Truer? Holier? All of these are questions in what I shall simply baptize the "Ethics of Love."[77]

The New Theory of Love is not a theory in the Ethics of Love, nor does it, by itself, entail such a theory. That is, NTL neither is nor directly entails a normative theory of love. On the other hand, NTL is far from being incompatible with (all) normative theories of love. Rather, it allows (and indeed insists upon) distinctions that normative theories of love should find useful. For, according to NTL, any actual case of love or enjoyment is distinguishable from any other by (1) the qualities that are loved or enjoyed in it and (2) the ways those qualities are reproduced. And both of these are sufficiently numerous and various to satisfy any normative concern.

It has been no part of my intention, therefore, to devise a theory that allows philosophy to shirk normative questions of love. It is simply that, in order to answer such questions most perspicuously—even to ask them properly—one could well use a maximally general theory of *what love is*. I claim that NTL is such a theory. Of course, in order both to be as comprehensive as possible and to avoid covertly injecting normative elements into my theory, I have tried to be ultimately latitudinarian in defining the subject matter of NTL—the set of phenomena to which it is applicable. Thus, to take only two kinds of examples, I have countenanced as part of that subject matter relations with other persons that are extremely self-centered, even selfish, and relations with art in which art becomes merely the vehicle for one's own self-absorbed fantasies. There are many theories—and intuitions—that would exclude the former as not being ("true") love of another and the latter as not being ("true") love of art. While my own intuitions may well agree with both of these exclusions, I have nevertheless felt it important, in the interests of generality, to ignore such intuitions in defining the subject matter of NTL. The important *normative* considerations behind such intuitions are capturable, I maintain, not *by* the terms of NTL exclusively, but by using the terms of NTL along with other considerations.[78] By defining its subject matter in such a latitudinarian way and in nonnormative terms, then, I am not implying that all the forms of love and enjoyment that NTL comprehends are, normatively speaking, on a level.

It is even possible, therefore, that when the New Theory of Beauty and the New Theory of Love are, together, followed to their distant horizons, they will there produce an Ethics of Love and Beauty that will answer many normative questions in the philosophy of love. Whether (my) time, energy, and brains will suffice to follow them there, I can hardly say.

37. *The Touch of Experience*

My qualifications, interpretations, and applications of NTL are finished. But its explication and justification are not. Two big questions about the formulations of NTL in Section 25 need answers. According to those formulations, reproductions of experiences of a quality are definitive of the Love of that quality only insofar as the desire for such reproduction is both aroused and satisfied in and by that very reproductive activity. I must specify, thus, the conditions under which the reproduction of an experience of a quality will both arouse and satisfy a desire for such reproduction. Second, I must try to explain *why* such conditions so arouse and satisfy. The latter explanation will

191

also complete my answer to the question that began this inquiry, namely, What is pleasant about enjoyment (that is, Love)?

As a prelude to addressing these two issues, let me distinguish and relate two key notions involved in NTL: "expansion experiences" and "reproduction." Note first that although each of my expansion experiences necessarily involves the *multiplication* of an experience of a quality, not all such multiplication is brought about by reproduction. For to reproduce an experience of a quality, I must do something *in order to* produce another such experience. Thus the fragility of an insect, the delicacy of a leaf, might suddenly "flood" me when I am in an especially sensitive mood and before I have a chance to do anything to encourage (or discourage) it. Anger, or sadness, may suddenly sweep over me unawares without my being conscious enough of it either to allow it to grow or to think of checking it. A more complex example of expansion—actually of what I call a "derived" expansion experience—without reproduction can occur when, for example, I notice persons in my vicinity infecting one another with a single quality, friendliness, say. Their friendliness might very well "expand" before my very eyes before I take note of it, become interested in it, and *then* quite deliberately *follow* the progress of their increasing friendliness.

On the other hand, some reproduction of experiences of qualities does not involve in any way expansion experiences of those qualities. *Simply* continuing to look at, hear, or feel some quality, while it may reproduce the respective experiences, does not necessarily produce an expansion experience. Similarly, simply *returning* to glimpse or otherwise experience a quality that you have experienced—even in the immediate past—in an expansion experience may not be a *continuation* of that expansion experience, but it will be a case of reproduction, whether or not the past expansion experience was the result of reproduction. Thus, for example, I may catch sight of the exquisitely delicate flower, have that delicacy expand through me (nonreproductively), return to view the flower again (reproduction), and then allow that delicacy to expand through me (this time reproductively). Indeed, most cases of enjoyment, especially enjoyment of complex activities, enjoyment of activities that continue for a while, and enjoyment that itself lasts a (relatively) long time, are complex mixtures of reproduction that produces expansion experiences and reproduction that does not. Such cases of enjoyment (of a given quality) may also be more or less immediately preceded by an expansion experience of that quality that is *not* a case of reproduction.[79]

I am now in a position to state the conditions under which reproduction of an experience of a quality will both arouse and satisfy a desire to reproduce that experience. There are two: (1) a large portion of the experience that is *reproduced* must be (nonderived) expansion experience; and (2) a large portion of the experiences that are *reproductions* must be (nonderived) expansion experiences.

I have little argument to make in favor of appending these two conditions to NTL; they simply seem to me to conform with our experiences of love and enjoyment. I do point out, however, that the conditions jointly imply that the *mere* perception, remembering, or fantasizing of some quality, no matter for how long or how repeatedly, will not count as a case of love or enjoyment. They imply that all such cases must include a substantial component of what, pretheoretically, we might call "feeling." Such "feeling," then, is what NTL elaborately interprets as (nonderived) expansion experiences.[80] That the above two conditions obtain universally in love and enjoyment will, I hope, seem fairly obviously true to anyone with an adequate comprehension of the phenomenon and concept of "expansion experiences." Counterexamples to the conditions may, of course, prove them wrong or in need of modification, but I can think of none at present.

But why, after all, should my expansion experiences of a given quality produce in me a desire to have more of them? For that is what the two conditions amount to. My answer, at its simplest, is that the experience of a quality expanding through me *feels good*, that is to say, *is pleasant*. To substantiate this answer I shall first try to describe more clearly what such an experience feels like and then try to say why that is pleasant.

In expansion experience there is a *twofold* "movement." On the one hand, there is the expansion of the *quality experienced*. It is this "movement" and its characteristics that I have elaborately analyzed in earlier sections. I call attention now to a second sort of "movement" in expansion experiences; that is the "movement" of my experien*cing* of the quality. For just as the quality seems, in our experience, to "move" into, through, or out of us, so—and necessarily it seems to me—does the locus, as it were, of the experience of it "move" with it. Another— possibly redundant—way of putting this point is that as we experience a quality in different "locations" in us and in different experiential modalities, we also *feel ourselves so experiencing it*. I do *not*, however, mean that we are self-reflectively aware of ourselves so experiencing the "moving" quality. Such self-reflective awareness, I shall argue, is not a necessary concomitant of an expansion experience. Rather, this sense of the locus of our experiencing itself moving is an unavoidable accompaniment of our having the expansion experience. To take a perhaps distant—but perhaps not so distant—analogy, it is like the sounds of various material elements in an audio system (such as tape hiss) themselves being audible along with the music. Or to take possibly closer analogies, it is like our sense of our eyeballs moving as our gaze sweeps a room, or of the lenses of our eyes changing shape as we simply alter our focus from far to near or back again.

Now, if we try to describe in a general way the "movement" of the experiencing itself in expansion experiences, we find several features that are important in my explanation of the *pleasantness* of such experiences. These features remain constant in all experiencings of the expansions of qualities, regardless of the particular quality that is being experienced as expanding. The first feature is that our experiencings seem to "move" in and through the body. Sometimes such "movement" seems to go in particular "lines of direction" through the body; sometimes it goes in several "directions" at once; sometimes the "lines" blend into a movement like a diffusion. But, second, whatever the "directional" character of the "movement," such "movements" are capable of reaching any "part" of the body, either sequentially or simultaneously. Although most such experiences do not feel as though they touch "all" parts of the body, it sometimes happens that an expansion experience is, at its greatest extent, "had" in (what feels like) "all" parts of the body. Finally, the "movement" of experiencing is felt as easy and smooth, on the one hand, and as light, soft, or gentle, on the other. The particular descriptive words are not important here; the "tone" I am trying to describe is. This "tone" is the opposite of rough, bumpy, jerky, hard, difficult, hesitant, loud, harsh, or noisy. This is so even when the quality that the expansion experience is *of* is itself a "hard," "difficult," "rough," or "noisy" quality—like anger, boldness, enthusiasm, vivacity, or energy.

Now, that the "tone" of the movement of our experiencing should have these particular qualities or this range of qualities is, on general grounds, quite to be expected. First, we should not expect the having of an experience *generally* to feel like what the experience is of. Second, we should expect that the means of getting "information" would not, in general, be such as to interfere or threaten to interfere with that information itself. Hence the "easyness" or "lightness" or "softness" of the experiencing as such. Nor should we expect those means to compete with the information it is the means to. Were the very *having* of an experience itself "noisy" in quality, it could well obliterate the quality which is the content of the experience. But a "gentle" or "soft" quality obviously does not present that threat to "noisier" contents. And it simply blends in with experienced qualities—like gentleness or smoothness—that it more closely resembles or harmonizes with. There is yet another reason why we should expect the "movement" of our expansion experiencing as such to have relatively unobtrusive "tonal" qualities. As organisms, we have no need or desire, generally speaking, to pay attention to the qualities of the comings and goings, as such, of our experiences. Novelists, poets, and philosophers do sometimes have such desires, but they seem to have no survival value.

As I shall presently argue, the above combination of features of the "movement" of our experiencing as such in an expansion experience makes it "feel good." And this pleasantness motivates the desire to continue or repeat such movement. To such a line of argument, however, the following objection might be raised: The "tonal" qualities of the "movement" of experiencing as such are admittedly, and for good reason, unobtrusive. Being so unobtrusive, they may readily go unnoticed. And, in fact, we are rarely aware of such "tonal" qualities of our experiencing expansions, just as we are rarely aware of the qualities of our experiencings in general. But if we are only rarely aware of these allegedly pleasant features, such pleasantness cannot arouse the requisite desire in most cases of love and enjoyment.

Now, if by "being aware" of these features or of their pleasantness one means being self-reflectively aware, "pointing them out" to oneself, "taking note" of them at their occurrence, scrutinizing them, or being able to recall them to memory once past, then it is true that such "awareness" rarely accompanies expansion experiences. But such awareness is also not necessary to arouse the desire in question. For there are many occasions on which we "find" certain features of the world unpleasant and this unpleasantness moves us to some action without our being "aware" either *that* it is those features that we find unpleasant or *that* we find anything unpleasant at all. We may simply act to avoid the feature we find unpleasant, and this avoidance may be the only evidence—to ourselves or to others—of the registration upon us of the unpleasant feature *as* unpleasant. We may thus avoid, or try to, certain rooms, or certain persons' houses, or certain restaurants for even a longish time without even "taking note" *that* we are doing so, much less understanding why we are doing so. We may finally notice our own behavior and even succeed in analyzing the specific features of those places that we find unpleasant in them—and *have found* unpleasant "all along."

My counterargument, of course, does not imply that the "tonal" features of our experiencing expansions, even if pleasant—a point I have not argued yet—actually do, in all cases of love and enjoyment, arouse in us the required desires; at most, it implies that they could do so. How could one answer those who profess that in some cases of enjoyment or love—when what is being enjoyed is, say, a towering rage, the competitiveness of a rough-and-tumble game, the energy of strenuous physical exercise, the passion of sex—they simply have not experienced any of the alleged features of expansion experiencing as such? To such objections, I can hope to say a few things that may *remind* others of experiences they have had but not paid any attention to. Accordingly, I submit that even in cases of intense enjoyment, when attention is, for the most part, clearly and appropriately *not* on features of our experiencing, but on the qualities experienced, there are occasionally the briefest moments in which the former come very vividly to our reflective consciousness. In all activities, even the most energetic, even those whose object or objective devours nearly all attention, there are tiny moments of pause, or of self-reflection, of self-illumination. At these times during the intensest enjoyment we sometimes "catch" how we are feeling. And at some of those times we can feel the "*wash*" of certain qualities being enjoyed—anger, enthusiam, energy, passion—go through us, touching every "part" of our bodies on the "inside" as it were, and enlivening us all over, making us know that we are "all there," that we are, in the most complete and intense way possible, participating in the present activity, for we seem clearly to be aware of it "everywhere in us." Such experiences are the ultimate form of the ones I am analyzing here.

Notice, however, that the above argument supposes that if we can notice such experiencings *sometimes* during even intense enjoyment, the experiencings are *always* there during love or enjoyment, even when they are not self-reflectively "caught." But to think otherwise, it seems to me, is to suppose, absurdly, that what the searchlight of reflective consciousness illuminates, as and when it illuminates it, is all there is to our experience. I obviously cannot *argue* the point here, but the latter supposition seems to me no more plausible with respect to our experiencings than it is with respect to the real world in general, of which our experiencing is, I take it, simply one part.

38. *Anteclimax*

But why, finally, *is* the experiencing of expansion pleasant? What is pleasant about the facts (1) that such experiencing is felt as *"movement"* through the body, (2) that it can be felt "in all parts" of the body, (3) that it is felt as "smooth" or "easy," and (4) that it is felt as "soft" or "gentle"? We might think that no more complex answer is called for here than to ac-knowledge that to feel smoothness and gentleness in many places "in" our bodies and sometimes even "all over" simply *is* pleasant, and that to inquire further into what is pleasant *about* that is either to get no answer at all or to go in circles, that is, to get a repetition of NTL. I think, however, that the question can profitably be pressed further. For there exists, for us, a par-adigm of pleasantness and desirability to which the experienc-ing of expansions is comparable.

A lover is caressing your entire body—a sensual (and de-sired) lover, so that, instead of resisting, you yield to the ca-ress. You "take it in" and try to feel it as deeply as possible. Thus you accept the caress and move into it. And you thus not only feel the caress, by the sense of touch all over your body, but as your accepting response *follows* the movements of the caress you feel that responding receptivity itself "move" wher-ever the lover's caress moves. But as it "moves," your response does not simply stay near the surface but goes deeply "into" the body. And the quality of the response, moreover, as a re-sponse to the smoothness and gentleness of the lover's caress, "reproduces" that smoothness and gentleness.

Now *imagine* that "same" caress, whether in retrospect, in prospect, or in despair. In your imagining there is no feel of the lover's touch *on the surface* of your body. But there *is* the feeling of your *response* to that imagined caress—the feeling within yourself as you imagine the caress moving over your body, in all of the corresponding "places" and to all the depths appropriate to its (imagined) power. There is within you the feeling of the smoothness and gentleness of the (imagined) caress. In other words, *imagining* such a caress is *actually* to feel at least some of the same (roughly speaking) feelings of *response* that you might have if the caress were real. Call such a pattern of feeling the "inner form of being caressed."[81] An inner form of being caressed may, thus, accompany both the experience of actually being caressed and the experience of imagining being caressed.

Now, it is important to see that the experienc*ing* of an expansion is *not* either the experience of a caress or an instance of the inner form of being caressed. For the experiencing (as such) of an expansion is not itself an expansion experience, but a necessary aspect of such an experience. It should be clear, however, that experiences of (real) caresses of the sort described above, and *a fortiori* cases of the inner form of being so caressed, are in significant portion *comprised* of expansion experiences. The qualities that are expanding are smoothness and gentleness. Furthermore, according to my analysis of expansion experiences, the smoothness and gentleness I feel in me in the inner form of being so caressed are qualities of my own act-beginnings, whether those acts are involuntary or are deliberately started and encouraged. In the experiencing (as such) of an expansion, however, we are, relative to our act-beginnings and even to our reproductive "acts," *passive*. For such experiencing simply "happens" to us, as it were, as a necessary accompaniment of the expansion experience as a whole. But in fact, this sense of being passive marks, from another angle, a similarity to instances of the inner form of being caressed. For passivity is, of course, crucial in such experience as well; that is one of the important distinctions between the inner form of *being ca-*

ressed and what we can think of under the rubric "the inner form of caressing." In both cases—experienc*ing* an expansion and an instance of the inner form of being caressed—we feel ourselves passive before, and merely receptive to, qualities from some "other." In a real caress the qualities really come to us from another; they are the lover's qualities in his caress. In an instance of the inner form of being caressed when we are not actually being caressed, the qualities are imagined by us as coming to us from another; so the "other" is an imagined "other." But in our experienc*ings* of expansions, the qualities are only *felt as if there were some "other" "within" us*, and this "other" is precisely the expansion that is taking place (even if partly as a result of our own efforts) within us.

Despite the differences, then, between the inner form of being caressed and the experiencing of an expansion, there are these analogies: In both we are *passively receptive* to certain qualities. These qualities are easyness and gentleness. The qualities are qualities of a "movement" "in" and "through" the body. This "movement" is *capable* of being felt "anywhere" as well as "everywhere" "in" the body. It is on the basis of these parallels with the inner form of being caressed (easily and gently) that I now proceed to the next step in explaining the pleasantness of experiencing expansions within us. The inner form of being caressed gently and easily, whether the "caress" is real or imagined, is pleasant. Experiencing an expansion is in essential respects *like* the inner form of being caressed easily and gently. Therefore, experiencing an expansion too is pleasant. This explanation explains the pleasure in enjoyment or love *in general* by seeing it as (very like) a *particular kind* of enjoyment. For that is what an instance of the inner form of being caressed easily and gently is: the enjoyment of the gentleness and easyness of a (real or imagined) caress.

Now, some may see in this form of explanation an uncom-

fortable circularity. For if NTL is a general theory of Love, then
it should comprehend that Love which is embodied precisely
in the inner form of being caressed easily and gently. But if the
pleasantness of all Love is explained in terms of the latter, then
it is explained in terms of a part of what is in need of explanation in the first place. Such circularity, it seems to me, however, does not impair the persuasiveness of the explanation, for
these reasons: The domain of Love, as NTL comprehends it, is
immense. Whereas it is generally agreed that Love is pleasant,
the source of pleasantness is obscure. But some forms of Love
are so indubitably, clearly, and universally held to be pleasant
that they become paradigms of pleasure. If, then, the source of
pleasantness of Love in general turns out to be that all of its
forms are (or are very like) the paradigmatic pleasure, then the
obscurity is cleared away. That the source of the paradigmatic
pleasure remains thus undiscovered is not bothersome precisely
because the pleasure is paradigmatic. In short, if we have been
shown to our satisfaction that all forms of love and enjoyment
are ultimately like ways of being caressed (which is roughly
what I am claiming), then we should feel we know why they
are all pleasant.

But although I believe that the above explanation is both
logically and psychologically secure, I want still to give another one. This second explanation will make up for some of
the deficiencies that some might see in the first.

39. *Anticlimax*

Experiencing an expansion is, in just the ways that it is like
the inner form of being caressed easily and gently, such as to
generate sexual feelings. Many cases of such experiencing actually do generate such feelings; many do not. But even those

that do not, fail to do so only, as it were, because of accidents of time and place; they do not last long enough, they are not "located" in the right places, or both. In these ways, too, experiencing an expansion is like the inner form of being caressed easily and gently. Furthermore, even when the experiencing of an expansion does not explicitly generate sexual feelings, the *form* of such experiencing—that is, precisely those features that it shares with the inner form of being caressed easily and gently—is such as to suggest to us, in the experiencing, the *possibility* of such feelings; the form of the experiencing holds out, as it were, the "promise" of such feelings. In this respect, too, the experiencing of an expansion is like the inner form of being caressed easily and gently. Now, since sexual feelings are pleasant, so, in the absence of an outweighing unpleasantness, is that which generates them, or holds out the promise of doing so. Since there is no such outweighing unpleasantness in experiencing an expansion,[82] experiencing an expansion is therefore pleasant.

The crucial notion in this argument is "sexual feeling," and it needs, therefore, a definition. Sexual feelings are, in my conception, bodily sensations, but they are *not* felt on the surface of the body. They are felt, rather, "in" certain "locations" in the body. They are felt, specifically, "in" the obviously sexual "parts" of the body as well as "in" those "parts"—which often vary from person to person—called "erogenous." Sexual feelings may, but need not, be accompanied by externally observable movement or behavior. Sexual feelings are themselves neither sexual desires nor feelings of sexual desire, although both of the latter will have sexual feelings as components. I mean by "sexual desire" what, I take it, is usually meant, namely, the desire to have sex with someone or to come to orgasm. My restriction on the term "sexual feeling" to exclude sexual desire and the feelings thereof is not, of course, entirely in accord with common ways of using the term; for "to have sexual feelings for or towards someone" commonly means precisely to have sexual desire for or, at least, sexual inclinations towards that person. Because of this discrepancy between common usage and my own, it is of great importance to keep this restriction in mind. Failure to do so will make my argument appear not only grossly unsound, but outrageous as well. For I am far from wanting to claim that experiencing an expansion—which, I maintain, necessarily occurs in *all* cases of love and enjoyment—always generates either sexual desire or feelings thereof towards what is loved or enjoyed.

What I am calling sexual feelings are, furthermore, *pleasant* bodily sensations felt "in" sexual or erogenous parts of the body. Of course, this proposition makes the pleasantness of sexual feelings in a way a matter of definition. But not, I think, in a way that hurts my argument. For the force of the proposition is not simply to *label* something as "pleasant." Rather, it is to distinguish, within a class of sensations felt "in" sexual and erogenous "parts" of bodies, a subclass of them which are the pleasant ones—pleasant not simply "by definition," but actually—and assert that what I am (indeed) labeling "sexual feelings" are in that subclass. And, finally, the class of orgasmic feelings—that is, these feelings that characteristically accompany orgasms—are explicitly excluded from what I am calling "sexual feelings." This exclusion is related to the above exclusion of sexual desire from the class of sexual feelings, though it does not, of course, amount to the same thing. I exclude orgasmic feelings partly because, in the vast majority of cases of love and enjoyment, there is (as I hope will become evident) not the slightest probability of such feelings being generated by the relevant expansion experiences. But my more important reason is that, even in cases of love and enjoyment in the course of which orgasm appropriately, relevantly, or expectedly occurs, feelings of orgasm are at best irrelevant to and at worst disruptive of the love or enjoyment *of qualities*, except, of course, when the orgasm itself is an object, via its own qualities, of enjoyment. Later I shall try to show why this is so. But for now it should be clear why, if it *is* so, I would want to exclude orgasmic feelings from the class of sexual feelings that, I maintain, are generated precisely by the love and enjoyment of qualities.

In sum, then, what I am calling sexual feelings are pleasant sensations that occur "in" sexual or other erogenous parts, but that are feelings neither of desire nor of orgasm. Because of the latter exclusions, however, some may ask by what right (apart from my right to use words as I please) I call such feelings "sexual." My answer is that the feelings occur "in" parts of the body that are sexual in nature, or that are related to the latter, as are erogenous parts. Erogenous parts are related to the explicitly sexual parts in that a pleasant stimulation of them typically stimulates explicitly sexual parts. By parts "sexual in nature" I mean simply parts that are, or are closely related in use or location to, parts naturally involved in sexual reproduction.

Some might be inclined to dispute that there are pleasant feelings "in" sexual parts that are feelings neither of desire nor of orgasm. To them I say the following: First, it is a plausible and not at all new idea (though perhaps plausible in large part because it is not a new idea) that one is liable to ignore one's own feelings—and especially sexual feelings—if one thinks them irrelevant, inappropriate, or improper. Now, if one thinks (as many people seem to) that sexual feelings *are* irrelevant, inappropriate, or improper in most aspects of one's life precisely because sexual *desire* is irrelevant, inappropriate, or improper in one's life in general, then the sexual *feeling* one has might easily be ignored unless it occurs in clear cases of what is thought of as relevant, appropriate, and proper sexual *desire*. The consequence would be both to solidify the connection between sexual feeling and sexual desire in one's mind and to restrict enormously the (recognized) play of sexual feelings in one's body.

Second, even in contexts in which sexual desire is relevant, appropriate, and proper—for example, even when we are actually being caressed easily and gently by others sexually "available" to us physically, psychologically, legally, morally, and spiritually—we may have sexual feelings that are *not* sexual desires. I, at least, have a difficult time believing that such feelings do not occur in all except the most "driven" persons— driven to achieve, to score, to prove themselves, or simply to repeat compulsively the orgasmic act. The feelings I have in mind here are simply those pleasant stimulations in sexual and erogenous parts that do not (perhaps "yet") constitute our being "turned on"—pleasant stirrings that we are content to allow to come (and perhaps go) without "reading" them either as a "call to action" or as a "call to judgment or repression."

Third, precisely the "current of consciousness" that runs "through" us in an expansion experience often runs "into" and "through" sexual and erogenous parts of our bodies. And even when it does not, we recognize at some bodily level of awareness that it could do so yet, or might have done so. And the qualities of that "movement," namely, easyness and gentleness, are such, after all, as to stimulate pleasant feelings in those parts that are predisposed to feel such stimulation, as are sexual and erogenous parts. Just as the easyness and lightness of a caressing movement that is imagined to flow over us and the "response" to which is thus felt within us can so stimulate those parts, so can the easyness and lightness of the "move-ment" felt within us of our own experiencing stimulate them. That it in fact does and, further, that such stimulation does not count as feelings either of sexual desire or, least of all, of or-gasm, I leave to be confirmed (or not) by the readers' experi-ence.

Assuming that in cases of love and enjoyment our experienc-ing expansions of qualities does generate sexual feelings within us, how do we thereby explain the *pleasantness* of love and en-joyment? The generation of sexual feelings works thus: In en-joying or loving any quality we reproduce experiences of that quality in large part by generating expansion experiences of that quality "in" and "through" ourselves. In such reproduc-tion, the very experiencing of those expanding qualities in turn "moves" "in" and "through" us, at each moment either stim-ulating sexual feelings or holding out the promise of them. But since sexual feelings are pleasant, so are their anticipations (the promises held out). Such pleasures thus move us to desire more of them, and "more" of them satisfy the "preceding" desires precisely for "more." At each moment during love and enjoy-ment there is in us some pleasure generating and satisfying desire for "more" of it.

I want now briefly to explain why orgasmic feelings must be either irrelevant or disruptive in this picture of enjoyment, and hence why I exclude them from the class of sexual feelings that explain the pleasure of Love. Orgasmic feelings, though they vary enormously among themselves, nevertheless have a certain "structure."[83] The structure is an upward rising, a "peaking" or "topping," and then a downward falling. There is a begin-ning—the "approach"—then the moment of no return, the "going over the top," the "fall," with its several surges that subside in intensity, the "afterglow," and the end. Such a form or structure of pleasure does *not* fit into the pattern of continuity of experience and of pleasant feeling presupposed and exhibited by occurrences of love and enjoyment. In such occurrences there is no such structure, no beginning, middle, and end. Rather, there is a sameness of structure *all through* the occasion of Loving, no matter what its duration. The fact remains, furthermore, that orgasmic feelings are hardly ever *immediately* repeatable, which they would have to be to fit into the pattern of Loving. Therefore, even when orgasmic feelings occur during the enjoyment of qualities, they cannot themselves be *part* of the pleasure of the enjoyment. This is not to say that orgasmic feelings cannot be pleasant or cannot themselves be enjoyed during Love. But it is to say that such feelings will be at least irrelevant to, and possibly interruptive or even disruptive of, any case of Loving except the enjoyment precisely of the orgasmic feeling. The closest to an exception that I can think of is a case of Loving in which precisely what is being "loved" is the lover's *responsibility* in being a "good lover," the conception of which includes the responsibility to have satisfying orgasmic feelings. (This possibility may seem far-fetched, but some people I know can construe *anything* as a responsibility.) Even in this sort of love, however, the orgasmic feeling is itself not *part* of the enjoyment of fulfilling the responsibility to have it, even if it is essential to it. But neither is it irrelevant to or disruptive of it. Notice, too, that other forms of "responsible" love, such as having orgasms in order to fulfill one's marital duty to try to beget children, do not make the orgasmic *feelings* thereby more a part of that particular form of love. For whereas one can plausibly argue that (male) orgasms are a necessary means to the responsible attempt to beget, one might argue that the *feelings* of orgasm are quite incidental to the fulfillment of that responsibility. Indeed, some followers of the particular tradition in the theory of love that exalts responsible married love as the ideal form of love sound sometimes as if they *regret* that the execution of such love must bring with it orgasmic feelings.

As the last steps in constructing the New Theory of Love and my arguments for it, I have given two explanations for the pleasantness of Love. I take the two to be independent, mutually compatible, and equally good. I admit that some will likely find one or the other more convincing. In the first explanation, I trace the pleasure of Loving to parallels between the experienc*ing*, as such, of Loving and a certain kind of experience of a *caress*. In the second, I trace the pleasure to certain kinds of sexual feelings. In virtue of these two explanations, I believe I have uncovered two senses in which Love, *in all its multitudinous forms*, is fundamentally *erotic*. But a by-product of my analysis and arguments is that despite the erotic nature of Love, Love in general is not essentially sexual. It may be "fitting," given a generally evolutionistic explanatory framework and the brute fact that human beings must reproduce sexually to survive as a species, both that human beings have sexual feelings and that caressing behavior is often a prelude, via its stimulation of sexual feelings, to behavior that is sexual in intent and result. But strictly from the point of view of Loving, as NTL understands it, the fact of human sexuality is irrelevant.[84]

We can easily imagine that Loving might apply to sentient beings other than human beings as they are now constituted. Such beings must, at minimum, experience qualities, have expansion experiences, and be capable of pleasant feelings like the sexual feelings that can, I claim, be generated in experiencing expansions. But—and this is crucial—the feelings like sexual feelings need not *be* sexual feelings in the sense of pleasant feelings *felt "in" sexual parts*, since the beings need not reproduce sexually and therefore need not have sexual parts. We would not have much trouble accounting for the existence of creatures with highly developed feelings of pleasure but no reproductive "need" for them. We might, for example, imagine human beings evolving somehow, say by way of parthenogonidial mutants, into nonsexual beings who retain exactly the same feelings that formerly were properly called "sexual feelings," just as they might retain bodily parts indistinguishable in form and location from those which formerly were properly called "sexual parts," and the inclination and the ability to engage in bodily interaction—including all styles of copulation—with their fellow beings.

Under such conditions would Loving still be erotic? Well, we might not *call* it "erotic," "erotic" retaining all the meanings and associations it now has (if it *could* retain them all). On the other hand, we might not *want* to call it erotic either, because it would not be as much fun as it is now to say that Love is fundamentally erotic, but not essentially sexual. Nevertheless, Loving would *be* then just what the New Theory of Love says it is now, and it would be just as pleasant.

Notes

1. I say "probably," because Plato never worked out a *theory* of beauty, even though there are plenty of ideas relevant to a theory of beauty throughout the Platonic corpus. It is nevertheless possible to see the Platonic enterprise in the *Republic* as grounded in precisely a desire to develop an environment of total beauty for the citizens of the ideal state. Such beauty would encompass everything from the food they eat, to the artifacts they come into contact with every day, to fellow citizens of good character, to the very Forms themselves. Such an environment would thus work to preserve forms of beauty in the state and in the citizens and ultimately, therefore, to maintain the happiness of the citizens and of the state as a whole. The connection between beauty and this moral and political program is best, if still obscurely, seen in the early educational passages of Book III and most particularly at 400d through 402, at the end of which the connection with love, whose proper object is beauty, is brought into the picture.

2. Essentially Platonic ideas of love and beauty and their significance were prominent in Western civilization through the Middle Ages and early modern times. This was due chiefly, I think, to Augustine's incorporation of them into Christian thought. Augustine, at least the "optimistic" Augustine who comes through in parts of the *Confessions* and elsewhere, would have subscribed to the ideas in my first paragraph (while putting his own construction on them, of course)—this despite the fact that much in the Platonic notions of love and beauty ran counter to profound currents in Christian, and indeed in Augustine's own, thought. Already by the seventeenth century, however, such ideas were on the wane. They play no role in the thinking of the great rationalists and empiricists of the early modern period, so that by Kant's time, and in his own writings, they have disappeared almost entirely.

3. This is a large statement indeed, and one for which a case someday may be made. Such a case might be made along the follow-

ing lines, by borrowing some concepts that have been introduced into the historical study of the family. First, assume that middle-class persons are peculiarly success- or achievement-oriented. Next assume that a basically Freudian model of the family and child development applies to the bourgeois family, so that the achievement the bourgeois child seeks is, at root, to win the approval of his parents. Assume, moreover, that this approval is a substitute for forms of erotic gratification systematically forbidden to the bourgeois child by his parents. (For the details of this model and how it applies to the analysis of middle-class civilization, see Mark Poster, *Critical Theory of the Family* [New York: Seabury Press, 1986], especially chs. 1, 6, and 7.) Then, if beauty, or the love of it, can be correctly regarded as rooted precisely in erotic good feeling, as I argue in the final pages of this study, and this in turn can be identified with a Marcusan neo-Freudian "polymorphous eroticism," the characteristic achievement-orientation of the bourgeois type can be interpreted as being *necessarily* incompatible with the love and enjoyment of beauty. Indeed, in terms of my distinction below between extrinsic and intrinsic desire, the kind of ambition the middle class builds into its children is founded on extrinsic desire, whereas the love of beauty, I claim, essentially involves intrinsic desire.

Of course, what drives the lives of real human beings of whatever class and whatever historical period is in fact a mixture of intrinsic and extrinsic desire. Nevertheless, persons might lead lives dominated by one or the other, and the above claim is precisely that it is a mark of bourgeois civilization that persons in it are raised to lives dominated by extrinsic desires of a particular pattern.

4. In Descartes himself this desire is expressed as the determination, in his philosophical method and program, to admit no source of knowledge except the inner light of his own unaided reason. Thus he excludes in particular knowledge that comes from book learning, social and cultural traditions, or the ostensibly external world revealed by the senses.

5. This capsule history of the idea of the love of beauty presumes, of course, that a long string of philosophers from Plato to George Dickie were all addressing a common subject matter, with Dickie

finally alleging (apparently) that it doesn't exist (the "myth"). Such a presumption is far from uncontroversial, even though no controversy that I know of has raged about it. Rather, it is, I think, unquestioningly *assumed* that Plato and the long line of his followers in matters of love and beauty were talking about something *other* than what the eighteenth-century British psychological aestheticians, Kant, Schopenhauer, and the later tradition of experimental aestheticians, including Bullough, were talking about. Thus the encyclopedic Wladyslaw Tatarkiewicz, in tracing theories of aesthetic experience from the ancient world to present times, finds no place for Plato's *Symposium* in that history, although he sees the Platonist Shaftesbury as one of the twin sources of modern theories of aesthetic experience. See *A History of Six Ideas: An Essay in Aesthetics* (The Hague: Nijhoff, 1980), ch. 11. And so it seems in contemporary times irrelevant to the topic of love to discuss disinterested pleasure and the aesthetic attitude, just as it seems irrelevant to contemporaries to look to the *Symposium* for insight into aesthetic experience and aesthetic pleasure.

Now, it is difficult to say how one might *argue* that the subject matter of this whole row of philosophical theories is in fact "the same" (except of course for the modifications which the individual theories themselves make in that subject matter). Part of that argument would, I suppose, be constituted precisely by the sort of theory I am constructing in this book. Another argument, though, is the historical line that can be traced in the eighteenth century linking Kant (and hence those who come after him) and Plato. For it is Shaftesbury who, at the very end of the Platonic tradition of beauty, still accords to beauty the amplitude that it had for Plato. And it is he who can still identify love as the "contemplation of beauty" (*Characteristics of Men, Manners, Opinions, Times, etc.*, ed. John M. Robertson [Gloucester, Mass.: Peter Smith, 1963], vol. II, pp. 126ff.). And it is Shaftesbury who is admitted on all sides to be a main source of modern notions of the aesthetic attitude and aesthetic pleasure. He influenced Edmund Burke, who defines love as "aesthetic satisfaction . . . arising from the contemplation of the beautiful" (*A Philosophical Enquiry into the Origin of Our Ideas of the Sublime*

and Beautiful, ed. J. T. Boulton [London: Routledge, 1958], p. 91
[first published 1757]). In Burke's work already the extension of
"beauty" is narrowed down to all "sensible" things, and the "love"
of it is explicitly said to be different from desire (ibid.). Thirty-five
years after Burke's work first appeared came Kant's mature work in
aesthetics, which in many ways follows Burke, with the significant
exception that the term "love" is almost completely eliminated,
never to appear again in a theoretical text as a term necessary to the
analysis of "aesthetic" experience. (It does appear, unsurprisingly, in
the poetry of William Wordsworth, who uses it precisely to denote
our relationship to beauty. It may also have such a use in the work
of other poets, though I am not aware of it. In any case, such "ata-
vistic" usage does not impinge on philosophical work.) I emphasize
that the term "love" is *almost* entirely eliminated in Kant's work in
aesthetics, for although the term does not figure at all in Kant's technical analyses of aesthetic judgment or experience, Kant is capable
of the following statement: "The beautiful prepares us to love dis-
interestedly something, even nature itself; the sublime prepares us
to esteem something highly even in opposition to our own (sensible)
interest" (*Critique of Judgment*, trans. J. H. Bernard [New York: Haf-
ner, 1951], p. 108). There may well be other such casual uses of
"love" in the Kantian texts, but I have not encountered them.

Seeing modern concerns with aesthetic attitude and disinterested
pleasure as being in a line of descent from ancient concerns with the
love of beauty also enables us both to see remarkable changes in those
ancient concerns in the eighteenth century and to see those changes
as an effect of the ("antibeautiful") bourgeoisification of aesthetics.
For it is "Enlightenment" ideas that lie behind the middle-class revolutions of the late eighteenth century (the political revolutions and
the industrial revolution). But Shaftesbury, who represents the old
Platonic ideas of love and beauty, is by no means an Enlightenment
figure. By virtue of style and content of thought, as well as social
position, Shaftesbury belongs firmly to the *ancien régime*. It is perhaps
important, too, that the term "love" still remains in the work of
Burke, an apologist for the old regime. But in Kant, whose work is
a pinnacle of Enlightenment thought, we find both the old, full con-

cept of beauty and its coupling with the concept of love effectively extinguished.

(Ironically, it is precisely Shaftesbury and his fellow Platonists who are revived by some revolutionary and postrevolutionary romanticists. And it is via romantic poets and philosophers that strains of Platonism return to the mainstream of Western thought. In particular, the *amplitude* of the "aesthetic," or "the love of beauty," that I have stressed in the Platonic tradition comes back into twentieth-century philosophy in John Dewey and Alfred North Whitehead. Dewey's insistence that the "aesthetic" is ingredient in *all* experience and Whitehead's doctrine of the ubiquity of "feeling" are the true progeny—though poorly integrated into the modern tradition of the "aesthetic attitude" and apparently unaware of their ancestry in the tradition of beauty—of that old Platonic vision of the "vast sea of beauty" [*Symposium*, 210d].)

Naturally, to claim that all of these very diverse philosophers were addressing the same subject matter is not to suppose that their *theories* about that subject matter have much in common. And, in fact, my capsule history supposes that some of them have hardly anything in common. To claim that there is a common subject matter, furthermore, is neither to endorse nor to disagree with any of these theories about that subject matter, except possibly one. When George Dickie speaks of the "myth" of the aesthetic attitude, he may mean (though I am unsure about this) that the subject matter that these theorists thought they were talking about *does not exist*. For he says at the conclusion of *Art and the Aesthetic* (Ithaca: Cornell University Press, 1974): "If I am right, the experiences that derive from intercourse with aesthetic objects do not have any affective features which are peculiarly characteristic and which distinguish them from other experiences" (p. 198). I, on the contrary, following the Platonic emphasis on beauty, take the qualities upon which beauty depends to be the "aesthetic objects"—though aesthetic objects far more varied and all-pervasive than most modern aestheticians admit—and attempt in this study to define just the "affective features" of *certain* (though, to be sure, not *all*) experiences of those objects.

6. The array of hostile attitudes, thrown up by and since the

eighteenth century against the essentially Greek ideas I shall defend in this book, is formidable indeed. In addition to what we may call the "aesthetic" point of view, according to which beauty is severely restricted to a narrow range of human life, much removed from the erotic, there is the "moral" point of view, represented chiefly by Kant and his followers, which seeks equally to protect the moral life—what Plato might have called "the realm of moral beauty"—from "inclinations" of all sorts, and *a fortiori* from *erotic* "inclinations"; there are some Marxist points of view that, buying into the very bourgeois trivializations and privatizations of beauty they ostensibly criticize, can maintain that any concern with beauty is insufficiently "political" or "historical"; there are many "modernist" points of view that maintain that beauty is irrelevant to modern art, modern civilization, and modern life; and, finally, there are "structuralists" and "poststructuralists" of many stripes to whom the very notion of beauty and of the love of it would seem, I presume, simply too humane or insufficiently paranoid.

7. This represents a not uncontroversial view of the *Symposium*. Most commentaries on that work—and nearly every one that I know of by a philosopher—allege that Plato expressed in that work a definite *theory* of love. Such interpretations, however, are bought at the price of ignoring important parts of the text. It is not that Plato did not have some definite *views* about love, but the claim that they are worked together into a *theory* in that dialogue ignores the most salient feature, in my opinion, of the work. It seems to me that Plato has written there a text that deliberately foils all attempts to find in it a coherent theory. At the same time, it is a work that demands of its readers that they *try* to find such a theory in it. If I were writing a book for an audience of my own students and research associates and I were as literarily gifted as Plato, I might write just such a book. It is, in effect, a literary and philosophical love object. For it makes of its readers a coterie of lovers who, in instantiation of the Diotiman formula, "desire to possess it forever"—in just the way it is relevant to "possess" such an object, namely, *by reading, studying and thinking about* it without end. I suspect, however, that it would take another book to make good my claims about the *Symposium*.

8. It is not, I think, that there is nothing in our experience that the theorists of the "aesthetic attitude" were trying to talk *about*. It is simply that their theoretical attempts already presupposed a theoretical—probably even an ideological—determination of the distinctness of the narrowly "aesthetic" from other aspects of life. Such an assumed distinctness ultimately distorts and obscures whatever in our experience genuinely needs description, to such an extent that, as I think George Dickie has adequately shown in *Art and the Aesthetic* (though I believe he draws some wrong conclusions from the fact), modern "aesthetic attitude" *theories* are unsalvageable.

9. Consider, for example, the difference between the pagan Plato's (allegedly) "egocentric" model of the lover who in loving desires his own immortality and, say, certain Christian conceptions of the lover as (allegedly) completely other-regarding. Or the (again alleged) differences between the basically erotic, if nevertheless nonsexual, love of the *Symposium* and certain Christian conceptions of a completely non-self-gratifying love. Or between the essentially homosexual model of love and friendship in the ancient world and the Christian ideal of married love. Or between the predominantly pagan view of love between persons as essentially edifying and the predominantly Christian view of love as basically procreative. Or between an early modern aristocratic view of (heterosexual) love as predominantly sexual and a classic bourgeois view of it as predominantly emotional and affectional (on this point, see Poster, *Critical Theory of the Family*, especially ch. 7). Or between the notion of love that operates (and fails to) in the universe of *King Lear*, on the one hand, and that which operates in the world of Tristan and Isolt.

10. Even if philosophers have often assumed, rather offhandedly, that they are. See, for example, Immanuel Kant, *Critique of Judgment*, passim, but especially pp. 38–45.

11. I have many reasons for preferring this line of argument. One is that Kant, in casually identifying pleasure and enjoyment, also seems implicitly to identify enjoyment with what I am calling propositional pleasure (ibid.). A second reason is that, despite this implicit identification, Kant's concern to distinguish specifically aesthetic pleasure—what he calls "disinterested satisfaction"—from all

other kinds of pleasure is motivated, it seems to me, by some of the same intuitions about pleasure that I have. For despite our terminological differences, what Kant calls "disinterested satisfaction" is just a special case of what I would call "enjoyment." And what he thinks of as pleasures involving "interest" are what I count as propositional pleasures (cf. note 13 below). A third reason is that the most recent and careful theory of enjoyment that I know, namely, that of Richard Warner, either makes enjoyment out to be, in the last analysis, a kind of propositional pleasure or, at least, makes the *pleasure* of enjoyment to be that of propositional pleasure (see "Enjoyment," *Philosophical Review* 89, no. 4 [October 1980], pp. 507–26; this article has been incorporated into Warner's book *Freedom, Enjoyment and Happiness* [Ithaca: Cornell University Press, 1987] without essential changes). My fourth reason is the simplest: this line of argument will help throw into relief some important features of enjoyment that have often been overlooked.

12. I give some arguments for this move, as part of a more general claim about the reducibility of enjoyment, below in Section 6.

13. My statement here of the necessary conditions of propositional pleasure accords, I think, with Kant's characterization of the "satisfaction" he calls "interest": "The satisfaction which we combine with the representation of the existence of an object is called 'interest.' Such satisfaction always has reference to the faculty of desire, either as its determining ground or as necessarily connected with its determining ground" (*Critique of Judgment*, p. 38). The connection between Kant's second sentence here and my point about desire and propositional pleasure is obvious, I take it. Kant's first sentence is more problematic. But if we construe "object" in this sentence as the *state of affairs desired*, the "existence" of that object as that state of affairs *obtaining*, and the "representation" of that existence as the *idea* or *belief* that the state of affairs obtains, then we get precisely my point about propositional pleasure. Moreover, if we interpret Kant in this way, we can make plausible sense of what is (or has always seemed to me at least) a very obscure doctrine. I cannot honestly say, however, whether Kant himself meant here what I am interpreting him to mean, for his subsequent discussion of *examples* of what he means rather badly muddies these waters.

14. This qualification is necessary to eliminate the possibility

that I desired that *p* at some time in the past but stopped so desiring before I came to believe that *p*.

15. This qualification is necessary for the obvious reason that sometimes having a desire of ours satisfied can turn out to be nothing but unpleasant even though we are unaware of that until the desire is satisfied.

16. This is not to imply, however, that we cannot *enjoy* being in a situation in which the objective conditions of satisfaction of some desire of ours obtain, for we can. But insofar as we do enjoy being in that situation, our enjoyment thereof is not identical with the pleasant feelings that that situation (or, more precisely, our belief that that situation obtains) generates.

17. Note, however, that it is not pointless to direct oneself or another *to continue* to enjoy a thing. And note, furthermore, that it is not pointless to direct oneself to enjoy *on a particular occasion* what one enjoys *in general and for the most part*. The latter two uses of "enjoy" illustrate an important distinction that will figure throughout this study, namely, that between *occasional or occurrent enjoyment* and *dispositional enjoyment*. What I am currently arguing is, of course, that *occurrent* enjoyment is not identical with the pleasant feelings sometimes generated by propositional pleasure.

18. Thus enjoyment cannot be defined, for example, as follows: If a person S is engaged in some activity A, then S is enjoying A just in case S is pleased that S is engaged in A.

19. On this fundamental point I align myself with Plato, for whom love *is* essentially a kind of desire. My own way of putting this is, rather, that desire of a certain kind is an essential ingredient in enjoyment and love. On this score, I disagree with Kant and what he has to say about "disinterested satisfaction." For in calling the specific pleasure relevant to a judgment of beauty "disinterested," Kant is strongly *suggesting* that it is *not* "determined by the faculty of desire." As far as I know, Kant never explicitly states this, but that he believes it can reasonably be inferred from the fact that desire in no way figures in his analysis of "disinterested satisfaction."

20. I find Richard Warner's recent theory of enjoyment (see note 11) attractive precisely because it makes central a notion of desire as both aroused and satisfied by enjoyed activity. In fact, this part of his analysis of enjoyment started the chain of reflections leading to

my own theory, and I hereby acknowledge my debt to that analysis. What I find weak in Warner's theory, as will become clear in the sequel, is his conception of the object of this desire and his failure to recognize the dynamic or continuing nature of this desire-satisfaction "system." As I see it, Warner's theory leaves it a mystery why we should want to *continue* doing anything we are enjoying (like looking at gorgeous legs) that does not have a natural terminus, or why we should leave off with regret doing something that does have a natural term (like flying to Hawaii) once we have reached that term. Yet it would be inadequate for Warner simply to answer that we want to continue because the activities are *pleasant*. For as I understand Warner's theory, what is pleasant about them is that they satisfy a desire that they simultaneously arouse. But this satisfaction, so statically conceived, "happens" as soon as its corresponding desire arises. There seems to be, in short, no sensitivity in Warner's theory to central facts about our experience of enjoyment: our sense of loss *after* some occurrences of enjoyment and driving passion *during* our enjoyments.

Without referring to such experiential facts, Warner does deal, rather summarily, with a notion that is relevant to such facts. For Warner, the desire aroused and satisfied in enjoying an activity is precisely that that activity "occur." He explicitly rejects the hypothesis that this is a desire to *continue* the activity. His only reasons are based upon the single example of "enjoying writing the last word of an essay." He cannot understand what it would mean to want to *continue* doing the latter ("Enjoyment," p. 519; *Freedom, Enjoyment and Happiness*, p. 130). But first, I find it implausible that anyone should in fact *enjoy* writing the last word of anything; Warner may be confusing enjoyment here with being *glad that* one is writing the last word. Second, we may have the desire to do something even if it makes no practical sense to realize it or to try to realize it—like writing the last word over and over again or drawing out at great length the writing of the last word. Third, having such a desire does not commit us even to trying to satisfy it, much less to actually satisfying it. And anyway, in the case of writing the last word, one *does* normally continue to do it, and hence does satisfy such a desire, if only for an extremely short time.

21. Or rather he has Socrates relate that Diotima introduced it to the young Socrates. And Socrates does not relate any argument that Diotima gave for it, or that the young Socrates requested for it. I do not think this absence of argument is Plato's oversight, however. For the very absence of argument draws attention to this astounding proposition that the lover desires to possess the beautiful forever. It also draws attention to Diotima's dottiness and to her general untrustworthiness as a philosopher and thereby raises the question (as do many other details about Diotima) whether Socrates isn't making up the whole story about her instructing him. I do not mean to suggest by these remarks, however, that Plato does not take the connection between love and immortality seriously. I mean to suggest only that, as with everything else in that dialogue, he is indulging in high intellectual play with it.

22. I think that *one* of the things Plato is doing with the notion of the desire for immortality is introducing it as a reading of our more or less ordinary *experience* of love. And, for the reasons given, I think it is a misreading. It will occur to some that the notion of the desire for immortality also looks forward to the rather *extraordinary* experience of the lover of the *Beautiful Itself*, at the top of the ladder of love, and that in that context the desire for immortality *is* apt and accurate, because the Beautiful Itself is "immortal." This is a complex point, and it obviously depends on an interpretation both of the Beautiful Itself and of the love of it. But I think a case might be made, even here, that such a love involves merely a desire "with no term."

It may also occur to some that by "forever" Plato means not "everlastingly" but something like "timelessly." Thus the formula that Diotima and the young Socrates agree to would be "Love is the desire to possess the beautiful timelessly." Such an interpretation might indeed accord with my own interpretation of the desire, in enjoying *A*, to continue doing *A* with no stopping point "in mind." Unfortunately, such an interpretation does not yield any coherent interpretation of the consequence Diotima draws from her formula, namely, that the lover desires his own *immortality*. For interpreting this to mean that the lover desires his own timelessness does not accord with Diotima's *examples* of seeking "immortality," namely,

221

producing children, producing cultural monuments to be remembered by, and producing virtuous students (208b–210e).

23. See *A New Theory of Beauty* (Princeton: Princeton University Press), pp. 39–42, where PQDs are characterized as follows: "A generic feature of any PQD F is that it be possible for one 'object' to be more or less F than another 'object.' A specific feature of any PQD F is that the degree to which one 'object' is more or less F than another is not numerically determinable according to a single scale that can measure the degree to which any given 'object' is more or less F than any other 'object.' "

24. Cf. *A New Theory of Beauty*, pp. 41–43.

25. I take "object" here in the sense in which I use it in *A New Theory of Beauty*, namely, as anything that is (ostensibly) denotable by the subject of a sentence whose predicate is "beautiful" or a synonym.

26. Since according to the New Theory of Beauty qualities are, as it were, "bearers" of beauty, however, the connection between experiences of qualities and experiences of beauty is close. Indeed, I intend it to be. That connection represents one, but only one, link between the theory of enjoyment I am constructing and Platonic *eros* on the one hand and Kant's "disinterested pleasure" on the other.

Yet the very fact that the essential objects of Love are not "beauties" but *qualities* marks a big advance over nearly all other theories of love or aesthetic pleasure, in my view. It appropriately "loosens" the connection, frequently taken to be a *necessary* one, between love or aesthetic pleasure, on the one side, and beauty, on the other. For according to the New Theory of Love, the form of love, enjoyment, or pleasure that is *distinctively appropriate* to experiences of beauty is, nevertheless, *possible* with respect to qualities and other "objects" that are not experienced as beautiful. Furthermore, as I shall later point out, experiences of qualities, and even of beauty with respect to qualities, do not *necessarily* carry with them enjoyment, love, or pleasure and *a fortiori* do not carry with them enjoyment of, love of, or pleasure in those qualities or that beauty (see note 80). The New Theory of Love, however, does not simply "loosen" the connection between Love and beauty in these two ways; it also can account for the *special* "pleasantness" of beauty that all theorists seem to have intuited, without reducing it, as so many of those theorists have, to a *necessary* "pleasantness" (see Section 28 below).

In this respect, then, the New Theory of Love distinguishes itself from modern and recent theories of beauty that concern themselves with the relationship between beauty and some kind of "pleasure." The theories I have in mind are those of David Hume in "Of the Standard of Taste," Kant in the *Critique of Judgment*, George Santayana in *The Sense of Beauty*, and Mary Mothersill in *Beauty Restored* (Oxford: Oxford University Press, 1985). Not all of these theories allege or presuppose the *same* connection between beauty and some kind of pleasure, or allege or presuppose such a connection on the same grounds, of course, but all of them share the idea that the connection is a necessary one.

27. Perhaps—but I am only guessing—this is *another* meaning Kant had (dimly) in mind in saying that (to paraphrase somewhat) the existence of an object is irrelevant to aesthetic pleasure. This interpretation of Kant on this point at least accords better with his *examples* than the interpretation I gave in note 13. Cf. Kant, *Critique of Judgment*, pp. 43–45.

28. Cf. *A New Theory of Beauty*, pp. 121–26.

29. For the concept of "artistic acts" see my *Mind and Art* (Princeton: Princeton University Press, 1972), chs. 1–2. The concept was devised primarily to account for attributions of so-called anthropomorphic qualities to works of art. It is easily generalizable, as here, to accommodate all qualities. In *Mind and Art* I found no need to distinguish between the artistic act and the "originating act," as I do now. Part of the reason is that in many cases (and in fact in most cases that we know about) we have no access to an originating act. Part of my point in that book, furthermore, is that we need no such access, nor indeed even the assumption that there was such an act *with the same or similar qualities* as the "artistic act." Nevertheless, there *may* have been such an originating act, and if there was one, the artistic act is its track.

30. See *Mind and Art*, ch. 3, for my arguments and for extensive analyses of examples.

31. Some odors and tastes may seem to elude this category. Thus in *A New Theory of Beauty* I counted as qualities what we designate by such descriptions as "piney-smelling." Call this whole class of qualities "characteristic smell and taste qualities." Such qualities can be shown to fit the present category if we nominalize the quality and then make the quality that bears the *beauty* of the resulting "object" something like *vividness*. Thus, what is piney-smelling is construable as having a piney smell, and this piney smell may be construed as an "object" with the quality of vividness. As such, then, piney smells can be experienced as "asserting themselves" with forcefulness or strength.

32. It is no concern of mine to argue here the proper placement of such qualities in these categories. My claim is only that these categories exhaust the world of qualities for every human being. As will be obvious later, nothing in my theory of Love depends upon where in the world each quality is experienced as belonging.

33. The "aesthetic point of view" as characterized here is first adumbrated, I would say, by Plotinus, since he both identifies beauty and "being" (*Enneads*, V.8.9) and holds that even the lower levels of being, such as Nature, are basically "soul" and that the workings and products of Nature are the effects of "contemplation" (*Enneads*, especially III.8.4). This view of reality is inherited by medieval Christian theologians and metaphysicians, and surfaces again in the Cambridge Platonists, Shaftesbury, the poetry of Wordsworth and other writers of the romantic period, and the metaphysics of A. N. Whitehead. The connection between this point of view and aesthetics more narrowly conceived appears in the commonplace view that to see beauty in a natural thing is essentially to see the natural thing as a work of art. It also appears in the Kantian view linking beauty in an object with a "purposiveness" the object *seems* (to the judging subject) to have despite the *fact* that the object, as object of the judgment of taste, has no purpose. A succinct formulation of this point of view with respect to beauty occurs in a work by the eighteenth-century British aesthetician Archibald Alison cited by George Dickie in *Art and the Aesthetic* (p. 67): "The Beauty and Sublimity which is felt in the various appearances of matter, are finally to be ascribed to their Expression of Mind; or to their being,

either directly or indirectly, the signs of those qualities of Mind which are fitted by the constitution of our Nature, to affect us with pleasing or interesting Emotions."

My own description of our "worlds of qualities" is obviously another embodiment of this "aesthetic point of view," for its implication is that since beauty is dependent upon qualities, and all qualities have some relation to the qualities of sentient beings, beauty itself, at least insofar as it is experienceable by us, has connections, distinct from that experienceability itself, to the activities of sentient beings.

34. Because of this some readers may be tempted to call my method in this study "phenomenological" in the technical sense(s) of that term. But I do not claim such a description. One reason is my disinclination to tread on foreign turf, where my step would inevitably be unsteady. I have not been trained as a phenomenologist and am quite unfamiliar with the intricate methodological disputes of that tradition. So, while it may be true that some of the moves in these pages can be described as quite authentically phenomenological in some sense of the term, I do not intend to claim such a description. On the other hand, I have no motive for refusing to acknowledge such a description should it come my way.

I should, however, point out that whereas *some* of the present study is based on introspectively gained experience and on descriptions of such experience in its more or less "raw" state, by no means all of it is. My aim in this book is resolutely theoretical. And that means, for me, that I *also* give schematic *analyses* of "raw" introspective experience and attempt, as well, by the mediation of such analyses to construct a general *theory*, the warrants for which do not by any means consist solely of introspectively gained experience. In this crucial respect, then, my methods in this book do *not* accord with (my understanding of) at least the early phenomenological animus against the "constructivism" of the turn-of-the-century Neo-Kantians and (again my understanding of) the consequent desire to give only "pure descriptions."

I insert this methodological note as a partial response to David Carrier, who as a reader for Princeton University Press pointed out the need for some such "placement" of my enterprise. I take this opportunity also to thank Professor Carrier for his suggestions in general, which I believe have led me to improve on an earlier draft of this book.

35. Some of the literature on "empathy," may, *I think*, begin to do so. I do not mean here the phenomenological literature on empathy initiated, I believe, by Edith Stein. Nor do I mean the contemporary literature in counseling psychology. I refer rather to the literature on the aesthetic concept of empathy (*Einfühlung*) elaborated, though not invented, by Theodor Lipps. (For English-language works in this literature see Lipps, "Empathy and Aesthetic Pleasure," in *Aesthetic Theories: Studies in the Philosophy of Art*, ed. Karl Aschenbrenner and Arnold Isenberg [Englewood Cliffs, N.J.: Prentice-Hall, 1965], pp. 403–12, and Herbert Sidney Langfield, *The Aesthetic Attitude* [Port Washington, N.Y.: Kennikat Press, 1920].)

This work on empathy came out of an apparently rich and busy tradition of physiological-psychological aesthetics stretching from the mid-nineteenth century to the early decades of the twentieth. Vernon Lee and Edward Bullough, to name only two thinkers whose work is still fairly widely remembered and used, worked in this tradition. The philosophical ancestors of the tradition apparently include, prominently, David Hume. Though I have read in it sporadically, I can by no means claim to know the literature of this tradition, much of which has not been translated into English. I can say quite definitely that the present work does not have intellectual roots in this literature. I have nevertheless found interesting if vague connections between my concept of expansion experiences and some of these discussions of empathy. Thus the literature on empathy is clearly concerned to say *something* about the connections between what we feel (inside us) and what we perceive (outside us). Furthermore, it emphasizes what is called a "dynamic quality" in experience. Precisely what these connections are, what this dynamic quality amounts to, and, finally, what the precise significance all this has for aesthetics or philosophy in general, however, has not come through to me on the basis of my (admittedly meager) reading.

For nearly every paragraph of that reading reveals relentless confusions between issues, points, and intentions that are empirical and those that are philosophical, between the phenomenological and the neurophysiological or mechanical, between the descriptive and the explanatory, between the factual and the normative. Furthermore, it is never clear to me whether empathy relates primarily to perception, primarily to enjoyment, or to the connections between them. Nor is it ever clear to me whether "empathy" applies only to aesthetic feeling and perception or is more universal. Where it clearly addresses specifically aesthetic issues, the literature is further vitiated, in my view, by inadequate, incorrect, or unclearly defined notions of beauty and by an uncritical allegiance to incorrect and confused theories of the "aesthetic attitude." Nowhere in this literature is there, of course, any recognition of the concept basic to both my theory of beauty and my theory of Love, namely, properties of qualitative degree.

Nevertheless, I get a definite sense from the literature on empathy that its authors would have recognized the *phenomena* that I call "expansion experiences" as at least part of the subject matter they were investigating. And I, for my part, occasionally recognize some of their *descriptions* of such phenomena as descriptions I could (almost) agree with.

36. In either kind of case, recall, there may be what I am calling an arousal experience, since the latter is an experience of our emotion, mood, sentiment, or feeling growing great in us insofar as it is not, or *not yet*, expressed.

37. As does, for example, I. A. Richards in *Principles of Literary Criticism* (New York: Harcourt Brace, 1938). But though I take issue with Richards' terminology, I freely acknowledge that the basic idea of emotions, moods, sentiments, and so forth being attached to what I call act-beginnings was already familiar to him. I do not know, however, where the idea originated. This concept is thus not original with me, but I think the use to which I am putting it is.

38. The problem of the one-and-many, incidentally, persists however one might choose to individuate act-beginnings. Even if one were to insist—unreasonably, I think—that in an arousal there is only a single act-beginning, the problem would arise in a different way. One would be forced, by the raw character of arousal experi-

ences themselves, to distinguish "parts" of that single act-beginning and to recognize the "same" quality in each of the parts.

39. I also want to distinguish this sort of "motion" from another sort of motion experienced in arousals, namely, the motion we sense in our very *experiencing* of the mood or emotion as it moves through us. This is the "motion" of the "searchlight of consciousness" as it *follows* the "moving" *object* of that consciousness. I shall explicate this variety of experienced "motion" in later stages of this study, for it plays an important role in my theory of Love, specifically in my account of the pleasantness of Love.

40. I emphasize here that although we experience the impulses as being in our muscles, the actual material basis of these experiences (as determined neurophysiologically) may be impulses which occur in parts of the *central* nervous system. Thus I would want to claim that even a person who had lost the use of his legs (or lost his legs) might be able to experience a "preparation" to use his legs in an action with a certain quality. For the same reason I would want to claim that such a person might well be able to *imagine* performing an action with a certain quality that required him to move his legs in a certain way even when such imagining involves having actual feelings of movement in one's limbs. For the latter feelings require no actual movement and no actual limbs, just as the *quality* experienced in the feeling does not require that any actual quality "exist."

Thus, although my language may not always explicitly recognize it, whenever I speak of feeling something "in" or "through" a specific bodily part, I do not mean to imply that the experience actually occurs in or through that part. Where the experience *occurs* is determinable, if at all, by neurophysiology. I mean that, as far as the *content* of that experience (in the mode of feeling) is concerned, the feeling is *experienced as being* "in" such and such a part.

I am grateful to Anita Silvers, who as a reader for Princeton University Press brought this problem to my attention. I can only hope that these remarks adequately solve the problem. I am grateful to Professor Silvers as well for other, more general suggestions that have helped me, I believe, to improve on an earlier version of this book.

41. A "complete" act is a definite and elaborated expressive act;

an "incomplete" act is a movement that, even if externally detectable, is barely begun. Obviously, there are many stages of incompletion that we have experienced for any one of our completed expressive acts—no matter how one counts incomplete acts.

42. As indicated above in note 35, Lipps does seem to vacillate between these two interpretations of what *he* calls "empathy." While I choose the word "empathy" to name this variety of expansion experience chiefly in commemoration of earlier empathy theorists in aesthetics, I do not claim to be using it in their sense(s). Sometimes empathy theorists seem to use "empathy" to refer to the whole collection of what I call "expansion experiences," though without cataloging the members of the collection. At other times, they seem to imply that empathy is *like* the specific form of expansion experience that I am calling "empathies." For empathy is most often spoken of in that early tradition as a kind of projection of feelings onto things; it is a kind of "feeling into" objects. It is this latter sense of "empathy" that I seek to evoke.

43. It is important in this kind of case that the friend be perceived by you as not becoming merely "ceremonially" sad, that is to say, putting on a sad face as the proper thing to do. It is also important that the sad-making event not be a reason why your friend becomes sad independently of your sadness, as might be the case, for example, if the paper were coauthored by him. For in the latter two circumstances, it is likely that the sadness that you experience creeping over your friend would *not* be experienced by you as generated by the sadness welling out of you.

44. This is not to say, of course, that the other may not be manipulating the situation so that precisely the qualities of her deliberate actions may transfer *themselves* to some deliberate actions of mine.

45. I am thinking here of R. G. Collingwood, for whom the significance of calling the work of art an "imaginary object" is in part, I believe, that it evokes emotions that also are "imaginary." I can find no passage in which such a thesis is stated explicitly, but see *The Principles of Art* (London: Oxford University Press, 1938), passim, and especially pp. 144–51. I have in mind also Kendall Walton's

thesis in "Fearing Fictions," *Journal of Philosophy* 75, no. 1 (January 1978), pp. 5–27. Walton wants to deny that the emotions generated by attending to works of art are real emotions. Hence he speaks of being, in the presence of fearful representations, "make-believedly afraid" and refers to the feelings evoked by such representations as "quasi-fear-feelings." Although the last phrase muddies things a bit, I assume that Collingwood and Walton could agree with me that both when we are really afraid and when we are imaginarily or make-believedly afraid we can have genuine fear experiences, and even have them in some of the same experiential modes (which does not mean, of course, that they would be indistinguishable from one another in their character as fear experiences). And I presume that we all agree, furthermore, that when we are *really* afraid (whatever the conditions under which that happens), our fear experiences are *veridical*.

There is a long history of attempts to distinguish the emotional experiences generated by art from "real" ones; see Tatarkiewicz, *A History of Six Ideas*, pp. 327–28. I certainly have nothing in principle against such attempts, and the New Theory of Love is definitely not incompatible with them. I am nevertheless skeptical enough about the prospects for success of these attempts to want to make my own theory independent of them. For one thing, though such attempts are usually couched in terms of what *in fact* distinguishes representation-feeling from real feelings, there is almost always a normative point hidden in the attempt. That is to say, the *implicit* assertion is that one *ought not* to be really afraid of fearful representations; one *ought* to be only imaginarily or make-believedly afraid. Thus an aesthetician like Bullough, in making a similar point about "aesthetic distance," could ridicule the hypothetical "yokel" who cannot tell Desdemona's murder on the stage from a real murder and rushes up to save her. It is precisely this kind of ridicule that makes me think, too, that far from describing the "way things actually are" with respect to the emotional experiences evoked by art, attempts to insulate such experiences from "reality" may in part be covert attempts to universalize what are in fact the experiences or norms of a certain culture, historical period, social class, age group, or gender. As far as I know, however, no work has been done on the "relativity" of aesthetic distancing, so my thoughts remain mere speculative possibilities.

46. The scare quotes around "directionality" and "somewhere" show that, like other aspects of what is experienced in expansion experiences, this spatiality cannot be taken in an ordinary geometrically or numerically determinable sense. I shall not always use scare quotes to indicate such special spatiality, but when I do not, the context, I take it, will indicate it.

47. The reader may wonder how these five classes of qualities relate to the four categories of qualities distinguished in Section 9, which I claimed exhaust the world of qualities, at least for human beings. By now it may be obvious how those four categories mesh with my analyses of expansion experiences. For the four categories are (1) qualities of human acts experienced from the "inside," (2) qualities of the acts of "other" sentient beings, (3) qualities of the "tracks" of the acts of sentient beings, and (4) qualities in nonsentient "objects" that can be experienced as qualities in categories 2 and 3. From my analyses of expansion experiences, it is clear how qualities in all four of these categories could figure in one or more of the types of expansion experiences described.

48. I emphasize again that nothing substantive rides on this class division. More subtle sensibilities may well want to distinguish more or different classes of mental qualities based upon a finer or different discrimination of characteristic demeanor. The point is that there is *some* characteristic demeanor associated with the manifestation of mental qualities.

49. Thus I do not include here such qualities as the buttery taste of a Chardonnay wine or the nutty taste of Emmenthaler Swiss cheese, even though these are characteristic tastes. For the purposes of discovering expansion experiences with respect to such qualities, the qualities can be reduced to one or more other qualities like smoothness and richness or richness and dryness, which I think do *not* pose problems for my analysis of expansion experiences. I readily admit that characteristic tastes and smells of natural objects, like characteristic looks, feels, and sounds, are also very likely reducible

to other qualities. Nevertheless, an analysis of the former, unreduced qualities as they figure in expansion experiences will yield results that are interesting and suggestive for the overall picture of qualities that results from the very possibility of expansion experiences.

50. Another of my terminological *hommages*, this time to that whole medieval tradition that thought of *claritas* as one of the two or three marks of beauty. Thus, for example, according to Thomas Aquinas, "everything is called beautiful if it possesses the spiritual and physical lustre [*claritatem*] proper to its kind, and if it is constructed in proper proportion" (cited in Wladyslaw Tatarkiewicz, *History of Aesthetics* [The Hague: Mouton, 1970], vol. I, p. 259). Those who are closer to that tradition than I may, of course, think this *hommage* a trifling one indeed, considering the sometimes grandiose meanings that have been attributed to the term *claritas* by modern writers, such as James Joyce and some neoscholastic philosophers. I, however, do not pretend to know what medieval thinkers meant by *claritas* in this context. I doubt that anyone knows, although there are no doubt many who could do an immensely better *scholarly* job than I of trying to find out. I am merely using the term here in its obvious sense of "clarity" and hence include the qualities of visual and aural clarity and their near relatives in this class of qualities. It seems to me, furthermore—though I do not consider the point a substantive one—that characteristic tastes and smells of natural things (and perhaps characteristic "feels" as well) are also kinds of "clarity." Such tastes, smells, and feels are ways those things have of (clearly) signaling to human beings their presence and the characters of their being—for example, as pine, as strawberry, as carnation.

51. It may also appear, of course, as color and quality of skin or hair, but that is irrelevant to the immediate point.

52. Being wide-eyed does not, of course, mean having wide pupils. It means opening the eyelids wide apart and raising the brows; it means not squinting and peering.

53. Or at least through our heads. For especially with respect to qualities of *claritas*, I believe, the experiences of those qualities in us are often confined to our heads, for the good reason that such quali-

ties, being narrowly confined to one sense modality each, affect predominantly those parts of us involved in that sense modality, and all the qualities of *claritas* I have discussed involve sense modalities whose organs are located in our heads. This point obviously would not apply if characteristic feels (to the touch) are included.

54. My claim is neutral with respect to such explanations because I do not know what considerations could decide in favor of one or the other of them. The alert reader will have noticed that the two kinds of explanation I sketch out are a version of the empiricists' "associationism" and a kind of "*a priori*" explanation in the style of Kant. It does seem to me, moreover, that if the Kantian arguments in the first *Critique* that space and time are "pure forms of intuition" are sound, then there should be sound arguments for the existence—if that is the word—of an analogous "pure form of qualitative space" as well.

55. For this sort of confirmation, it is sufficient to imagine having *any sort* of expansion experience, since if distinct experiences of a quality can be components of an expansion experience of any kind, they can *ipso facto* be components of a Night of Love.

56. What this "allowing" precisely consists in, and how it works, is beyond me and, I think, beyond everyone at the present stage of knowledge. It is, however, a fact of our experience that we can somehow "acquiesce" in such feelings or "give way" or "yield" to them, often quite deliberately. Such acquiescence is not limited to qualities of emotion and mood in ourselves, but is a quite general feature of our experience of qualities and a chief means of producing such experience especially, as we shall see, as regards Love.

This phenomenon is, incidentally, probably what Plato had in mind when he had Agathon in the *Symposium* attribute "tenderness" and "softness" to love and deny to it hardness and rigidity (195c–e). I am certain, moreover, that Plato was aware of the phallic and contraphallic suggestions of this. Of course, it is hard to "prove" these points for the reason that anything about what Plato meant in that scintillating work is hard to prove. Many interpreters think that whatever Agathon the poet is made to say is not taken seriously by Plato, since Socrates later is portrayed as "refuting" Agathon. But since that "refuting" argument is obviously unsound and Socrates seems to know that it is, what are we then to make of Plato's view of Agathon? To be sure, Agathon's speech *is* frothy and clearly seems, on one level, designed to make absurdly false ideas seem the "better cause." Yet there are interpretations of nearly everything that Agathon is made to say that could render his speech plausible. (Agathon himself characterizes his speech as "half playful" while yet having some seriousness to it [197e].) My suggestion above is simply one of these interpretations. In my view, Plato is in this passage referring (via Agathon) to the yielding quality of the Love experience; stiffness and rigidity "of the soul" will work to prevent enjoyment. It seems fairly obvious to me, furthermore, that Agathon, in making this point, hopes to make a point about his own "yielding" qualities, since there is evidence in the dialogue that he is trying to seduce Socrates, and were he to do so, he would, as the younger partner, have to play the "yielding" role.

57. The term "reproduction" is another *hommage*, in this case to the Plato of the *Symposium*: "Love is the desire to reproduce in the beautiful," says Diotima, mysteriously of course. I use the term partly with the idea that Plato may have had in mind something like what I mean by the concept. Then again, he may not have. I also use the term in honor of the great fun Plato had with the idea of reproduction (sometimes translated as "generation") in that work.

58. This verb form sounds like decidedly awkward, if not incorrect, English. Remember, however, that "Love," strictly speaking, is not an English word. The grammar will sound more acceptable if "enjoy" is substituted for "Love." I admit, however, that when the English word "love" is substituted for "Love," which I shall later claim is possible in many cases, there are some apparent grammatical problems. How these problems are solved we shall see later.

59. I do not have any particular theorist in mind who might make such an objection. But, the notion of the "work itself" originated in the late 1940s and was popular for some time afterwards. The notion was due originally to the "New Critics" in literature, but was sometimes generalized by others to include all the arts. Thinkers who accept some version of this idea tend to believe that attention—

whether critical or appreciative—that strays from what they think of as the "work itself" is "aesthetically" irrelevant or improper.

60. This is another way of describing my disagreement with Richard Warner's theory of enjoyment (cf. notes 11 and 20). For as I understand that theory, it implies that we enjoy an activity we are engaged in precisely insofar as (and therefore "because") we are pleased that we are engaged in it.

I point out, furthermore, that on the basis of the consequences of NTL that I am here spelling out, any desire we have to reproduce an experience in a particular way—for example, to hike, to live in Laguna Beach, or to look at old photographs—is, according to the terminology introduced in Section 5, an "extrinsic desire" and not an "intrinsic desire." It fails to be an intrinsic desire, however, not because it fails to arouse a desire to continue hiking, living in Laguna Beach, or looking at old photos. For, in an *indirect* way, enjoyable hiking (and the rest) do arouse the desire to continue those activities; they arouse it via the enjoyable experiences they are the means to. Such desires fail to be intrinsic desires, rather, because they fail to arouse desires to continue those activities *indefinitely*. Hiking arouses the desire to continue hiking only as long as the hiking provides the enjoyable experiences it is (at the time) a means to.

61. This interpretation only *appears* to reduce a property of qualitative degree to one of quantitative degree. For although I have provided a way of distinguishing *an* experience, I have provided no way of counting such experiences. Indeed, because experiences are notoriously transient and because, in any case, distinguishing an experience as a constituent of another depends upon its "discernibility," experiences can be counted, it seems to me, only in the vaguest and most imprecise ways. The vagueness and imprecision are so great, in fact, that the notion of "counting" in such a context seems, strictly speaking, inapplicable. Or, to state the point in other terms, it is incorrect to speak of "more" or "fewer" experiences, and more accurate to speak of "smaller" and "larger" experiences, in which case the latter determinables are interpreted in a *qualitative* way, just as are "greater" or "lesser" when applied to qualities.

62. *The Sense of Beauty* (New York: Random House, 1955), p. 51.

63. One may legitimately wonder, of course, just how serious and dignified the word "love" is, considering that one may speak of "loving" drinking wine coolers or copulating on the beach at midnight. Indeed, it would seem that one can use "love" as a synonym for "enjoy," at least when one is *not* trying to be formal or dignified.

64. I certainly would not claim that what Plato and Aristotle meant by the phrase translated as "love of virtue" and its cognates is the same as what I mean by "the love of virtue," for the good reason that I am not confident that I know what they meant. I indicate here only a general affinity between the moral application of NTL and the moral thought of Plato and Aristotle. For an interpretation of the notion of the love of virtue in Aristotle, and to some extent in Plato, see M. F. Burnyeat, "Aristotle on Learning to Be Good," in *Essays on Aristotle's Ethics*, ed. Amelie Oksenberg Rorty (Berkeley and Los Angeles: University of California Press, 1980). It is interesting, incidentally, that in representing Aristotle's thought in this essay, Burnyeat has no compunction whatever in writing of "enjoying virtue." So far have we come since the "old days," under, I assume, the dour influence of Kant!

I am grateful to Gary Watson for providing the above reference. I take this opportunity also to express my thanks to Professor Watson for some interesting and helpful conversations about virtue.

65. I am not denying here that some theoretical account of dispositional enjoyment or dispositional love of virtue could be *constructed* on the basis of NTL. My claim is that NTL is explicitly formulated only as a theory of "occurrent Love."

66. No doubt there will be some sophisticates who deny enjoying works whose characters they identify with. To them I say two things: (1) Remember that NTL determines only that we enjoy the work *insofar as* we identify with a character; it does not demand that we enjoy everything about the work, that we enjoy the whole work *on balance*, or that we enjoy *the fact* that we enjoy identifying with a character. (2) There are complex theories that say (or imply) that we *ought not* to enjoy works whose characters we identify with or ought not to identify with characters and *a fortiori* ought not to enjoy it, on pain of being banausic (see, for example, T. W. Adorno, *Aesthetic*

Theory, trans. C. Lenhardt [London: Routledge, 1984], pp. 386–87, 474–75). Those who deny enjoying such works may simply be confusing what they think they ought to do with what they do. It is, of course, quite possible that some persons have so absorbed theories of what they ought not to do with respect to art that they in fact do not identify with any characters, and therefore do not *enjoy* identifying with characters.

67. For a discussion of this dimension of artistic and other works, see my *Mind and Art*, chs. 1–3.

68. This holds even if we are not always entitled to infer, on the basis of their works, that these real persons ever manifested those qualities other than in these works. To say that such qualities are the qualities of real persons is not, of course, to say that they are the "real" qualities of real persons, in the sense of being qualities those persons always and everywhere manifest. But then often the qualities we love in our friends are qualities they may manifest especially, or even only, when we are interacting with them. Cf. *Mind and Art*, especially pp. 26–46.

69. That model of love is preeminently what I would call a "pedagogical love"—one in which certain traits ("philosophical" traits like wisdom in the highest form of such love) are encouraged and intensified in the younger partner and realized and developed more fully in the older partner. But in the *Phaedrus*, though not in the *Symposium*, Plato admits that this sort of love may occur between lovers who are not (as are the highest and truest kind of lovers) "in the train of Zeus," but "in the train" of other gods. I take it that "being in the train of a god" means that the lovers share certain traits, such as warrior traits if they are in the train of Ares. The text does not specify what traits are included in the total set of traits found in the trains of all the gods. It is conceivable, but not likely, that Plato had in mind here the view that any and all personal qualities (in my sense) are legitimate bases for the sort of "pedagogical love" exemplified in its purest form by philosophical love. Cf. *Symposium*, 208e–212a, and *Phaedrus*, 252c–256e.

70. I stress the phrase "all cases of love *modeled on the love of human beings for other human beings*." For there are arguments that kinds of

"love" exist that are not so modeled. Thus, for example, Anders Nygren in his (in my view unaccountably) influential *Agape and Eros*, trans. Phillip S. Watson (Philadelphia: Westminster Press, 1953), maintains that "the" Christian idea of love (*agape*) is not so modeled. According to Nygren, *agape* is primarily and essentially the love of God for human beings. Other kinds of specifically Christian love, for example, the love of people for God or of people for one another, are derivatives of this original love. Nygren gives four characteristics of God's *agape*: (1) it is "unmotivated" by the worth of the beloved; (2) it is "indifferent to value" in the beloved; (3) it is "creative" of value in the beloved; (4) it is initiative of fellowship with God (pp. 75–81). Nygren believes that all of these features distinguish *agape* from love in the "Eros-tradition" of love. I think that claim is disputable with respect to all of these features except (4), although it would be a full-scale undertaking to argue this convincingly. But for Nygren, it is precisely feature (4) from which the *other* forms of *agape* are derived. For what distinguishes true love for God and true Christian love for others from *eros*-influenced models of such love is precisely the role of God in *causing* it (pp. 211–19). Furthermore, Nygren insists that *agape* includes *no* form of "self-love." What he means by this is not altogether clear, but I infer that the "erotic" character of Love developed in Sections 37, 38, and 39 below would be sufficient to brand Love as, at core, self-love. As Nygren says, "Eros is essentially and in principle self-love" (p. 216).

NTL does not comprehend Christian love as Nygren understands it. The question is, does this exclusion in fact limit the comprehensiveness of NTL? Nygren admits that many prominent and influential Christian theorists of love, such as Augustine, have worked out notions of Christian love heavily influenced by the *eros* tradition. Thus by excluding *agape*, as Nygren defines it, NTL does not by any means exclude all kinds of love historically considered Christian. More significantly, however, it is still possible (and, I claim, true) that all *actual* cases of Christian love *do* fall under NTL. Were Nygren to disagree and maintain that there have been (and are) at least some genuine cases of *agape*, he would have to produce examples of love in which God's causal agency has in fact operated, and I do not have the dimmest idea how he could do that.

But, some will object, it is not necessary to prove that there are *actual* cases of *agape* in order to limit the comprehensiveness of NTL. The very (logical?) possibility of *agape* is enough to do so. Is *agape* in Nygren's conception a logical possibility? If it is, then it is logically possible for a being with the properties of Nygren's God to *cause* a human being to love another. Even without knowing precisely what the properties of that God are (Nygren does not elaborate them in *Agape and Eros*), I have strong doubts about the (logical) possibility of *agape* and strong doubts therefore that Nygren's concept of Christian love limits the comprehensiveness of NTL.

71. Gregory Vlastos, in a well-known paper on Plato's idea of love, raises questions that can be construed as disputing this point. See "The Individual as Object of Love in Plato," in Vlastos' *Platonic Studies* (Princeton: Princeton University Press, 1973). I do not claim that NTL is identical, in whole or in part, with Plato's theory of love—if he *had* a theory of love. Nevertheless, some of Vlastos' criticisms in that paper apply to NTL. Vlastos, as I read him, does not deny that persons may be loved simply for their qualities. His ultimate points seem to be (1) that such love is not the most valuable kind of love for persons and (2) that therefore there is a kind of love for persons that goes beyond love of their qualities. Now, as I shall detail below in Section 32, I agree with Vlastos on point 2. And, as I shall point out in Section 36 below, Vlastos' point 1 is an issue in the "Ethics of Love," with which NTL is not directly concerned.

But Vlastos has several reasons, not all clear or clearly distinguished from one another, for believing (2). The one germane at this point in my argument is his complaint that the love of a person's qualities cannot comprehend love for the "whole" person, that is, love for the mixture of excellences and imperfections which constitutes actual persons. In this respect Vlastos seems to agree with Nygren that there is a love that is "indifferent to value" in persons. (ibid., pp. 32–34). In this respect, then, Vlastos' criticisms of Plato would seem to be criticisms of NTL as well. Now, I have my own reasons for thinking, like Vlastos, that a love for the "whole person," including his imperfections, is a possibility. But those reasons, detailed in Section 35, do not put such love at odds with NTL and, moreover, do not imply that such love is "indifferent to value."

Possibly another intuition, not at all clearly articulated, lurks behind Vlastos' unhappiness with Plato's notion of love. And that is
that the latter cannot comprehend love of the individual "as such." I
am not sure what this might mean, but I take one of its implications
to be that there is a kind of love of persons that is *not* reducible to
love of qualities because precisely what is loved about the person is
what is unique about the person. Now, such an objection may work
against Plato's theory of love; it certainly works against Vlastos'
interpretation of Plato's theory of love. I do not see, however, that it
necessarily works against NTL. For NTL does not imply that the
qualities loved in a person must be *shared* by other persons or even
shareable by other persons. For, after all, it is the lover in such an
"individualizing" kind of love who, according to NTL, determines
sameness of quality. And her love may be such—perhaps just because it is "individualizing"—that she *cannot* experience the beloved
qualities of her beloved as belonging to any other person.

The term "individualizing love" I take from Roger Scruton's book
Sexual Desire (London: Weidenfeld and Nicolson, 1986), where it is
discussed in the wider context of "individualizing thoughts" and the
"individualizing intentionality" of emotions and attitudes. Scruton
takes what I think is a basic intuition behind Vlastos' complaint
against Plato, expands on it, and analyzes it at some length. Scruton's conclusion, in the style of Kant though an anti-Kantian one, is
that such individualizing intentionality is a necessary ingredient in
interpersonal love, but that it is based ultimately upon a "metaphysical illusion" of personal individuality (p. 118). As an analysis of the
idea that what we love in another is his unique individuality, Scruton's work here is brilliant and the best thing by far in his book. I
construe Scruton's analysis as another way to support NTL against
an attack on its reduction program via the phenomenon of individualizing love. Unfortunately, that analysis is vitiated, as is nearly
everything else in Scruton's book, by the author's tendency to take
what is merely one form of a phenomenon such as desire, sexual activity, or love and universalize and normalize it as "the" form of it.
I do not find such a tendency in Gregory Vlastos, despite the latter's
view that individualizing love of a person is more "valuable" than
nonindividualizing interpersonal love.

72. NTL makes this "suggestion," of course, by insisting that duty and responsibility can, and ideally "should," rest on "feelings" and *hence* live in the domain of Love. I take this suggestion to be an anti-Kantian one. For I take Kant, in exorcising "inclinations" from the properly moral realm, to be excluding *feelings* of duty, responsibility, and "respect for the moral law as such" as acceptable ingredients in moral motivations. I take it, furthermore, that this exclusion is an implication of Kant's idea that the good will is, as such, determined only by "reason."

My emphasis on *feelings* of duty, responsibility, and (by extension) respect for the moral law as such (suitably cleansed of unrealistic rigidities, of course) and my attempt to integrate them into a basically non-Kantian theory of Love I see as an effort to reconcile a *style* of moral being that is Kantian in spirit (if not, as I say, strictly accordant with the Kantian letter) with the fundamental Hellenism of NTL.

73. The alert reader will notice that under what I call "acquisitive love" falls a great deal of what we recognize as love, marriage, friendship, and "relationships." Cynics will say that *most* of the latter are *nothing but* cases of acquisitive love. For, after all, we do not even have to be cynical to admit that most of us are, at one time or another, greatly self-deceived about the bases of our interpersonal relations. Notice that acquisitive love, as I define it, does not require that the participants acknowledge that their relationship is in any part acquisitive in my sense. My desire that NTL comprehend such love is a desire, in part, to comprehend cases of "love" and "friendship" according to *common usage*. It is also of a piece with my desire that NTL remain steadfastly nonnormative (see Section 36 below). My conception of "acquisitive love," furthermore, has much in common with one of the forms of friendship—"friendship for the sake of utility"—that Aristotle distinguishes in the *Nicomachean Ethics* (Bk. VIII, ch. 3).

74. These "directions" are, at this stage of the exposition, still incomplete. For although NTL says that we enjoy an experience of a quality by "reproducing" it, it specifies that we must do so in such a way that the desire to reproduce the experience is also aroused. The

241

final sections of the book will describe that way and, again implicitly, suggest how it may be contrived.

75. Though it also does not entail denying that the hurt of pain is enjoyable. I *suspect* that it is incoherent to speak of enjoying the hurt of pain, but I know no way of arguing this without a theory about the hurt of pain, which I do not possess. Some might object that "hurt of pain" is redundant, that a pain simply *is* its hurt. It seems to me that this issue is purely terminological. Nevertheless, were we to credit the objection, we would have to recast the point I am making about the possibility of enjoying pain. The point, recast, would be that it is possible—both in fact and according to NTL— to enjoy *painful sensations*, though possibly not the pain itself.

76. I should note, however, that such an analysis in no way limits the kinds of explanations that may obtain as to *why* a person might be inclined to experience certain negative qualities in (certain) partial ways. That is to say, the cause of a person's seeing unfeeling behavior as strong, for example, might be identified as one of any number of interesting psychological, social, or cultural factors. I should also point out that the analysis I am presenting here of loving or enjoying negative qualities is reminiscent of the analysis Augustine gives, in his discussion in the *Confessions* of the incident of his stealing pears (Bk. II, chs. 4–6), of loving vices by loving the "shadowy beauties" they may possess. But my own analysis emphasizes a Neoplatonic element more explicitly, and I think more clearly, than Augustine's characteristically rambling, though highly suggestive, remarks.

This "Neoplatonic" analysis of the "love of evil" is, of course, my interpretation of how the love of human imperfections is possible and my response to what I called in note 71 Gregory Vlastos' implicit criticism of NTL. I should think, however, that Vlastos' (and possibly Nygren's) response to this interpretation would be that it does not really account for the love of imperfections *as such* and therefore for the "true" love of actual, flesh-and-blood persons *as such*. I suspect that this sort of objection, which I cannot express well since I think it is ultimately groundless, must finally dispute NTL at its roots, namely, the reduction program on which it rests. For to say that one can and does love the imperfections of another "in themselves" and not with respect to any qualities (in my sense) that one perceives in them is to claim a kind of counterexample to that reduction program. But to make such a claim good, of course, one would have to argue that there is or can be a love of imperfection—of "evil"—that is in no way a love of "positive" qualities. I do not think such a "Manichaean" argument can be successfully made, and I know of no attempts to do so.

77. Nearly every philosophical work on love that I know, from Plato's to Roger Scruton's, is, in part at least, a work in the Ethics of Love. The ladder of love in the *Symposium*, for example, is precisely a *ranking* of types of love, though that with respect to which they are ranked is not completely clear. Augustine similarly ranks loves— with the love of God at the very top, of course, and all the others fastidiously arranged below that, with, presumably, the love of the "shadowy beauties" of vice itself at the very bottom. Aristotle's distinction between three basic types of friendship is, in part, a distinction between the best and less good types (see *Nicomachean Ethics*, Bk. VIII, chs. 1–6). Even Kant, who in his discussion of disinterested satisfaction did not think of himself as discussing love or (probably) even enjoyment, nevertheless draws a distinction between "pure" and "impure" judgments of taste, the latter being based partly on "charm" or "emotion" (see *Critique of Judgment*, pp. 58–59). Moreover, we can interpret the whole Kantian enterprise in the "Analytic of the Beautiful" as laying down conditions for *genuine* judgments of taste, as opposed to spurious ones that are presumably based upon "interest." (Mary Mothersill in *Beauty Restored* brings out this Kantian theme very strongly and uses it in her own theory.)

Of course, it goes without saying that the few philosophical works that deal with sexual love are concerned to rank its varieties, usually according to their "morality" or "immorality," their "naturalness" or "unnaturalness," their "normality" or "deviancy." Thus Roger Scruton in *Sexual Desire* not only explicitly discusses what he thinks of as sexual perversions but couches virtually all of his conclusions in terms of the "best" (my term) form of phenomena such as sexual desire, erotic love, the sexual act, and so forth, thereby implicitly categorizing all other forms of such phenomena as in some way deficient or defective. In a sense, therefore, Scruton's book is *nothing but* an ethics of (sexual) love, and it is so in a covert and therefore insidious way. I do not mean to imply that Scruton hides the fact that his is a thoroughly "moralized" view of sex and love; indeed he admits it with the same priggish aplomb that informs his entire book. It is simply that by stirring up a great deal of philosophical and scholarly dust he tries to give the impression that his moralized views are extracted from the "nature of things" (my term)—the "nature" of persons, of sexual desire, of "the" sex act. Hence his rhetoric is regularly the rhetoric of factual (or conceptual) assertion clothing the most moralized of premises and conclusions. There is, of course, a long tradition of such practice, and since Scruton is clearly not unaware of it in himself, he can hardly be unaware of its oppressive character.

However that may be, it still seems to me that Scruton's work, like most other work in the Ethics of Love, is, if properly redescribed, basically *compatible* with NTL. My hope would be, however, that NTL would encourage work in the Ethics of Love that would not be deceptive or oppressive, either of the writer or of her readers.

78. Thus, for example, if we wanted to lay down conditions for "true" love of another person, we might include the condition that the qualities that the lover loves be (1) the beloved's actual qualities, not her qualities as only imagined by the lover, (2) *not* qualities of the lover insofar as he is in the loving relationship, and (3) not merely qualities that the lover enjoys as a *consequence* of the actual qualities of the beloved, such as comfort and security enjoyed as a *consequence* of the beloved's benevolence or generosity. Similarly, if we were interested in one variety of normative theory of the enjoyment of art, we might seek to proscribe the reproduction of an art work's qualities in any experiential mode other than the (veridical) *perception* of qualities as they exist *in* the work. I hasten to add that I am not recommending either of these projects. I sketch them only as *examples* of how one might proceed in making "normative" distinctions using NTL as a base.

79. One might think that as long as the experiencer does not do anything to terminate the experience, all such cases of expansion ex-

periences are *ipso facto* cases of reproduction. On the contrary, I would argue that many expansion experiences, like many other perceptual experiences, take place before I have time to do *anything* either to continue having them or to stop them. They really do seem simply to "happen" to me.

80. It is an interesting implication of this point that certain cases of the "reproduction" of qualities that, I take it, actually occur in the appreciation and analysis of art do not amount to the enjoyment of those qualities or of that art. For we may locate, identify, describe, and analyze qualities, usually complex ones, in art and return again and again to those qualities (hence reproducing the experience of them) precisely for the purposes of locating, identifying, describing, and analyzing them, without such "reproduction" thereby counting as the "enjoyment" of them in terms of NTL.

Some theorists might, I surmise, want to go beyond this bare point and allege that the "enjoyment" of the qualities of art as described by NTL is even *improper* in our intercourse with art, possibly on the grounds that it is "sentimental," that it precludes proper "distancing," or that it precludes a properly "alienated" stance towards cultural forms that may seek to "co-opt," "manipulate," or otherwise deceive us. Such negative attitudes towards the enjoyment or love of art as NTL defines it may imply, as their positive counterparts, that the "proper" stance towards art and its qualities is purely descriptive, purely analytical, or purely critical.

Obviously I cannot engage such issues here; they belong to the Ethics of Love. I point out only that persons with such attitudes, while often professing some contempt and hostility towards the love and enjoyment of art (and possibly towards love and enjoyment in general), nevertheless often betray opinions about what it *is* acceptable and proper to love and enjoy, namely, the description, analysis, and criticism of art. Note, too, that to the extent that we enjoy describing, analyzing, and criticizing art but resist enjoying the qualities of the very art that we describe, analyze, and criticize, we may be using our intercourse with art and its qualities as an opportunity to enjoy qualities of *ourselves*, such as our perspicacity, cleverness, adroitness, or knowledgeability. The analogous use of intercourse with another in the sexual sphere has occasionally been regarded as despicable.

81. I am aware that caresses can be rough, passionate, greedy, and many other things besides smooth and gentle. I here concentrate on caresses with the latter qualities, however, precisely because I want a certain result. The result will not, I believe, be prejudiced by such a concentration.

82. There is no concurrent outweighing unpleasantness in the life of the person experiencing an expansion because, if there were, the person would simply *leave off* continuing the expansion experience.

This is probably the place to put to rest an uneasiness that some readers may have felt since I first described the experience of enjoyment. I have been alleging that the very structure of Love is the desire to reproduce the experience of a quality indefinitely, so that *as long as I am enjoying a thing* I have such a desire. This in turn implies that up to and including the "last" moment of enjoyment I have such a constituent desire. And this in turn implies that when my enjoyment is "over," for whatever reasons, there is some unsatisfied desire "left over" from the "last" moment of enjoyment. There is thus a kind of "frustration" built into my model of Love, just as (though, as I have explained, for slightly different reasons) it is built into Platonic *eros* in the *Symposium* (for if love is a desire for "immortality" and no lover is ever literally immortal, all desire constituent of love is ultimately frustrated desire). As I mentioned earlier, such "frustration" explains why we are often reluctant to break off activities we are enjoying, even when they have reached their natural terminus.

But—and here I address the "uneasiness"—this built-in "frustration" seems to *conflict* with another phenomenon of enjoyment, namely, the fact that we sometimes "tire" of the enjoyed activity and break it off of our own accord. On the face of it, my model of enjoyment does not allow for that. It seems to allow only for the possibility that some desire *stronger* than the intrinsic desire to continue indefinitely enjoying something will overpower the latter. Of course, the overpowering desire and the enjoyed activity may be such that the end of the enjoyment leaves no lingering regret and occasions no reluctance (as when I leave off enjoying the smell of a flower to save

246

my house, which has just caught fire). Hence my use of scare quotes above around "frustration"; the term denotes only the *fact* of an unsatisfied desire, not necessarily any *feeling* of frustration. But the possibility of *simply* becoming "tired of" or "satiated with" a particular enjoyment apparently remains inexplicable on my theory.

My response is this. There are no cases of "simply" becoming "tired of" or "satiated with" an enjoyment; all such (apparent) cases are in fact cases of *other* and *stronger* desires overpowering the intrinsic desire to continue indefinitely enjoying something. Often when we describe ourselves as simply "tired" of a thing, it is precisely because something else (another delectation, even doing the dishes) is at that moment, for any number of quite heterogeneous and possibly quite nonaesthetic reasons, more "attractive." After all, to say that an intrinsic desire is hidden in *every* case of enjoyment is not to say anything about how strong that desire is in comparison with the other concurrent desires in one's life. Even in the absence of overpowering "positive" desires, to *do* something else, however, there may be overpowering "negative" desires, to *stop* doing what I am now doing (and enjoying). It is just such overpowering "negative" desires that are crucial in understanding "core cases" of "getting tired" of doing something enjoyable. For everything enjoyable, even smelling a rose, requires some physical activity and some bodily part(s). Bodily parts literally tire, and as they tire, it becomes more and more unpleasant to continue an activity that requires their use. Sooner or later this unpleasantness becomes an "outweighing unpleasantness" that generates a "negative" desire to *leave off* doing the enjoyable actvitity, a desire that overpowers the intrinsic desire to continue the enjoyed activity indefinitely. Of course, we need not resort to mere bodily fatigue to motivate such overpowering "negative" desires. There is mental fatigue, too. Thus however much we may be enjoying thinking about a philosophical project, there comes a time when we are mentally exhausted. And such exhaustion generates the desire to leave off doing the philosophy.

I am grateful to Anita Silvers for bringing this issue to my attention.

83. I can speak here only of male orgasms. Whether female or-

gasms have a similar structure I do not know. I hereby welcome attempts to fill the gaps in my knowledge.

84. The distinction between the "erotic" and the "sexual" that NTL leads us to has some interesting, if difficult to track, implications with respect to an "issue" about love that is both extremely vague and highly resonant, intellectually and emotionally speaking. It is an issue that is sometimes raised in contexts, such as the discussion of sexual politics, that encourage sloganeering and other untidy modes of thought. That is the issue of whether human love has its "origins" in sexuality, that is, the fact of human sexual reproductivity and its (alleged) attendant instincts, activities, attitudes, and social arrangements, or whether it has its roots in activities of "nurturing," in the broadest sense. This distinction of "origin" is sometimes cast in terms of a contrast between a masculine view of love and a feminine view. Casting the distinction in this way is erroneous if it implies that only men have, or can or should have, an interest in sexual reproduction and only women have, or can or should have, an interest in nurturance. If the masculine-feminine contrast is meant to describe a "stylistic" difference, however, there may be more validity to the description. For the description could then be used to call attention to attitudes of competition, violence, and "conquest" that surround sexual reproduction, both in nonhuman animals and in much of human society, as well as to the fact that it usually falls to the male to bear the burden of having and maintaining these attitudes. Conversely, the description could be used to call attention both to attitudes of care, protection, and nourishing that are presupposed in "nurturance" and to the fact that, in many nonhuman animals and in human cultures, such attitudes and activities are found predominantly in, or have been assigned predominantly to, females.

Notice, however, that the masculine-feminine contrast is not the only "resonant" description that might apply to this distinction between views of the "origins" of love. I can also think of the following ways of describing the contrast, which I shall neither discuss nor justify here: Aristotelian-Platonic; religious-spiritual; conservative-radical; heterosexual-homosexual. And there are probably several more that are equally intriguing and promising.

But whatever the proper description—and ramifications—of this distinction between views of love, no reasonable interpretation of NTL could allege that it finds the "origin" of love in the fact of sexual reproduction. On the other hand, NTL arguably finds all love to be a sort of "nurturance," if the latter is understood in a suitably general way. For according to NTL, the essence of love is that the lover seeks ways for the beloved (quality) to "grow" and to "flourish." Moreover, the pleasure of love is, according to NTL, not traced to orgasmic pleasure, with its presupposition of a genital sexuality presumably required in the pursuit of sexual reproduction. Rather, it is traced to feelings of an "overall caress"—reminiscent both of the parental embrace of the helpless infant and of the all-enveloping nurturance of our prenatal situation in the womb.

I remind the reader here, however, that in speaking of the "origin" of love I refer to "logical" or "theoretical" origins, and not necessarily to biological or evolutionary origins. About the latter, NTL neither makes nor implies any claims.

Index